air

FLYING MACHINE

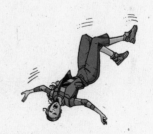

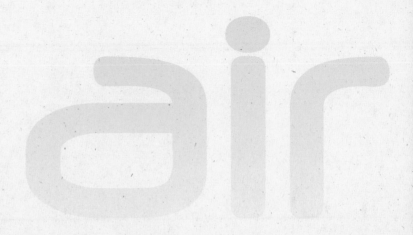

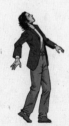

FLYING MACHINE
G. Willow Wilson Writer
M. K. Perker Artist
Chris Chuckry Colorist
Jared K. Fletcher Letterer
AIR created by Wilson and Perker

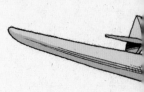

aren Berger SVP-Executive Editor & Editor-original series
ornsak Pichetshote Associate Editor-original series
eorg Brewer VP-Design & DC Direct Creative
ob Harras Group Editor-Collected Editions & Editor
obbin Brosterman Design Director-Books
uis Prandi Art Director

C COMICS
aul Levitz President & Publisher
ichard Bruning SVP-Creative Director
atrick Caldon EVP-Finance & Operations
my Genkins SVP-Business & Legal Affairs
m Lee Editorial Director-WildStorm
regory Noveck SVP-Creative Affairs
teve Rotterdam SVP-Sales & Marketing
heryl Rubin SVP-Brand Management

AIR: FLYING MACHINE

Published by DC Comics. Cover and compilation
Copyright © 2009 DC Comics. All Rights
Reserved.

DC Comics, 1700 Broadway, New York, NY 10019
A Warner Bros. Entertainment Company
Printed in Canada. First Printing.
ISBN 13: 978-1-4012-2483-7

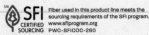

A Brief Layover by G. Willow Wilson

When I ran into Blythe a few weeks ago, she looked agitated. I was on my way to meet M.K. in Istanbul—where he was hard at work on cover sketches—but found myself delayed in Amsterdam by an early snowstorm. I saw her hurrying down the terminal as I stood pondering an Old Master still life in Schiphol's art gallery, jetlagged and slightly nauseous. She was a flash of ochre and red out of the corner of my eye, zigzagging through the crush of passengers like she'd done it a thousand times. Which I guess she has.

She stopped when I called her name and looked at me with a harried expression. I made my way toward her through the crowd.

"You seem like you're in a hurry," I said unnecessarily.

"Yeah." Blythe tucked a strand of hair behind her ear and looked around. "I kind of am. There's this—I just got back from somewhere and now I'm on my way to Mexico City. With my boss. But it's not for work. At least—not exactly."

"What ever happened to your boyfriend?" I asked, thinking I was making polite conversation. "What's-his-name. You haven't mentioned him in awhile."

Blythe looked a little stricken. "You mean... Zayn?" she said.

"I thought his name was Manuel?"

"Oh." She clapped one hand over her mouth. "It might have been."

At that point I knew I was getting into strange and possibly indelicate territory. The Blythe I knew wore her heart on her sleeve—always open because she had no reason not to be. Though most of our mutual friends wrote her off as somewhat ordinary, I had a sneaking suspicion there was a lot more going on in that girl's head than she let on. There were worlds we didn't see, floating behind those innocuous Slushie-blue eyes. This strange new Blythe—of secret appointments and anonymous boyfriends—seemed to confirm my guess.

"Are you, I mean, okay?"

Blythe chewed her lip. "Yeah. No. Do you think it's possible to fall in love with someone you don't really know? I mean, someone you've only seen a few times?"

For some reason, I wasn't surprised by the question. "Yes," I said. "I think it's not only possible, but a good sign."

She seemed satisfied by my answer. "Listen," she said after a pause. "If you don't see me again for awhile, I don't want you to worry. There are a lot of things going on in my life right now that I can't explain. But I'm handling them. Okay?"

"Okay," I said uneasily. Blythe smiled and waved over her shoulder as she continued on her way.

As soon as I reached Istanbul, I started digging around to figure out what "things" Blythe alluded to. But after a few phone calls and judicious Google searches, I was even more uneasy. It seems that Blythe was not the same after she helped foil that hijacking by the Etesian Front. Just before I saw her, she disappeared for several days to a place called Narimar—which, when I looked it up, didn't appear to exist. A few days after our chance encounter, her boss at Clearfleet returned from Mexico City without her, and wouldn't say where she was. A friend in the defense industry told me a rumor that an Aztec artifact—something to do with the cult of the Feathered Serpent—went missing around the same time Blythe started acting strange. It was unclear why this artifact was so important. Unclear that Blythe was connected to it in any way. Yet I couldn't get it out of my mind, and had the strangest feeling I'd seen a feathered serpent somewhere before. Finally I remembered where: on the tails of all the Clearfleet planes. It's their logo.

It can't be a coincidence.

I have not seen Blythe since that snowy afternoon at Schiphol Airport—at least, not in waking life. She did come to me in a dream. I was sitting on a lawn chair in the sky, contemplating a cube within a sphere—within a cube, within another sphere, ad infinitum. A young Arab boy in a soccer uniform approached me.

"Do you know what it means?" he asked, in Blythe's voice.

"No," I said, "What are you doing in this body?"

"I don't know," he—she—said miserably, "It has something to do with what Amelia told me, but I can't remember what."

"Amelia?"

"Earhart."

I woke up feeling humbled. I always thought my writer's life was glamorous and unusual, but Blythe—a flight attendant with a fear of heights—inhabits something bigger: a world I can neither see nor understand, a rarefied sky, where the horizon between the real and the merely possible vanishes. Blythe is off on the adventure of a lifetime. (Maybe several lifetimes, if my dream means anything.) What she finds in the wild blue yonder will amaze us all.

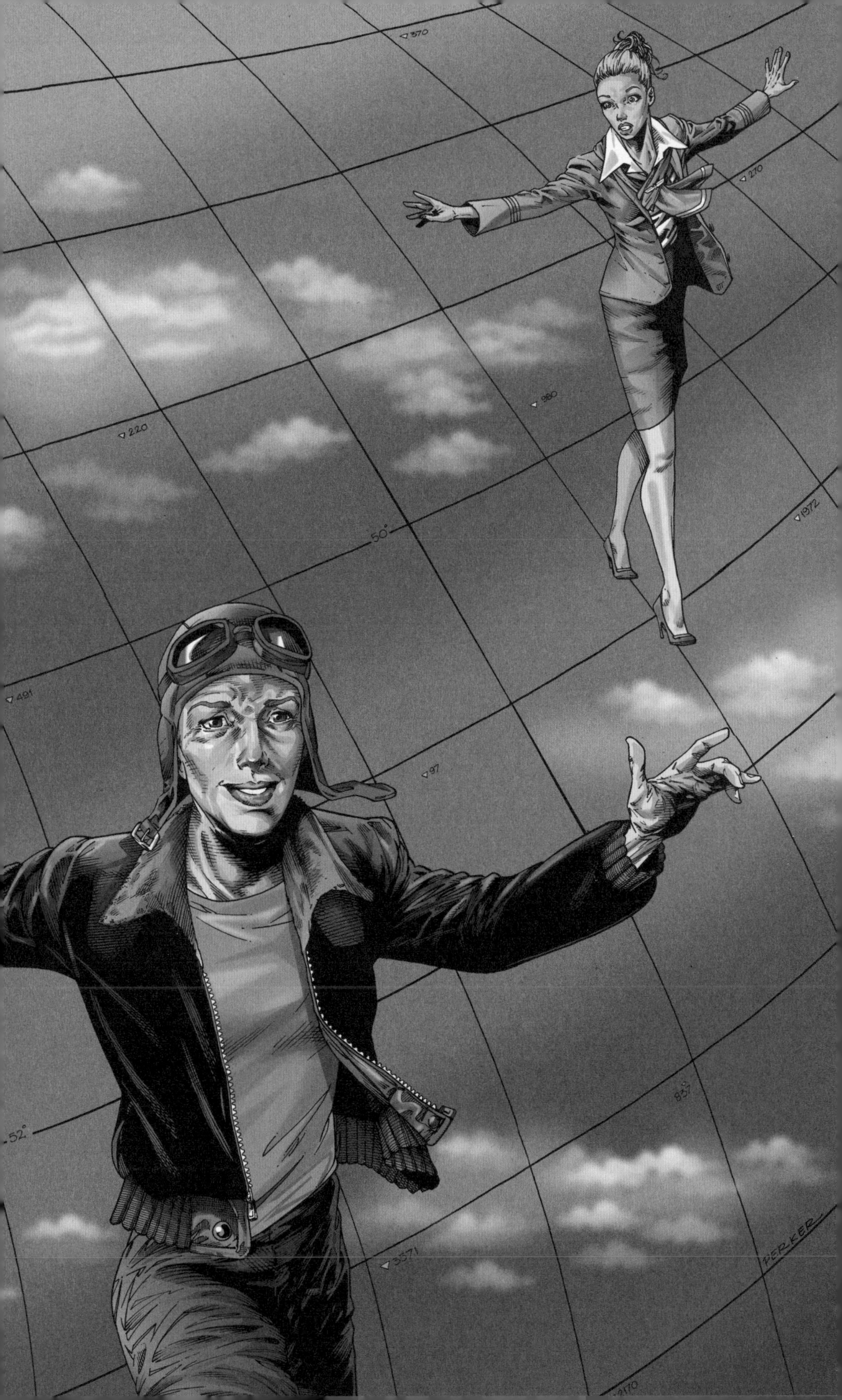

370
270
220
980
1972
50°
491
97
52°
837
3371
PERKER

AMELIA... *EARHART?*

GOOD THING YOU THREW UP *BEFORE* NORTHFIELD INTRODUCED ME. MOST PEOPLE THROW UP *AFTER.*

THE--

--AMELIA EARHART?

PLAIN OLD "AMELIA" IS FINE.

DON'T WORRY, ALL YOUR QUESTIONS HAVE ANSWERS.

YOU'RE NOT *DEAD?*

LIKE THAT ONE. BUT FIRST LET'S COLLECT NORTHFIELD.

I'M GONNA USE THAT GIRLY-BOY *HAIR* OF YOURS TO FLOSS MY--

JOHN, PLEASE. THEY WERE JUST FOOLING AROUND.

WE ARE VERY SORRY.

VERY SORRY. IT WON'T HAPPEN AGAIN.

LET'S GET YOU A STIFF DRINK.

HMMPH. GYPSIES.

...TINY STATE OF NARIMAR HAS ENTERED INDEPENDENCE TALKS WITH INDIA AND PAKISTAN.

LONG A CONTROVERSIAL TERRITORY, NARIMAR HAS--

KISTAN

NARIMAR

INDI

NEWS 1

HOW...?

WHAT'S THAT?

NOTHING. I'LL TELL YOU LATER.

THREE PLEASE, FRONSAC.

AVEC PLAISIR, MADAME.

SO AMELIA EARHART JUST SAVED MY LIFE. I REALLY DON'T KNOW HOW TO *PROCESS* THAT.

YOU'RE OUR SHOT AT KEEPING THE MOST IMPORTANT ARCHAEOLOGICAL FIND IN HISTORY OUT OF THE HANDS OF CRIMINALS AND TYRANTS. I WASN'T GOING TO LET YOU DIE ON SOME *JOY RIDE.*

BUT BEFORE YOU CAN FIND THE DEVICE, YOU'RE GOING TO HAVE TO LEARN TO PILOT A HYPERPRAX AIRSHIP. AND THERE'S NO ONE BETTER TO *TEACH* YOU THAN AMELIA HERE.

HOW ARE *YOU* INVOLVED WITH ALL THIS? AND WHAT'S THE STORY WITH YOU BEING *ALIVE*?

HOW I'M INVOLVED, HOW I DISAPPEARED AND HOW I'M STILL ALIVE ARE ALL *ONE* STORY, BLYTHE.

"BUT LET'S GO BACK A LITTLE FURTHER."

"IN 1927, THE FIRST HYPERPRAX DEVICE WAS DISCOVERED AT AN AZTEC RUIN IN MEXICO."

"WHEN THE ARCHAEOLOGISTS HEADED BACK TO THE *U.S.* WITH THE DEVICE, SOMETHING *STRANGE* HAPPENED."

"ONE MOMENT, THEY WERE FLYING ALONG THE MEXICAN COAST..."

"...AND THE NEXT, THEY FOUND THEMSELVES OVER RIVERTON, IOWA, THE TOWN WHERE ONE OF THE ARCHAEOLOGISTS WAS BORN."

"HE SAID HE'D BEEN SLEEPING AND *DREAMED* OF HOME."

THE GOVERNMENT IMMEDIATELY *CONFISCATED* THE DEVICE AND BEGAN STUDYING IT.

"BECAUSE OF WHAT HAPPENED TO THE ARCHAEOLOGISTS' PLANE, THEY SUSPECTED THE DEVICE COULD GIVE RISE TO A NEW METHOD OF *FLIGHT.*

"THEY WERE *RIGHT.*

"BUT THEY DISCOVERED THAT HYPERPRAX AIRCRAFT COULDN'T BE PILOTED BY JUST ANYBODY. IT TOOK AN *INBORN* SKILL.

"AND THAT SKILL WAS MORE COMMON IN *WOMEN.*

"SO THE NINETY NINE WAS FORMED: A SOCIETY FOR WOMEN AVIATORS. WELL, THAT'S WHAT THEY *CALLED* IT. THE REAL AIM WAS TO TRAIN WOMEN HYPERPRACTS AS PILOTS.

"IN 1937, I WAS CHOSEN FROM AMONG THE NINETY NINES FOR THE MOST AMBITIOUS FLIGHT IN HISTORY: CIRCUMNAVIGATING THE GLOBE IN A HYPERPRAX AIRCRAFT.

"THAT WASN'T WHAT THEY SOLD THE *PUBLIC,* OF COURSE--TO THEM, I WAS SETTING A RECORD FOR *WOMEN,* NOT *HUMANITY.*"

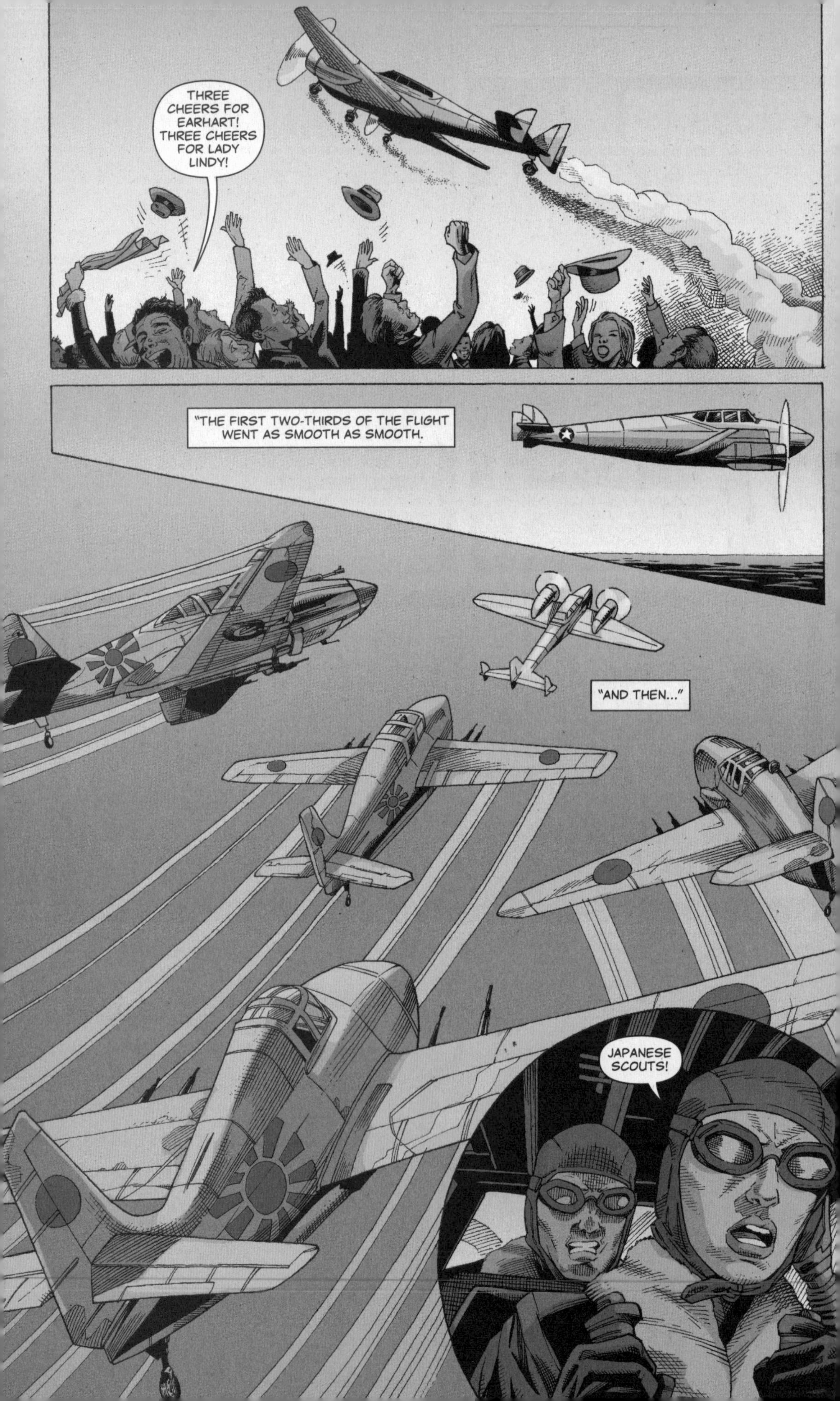
THREE CHEERS FOR EARHART! THREE CHEERS FOR LADY LINDY!
"THE FIRST TWO-THIRDS OF THE FLIGHT WENT AS SMOOTH AS SMOOTH.
"AND THEN..."
JAPANESE SCOUTS!

DAMN IT,
DAMN IT--

"DURING HYPERPRAX FLIGHT, THE ONLY THING KEEPING YOU ALOFT IS YOUR *MIND*. BEYOND THAT, ALL YOU HAVE IS A TINY BACK UP MOTOR. IT REQUIRES CONSTANT FOCUS."

NNGH--

AMELIA!
AMELIA!

"AND I *LOST* MINE."

"MY GAUGES STARTED GIVING ME FUNNY READINGS."

WE ARE RUNNING NORTH AND SOUTH--

AARGH!

"I FOUND MYSELF SLIDING ALONG A STRANGE HORIZON-- THE WORLD WAS STILL THERE, BUT IT WASN'T ANY WORLD I RECOGNIZED. MY COPILOT HAD DISAPPEARED. I WAS ALONE."

...AND?

AND I THOUGHT THAT WAS *IT* FOR ME. I HAD SLIPPED BETWEEN THE SEAMS OF WHAT WAS REAL AND WHAT I *MADE* REAL.

"I FLEW FOR--WELL, FOR A VERY LONG TIME. AND THEN SOMETHING HAPPENED."

NO!

"I CAME TO THE EDGE OF THE WORLD.

"IT WAS THE *STRANGEST* THING I HAD EVER SEEN. BUT SOMEHOW I FINALLY *UNDERSTOOD* WHAT HAD HAPPENED TO ME. AND I KNEW WHAT I HAD TO DO TO GET HOME.

"I THOUGHT ABOUT WHAT THE FIRST EXPLORERS MUST HAVE DONE WHEN THEY SAILED TO MEET THE HORIZON.

"LOOK BEYOND IT TO THE *NEW* HORIZON...

"...AND MAKE A NEW MAP."

"POOF. THERE I WAS. BACK.

"BUT NOT OUT OF DANGER.

SON OF A *BITCH!*

"THE SKIES HAD GOTTEN A LOT MORE *CROWDED* WHILE I WAS AWAY.

"AND THAT WASN'T THE *ONLY* THING THAT HAD CHANGED.

I'D BEEN LOST *FORTY-SIX* YEARS, BUT I HADN'T AGED A DAY. I DECIDED TO LIE LOW--I DRIFTED. IN THE EARLY 90'S, I HELPED BUILD SKY 1. BEEN HERE EVER SINCE.

UN-FUCKING-BELIEVABLE.

SO WHAT HAPPENS NOW?

NOW YOU LEARN. LET'S GET BACK TO THE PALACE AND LOOK AT A *MAP.*

THE MOST IMPORTANT THING TO REMEMBER ABOUT HYPERPRAXIS IS THIS.

SYMBOLS EXIST INDEPENDENTLY OF THEIR *MEANINGS.* IN OTHER WORDS, THE MAP--

--IS THE *TERRITORY.*

WHO TOLD YOU *THAT?*

ZAYN. THE GUY WE'RE *LOOKING* FOR.

HEY! IT'S *BACK!*

WHAT'S BACK?

NARIMAR (disputed)

NARIMAR! IT'S LIKE IT NEVER DISAPPEARED...

DISAPPEARED? YOU LOST ME, HONEY.

OKAY. *FIFTY YEARS* AGO, THEY TOOK THIS PLACE OFF ALL THE MAPS AND GAVE THE LAND THAT BELONGED TO NARIMAR TO OTHER PEOPLE.

ONLY NARIMAR WENT ON *EXISTING*-- BUT YOU COULDN'T GO THERE, AND THE PEOPLE THERE COULDN'T LEAVE.

BUT SOMEHOW ZAYN--THE GUY WITH THE DEVICE--ENDED UP THERE, AND THE ETESIANS FOLLOWED HIM, AND I FOLLOWED THEM.

AND NOW THAT WE'RE *ALL* BACK, NARIMAR IS ON THE MAPS AGAIN!

I AIN'T NEVER HEARD OF A WHOLE *COUNTRY* BEIN' REINTERPRETED LIKE THAT.

IT COULD BE THE *DEVICE* IS MORE POWERFUL THAN WE THOUGHT.

...OR *BLYTHE* IS MORE POWERFUL THAN SHE THINKS.

EITHER WAY, YOU'RE MORE THAN READY FOR YOUR FIRST *HANDS-ON* FLYING LESSON.

IF YOU NEED US, WE'LL BE IN THE ENGINE ROOM.

DON'T YOU GIRLS GO RUININ' MY BEAUTIFUL BOAT!

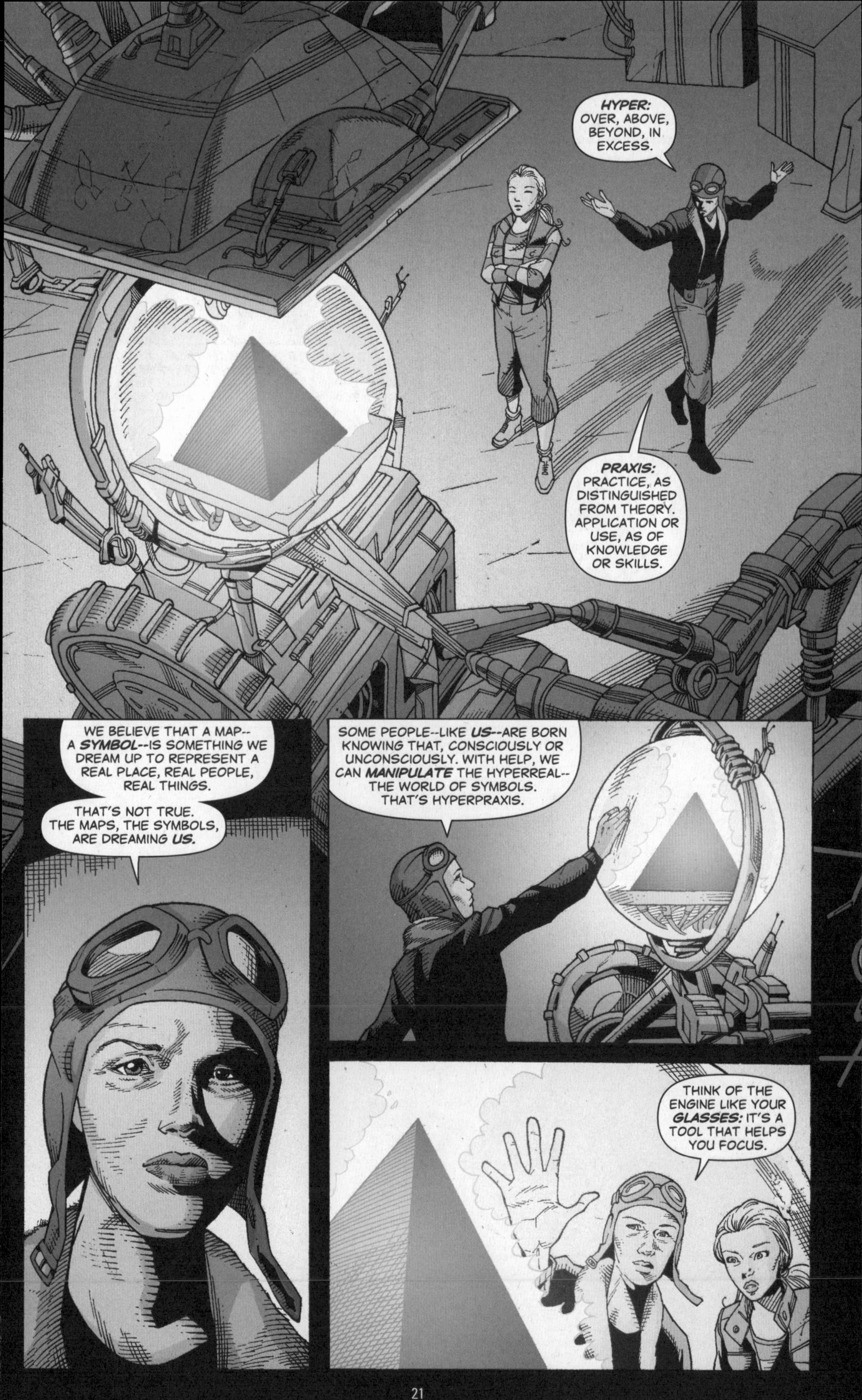
HYPER: OVER, ABOVE, BEYOND, IN EXCESS.
PRAXIS: PRACTICE, AS DISTINGUISHED FROM THEORY. APPLICATION OR USE, AS OF KNOWLEDGE OR SKILLS.
WE BELIEVE THAT A MAP-- A SYMBOL--IS SOMETHING WE DREAM UP TO REPRESENT A REAL PLACE, REAL PEOPLE, REAL THINGS.
THAT'S NOT TRUE. THE MAPS, THE SYMBOLS, ARE DREAMING US.
SOME PEOPLE--LIKE US--ARE BORN KNOWING THAT, CONSCIOUSLY OR UNCONSCIOUSLY. WITH HELP, WE CAN MANIPULATE THE HYPERREAL-- THE WORLD OF SYMBOLS. THAT'S HYPERPRAXIS.
THINK OF THE ENGINE LIKE YOUR GLASSES: IT'S A TOOL THAT HELPS YOU FOCUS.

NOW YOU'RE GOING TO MOVE THE PALACE. MAKE YOURSELF QUIET, AND THINK OF THE *ENGINE*.

DO I HAVE TO *TOUCH* IT OR SOMETHING?

NO. AT FIRST IT HELPS TO BE CLOSE TO IT, BUT WHEN YOU GET GOOD AT THIS YOU WON'T EVEN NEED THAT.

"THE UNIVERSE IS *MECHANICAL*. A MACHINE MADE UP OF *REPRESENTATIONS*. DON'T THINK OF MOVING THE PALACE. THINK OF REINTERPRETING WHAT LIES AROUND IT."

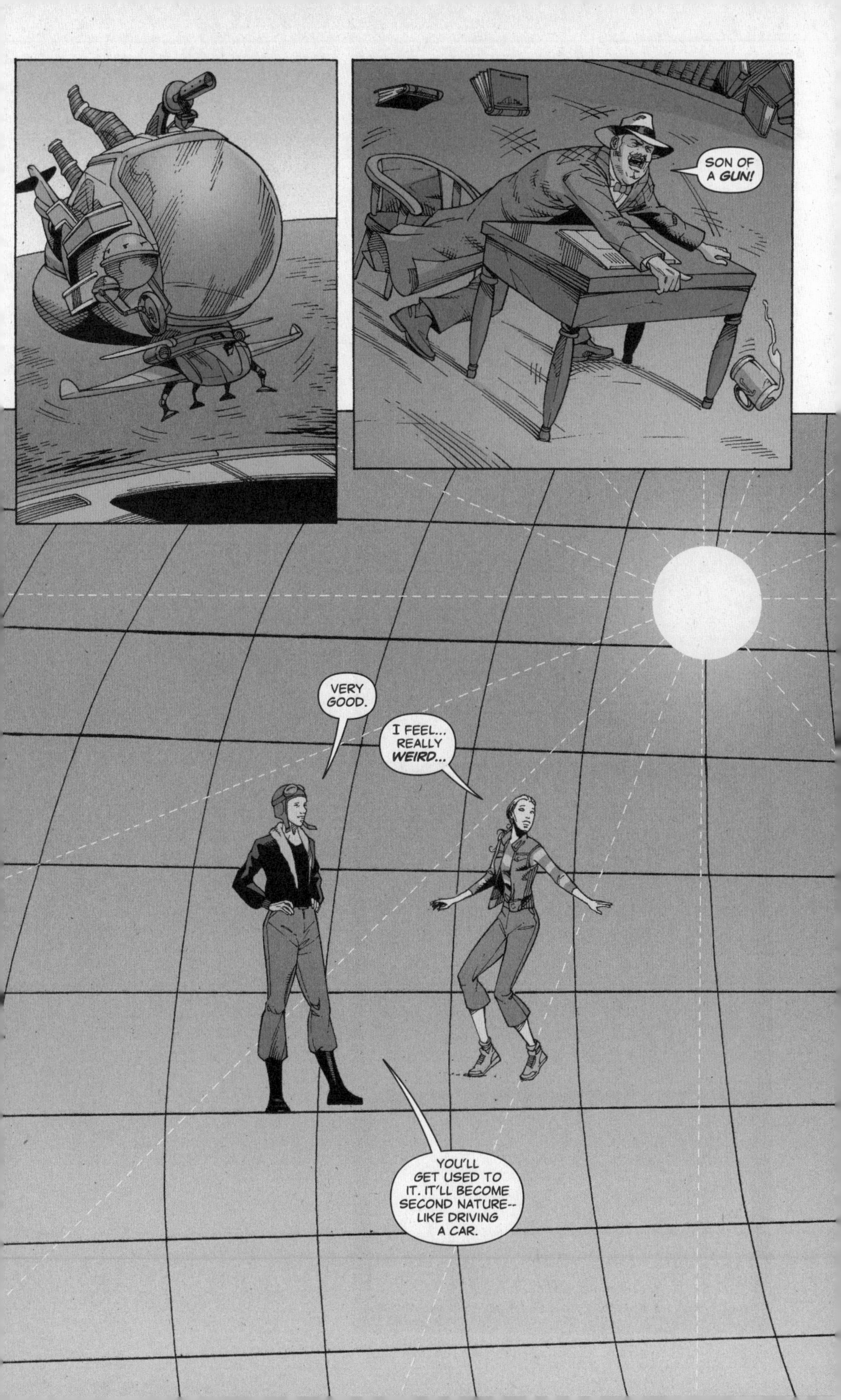
SON OF A GUN!
VERY GOOD.
I FEEL... REALLY WEIRD...
YOU'LL GET USED TO IT. IT'LL BECOME SECOND NATURE-- LIKE DRIVING A CAR.

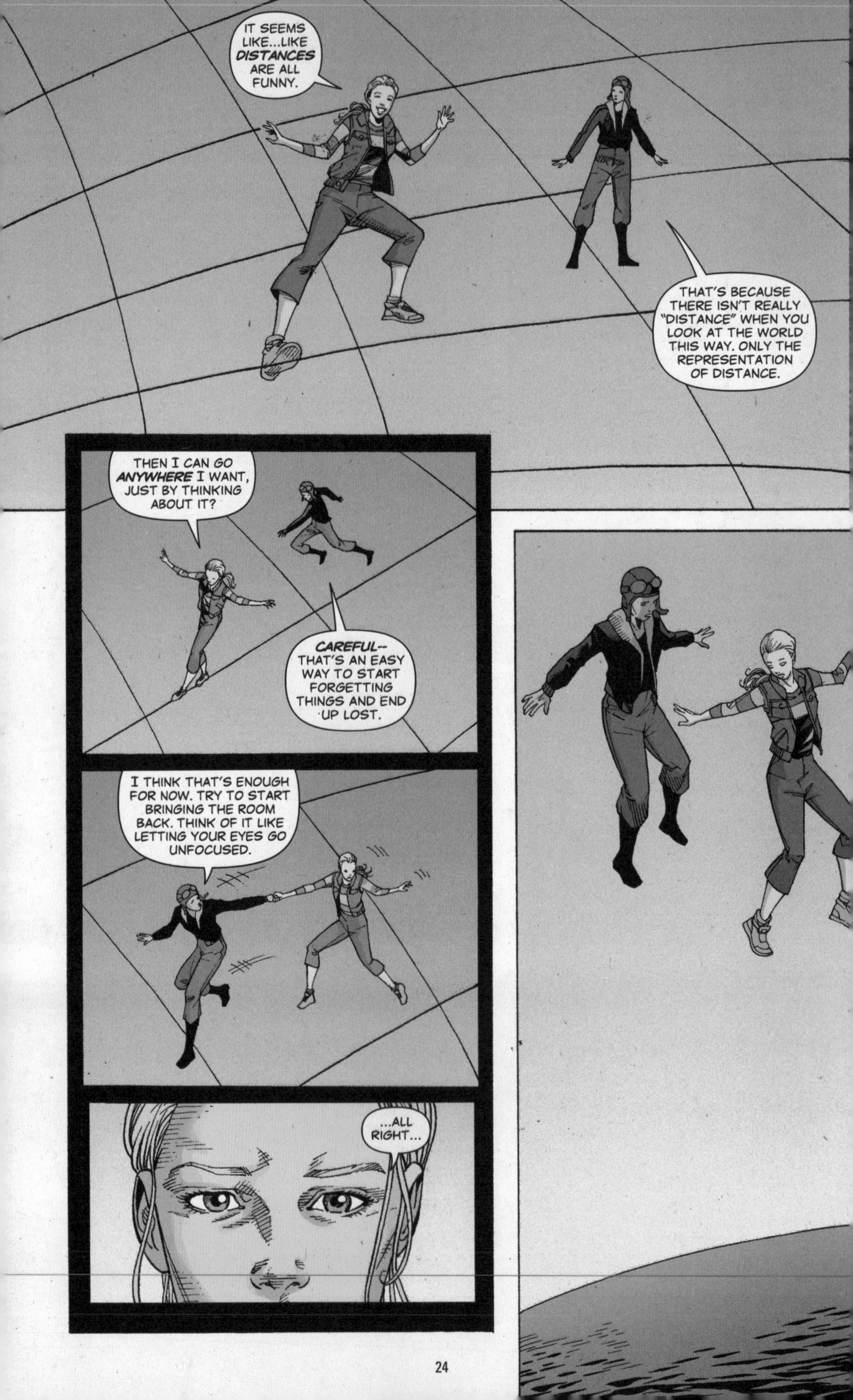
IT SEEMS LIKE...LIKE DISTANCES ARE ALL FUNNY.
THAT'S BECAUSE THERE ISN'T REALLY "DISTANCE" WHEN YOU LOOK AT THE WORLD THIS WAY. ONLY THE REPRESENTATION OF DISTANCE.
THEN I CAN GO ANYWHERE I WANT, JUST BY THINKING ABOUT IT?
CAREFUL-- THAT'S AN EASY WAY TO START FORGETTING THINGS AND END UP LOST.
I THINK THAT'S ENOUGH FOR NOW. TRY TO START BRINGING THE ROOM BACK. THINK OF IT LIKE LETTING YOUR EYES GO UNFOCUSED.
...ALL RIGHT...

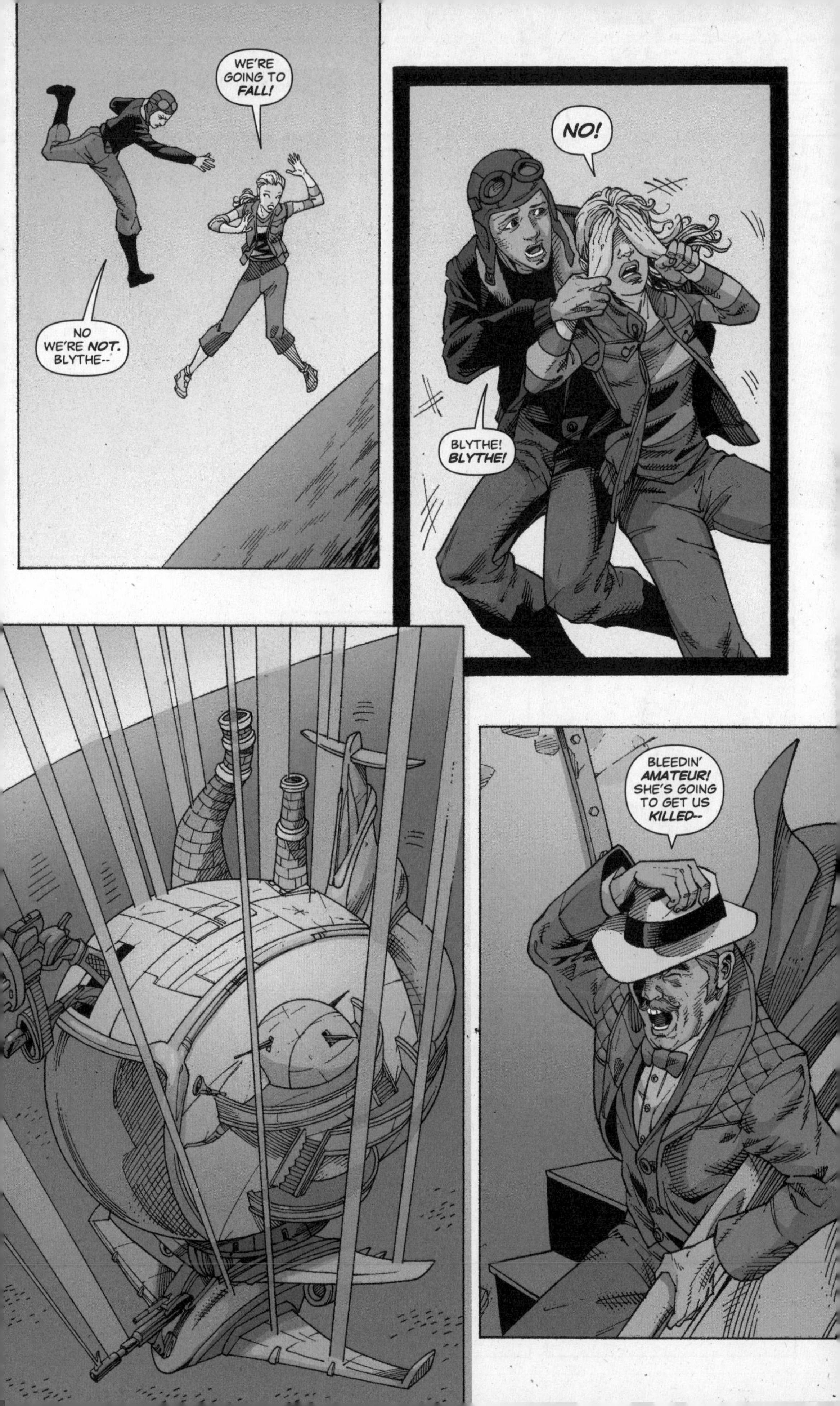
WE'RE GOING TO **FALL!**
NO WE'RE **NOT.** BLYTHE--
NO!
BLYTHE! **BLYTHE!**
BLEEDIN' **AMATEUR!** SHE'S GOING TO GET US **KILLED--**

DAMMIT EARHART!

SHE PANICKED--

OF COURSE SHE PANICKED! SHE'S AFRAID OF *HEIGHTS!*

STOP, MAKE IT STOP--

AREN'T YOU GLAD THIS ISN'T A SALMAN RUSHDIE NOVEL?

ZAYN! YOU'VE GOT TO HELP ME--

WHY? YOU'RE NOT IN DANGER.

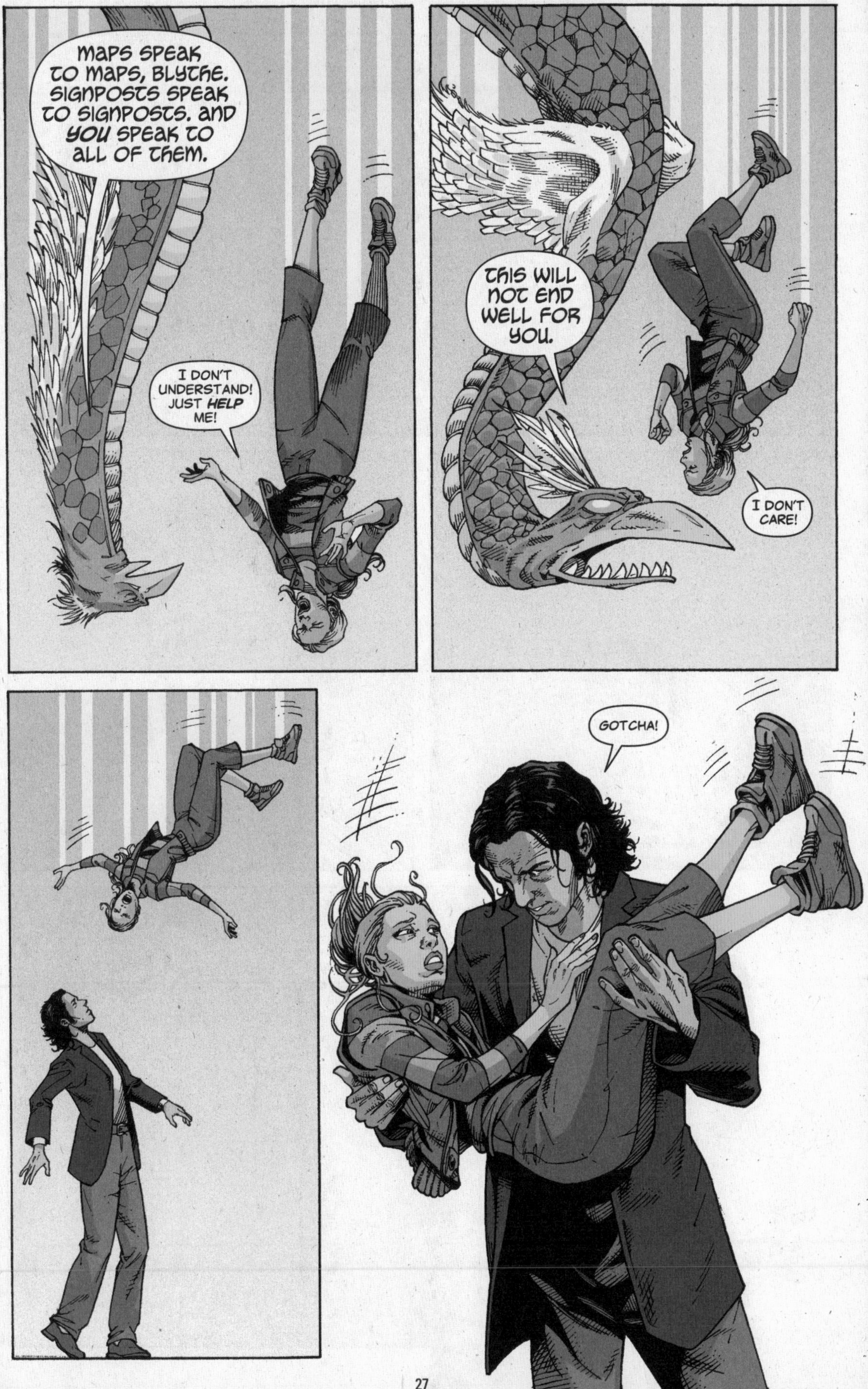
MAPS SPEAK TO MAPS, BLYTHE. SIGNPOSTS SPEAK TO SIGNPOSTS. AND YOU SPEAK TO ALL OF THEM.
I DON'T UNDERSTAND! JUST HELP ME!
THIS WILL NOT END WELL FOR YOU.
I DON'T CARE!
GOTCHA!

NN!

WHAT THE FUCK...WHAT'S GOING ON?

ZAYN! WAYNAK YA HABIBI?

AAH!

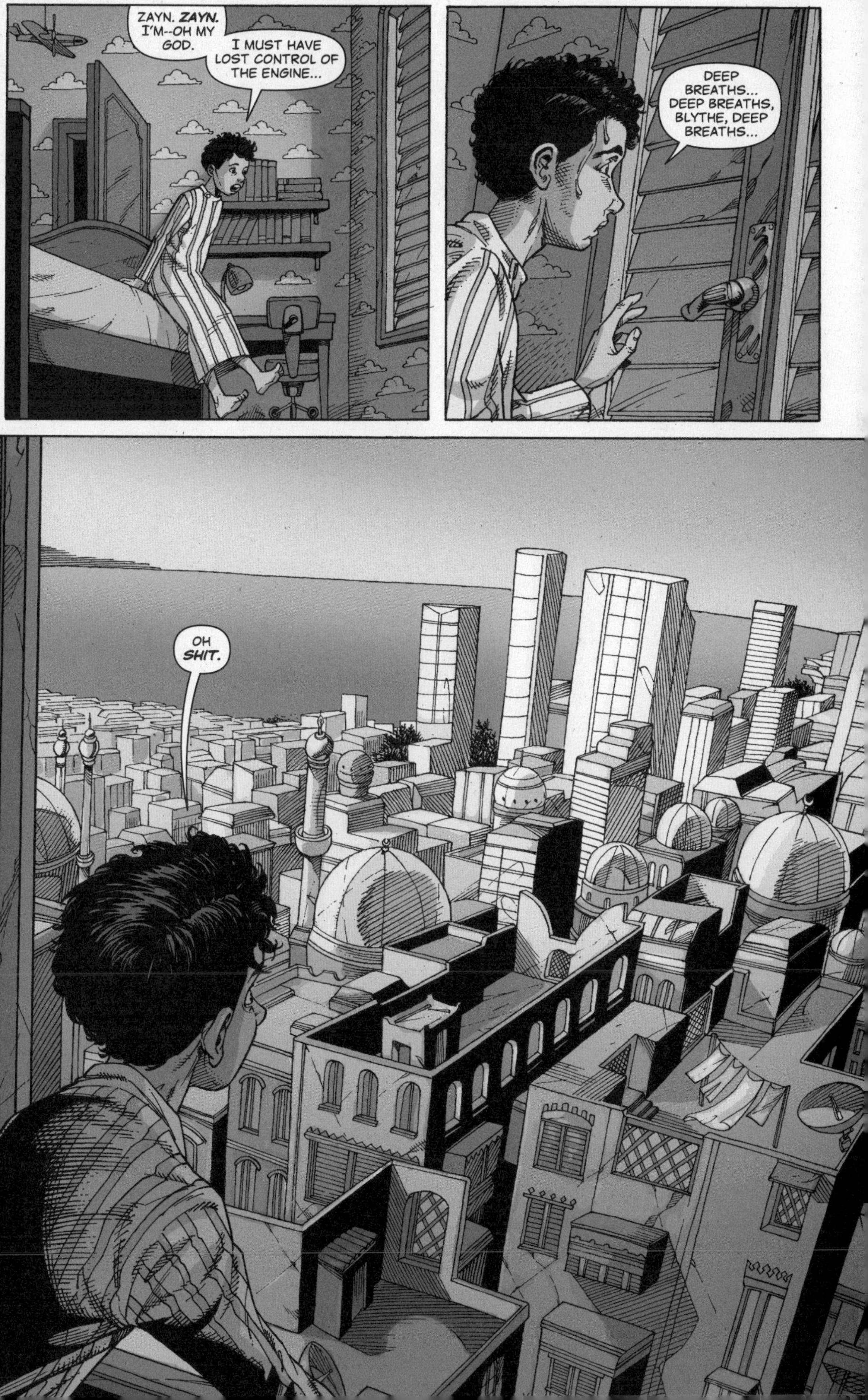
ZAYN. ZAYN. I'M--OH MY GOD.
I MUST HAVE LOST CONTROL OF THE ENGINE...
DEEP BREATHS... DEEP BREATHS, BLYTHE, DEEP BREATHS...
OH SHIT.

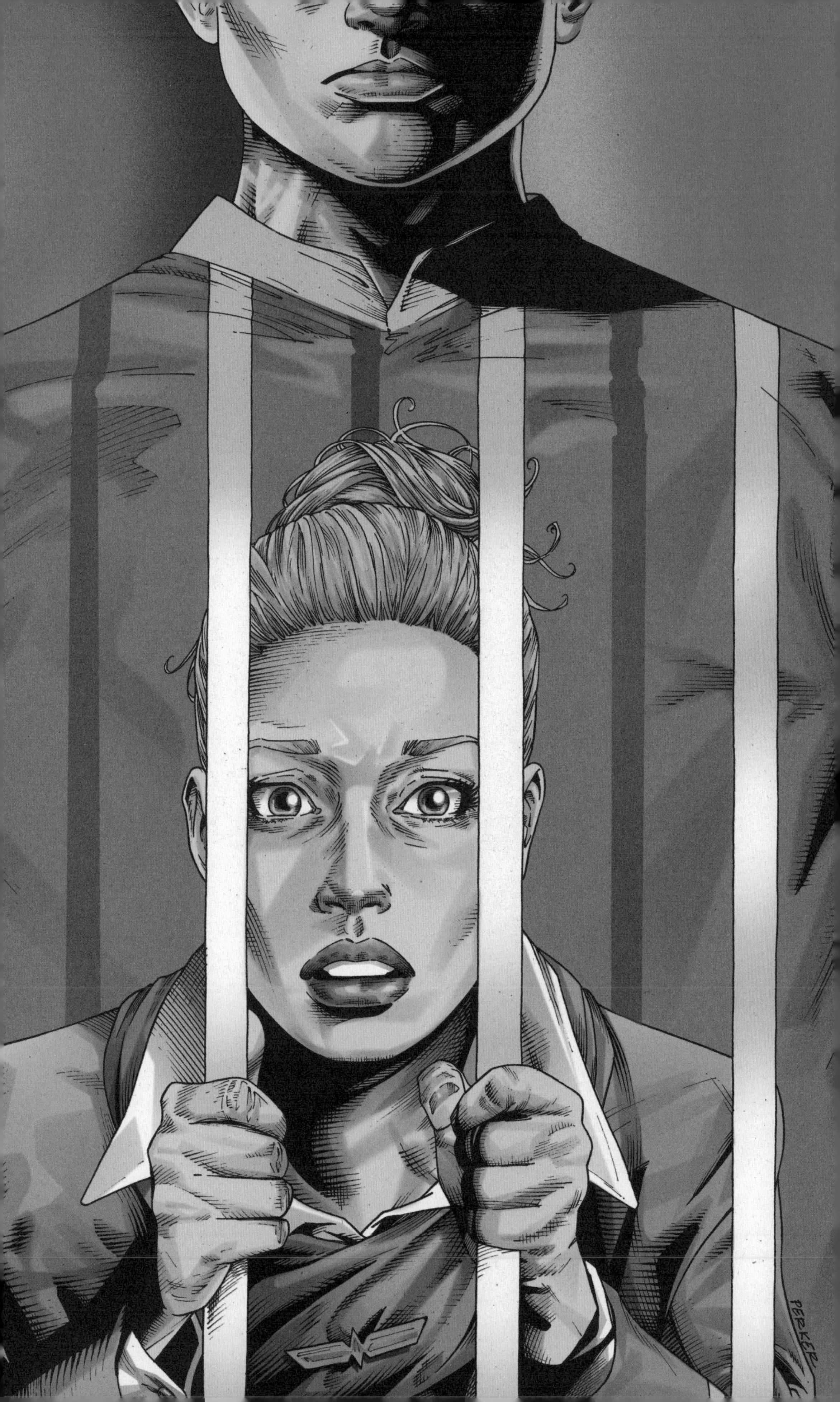
PERKER

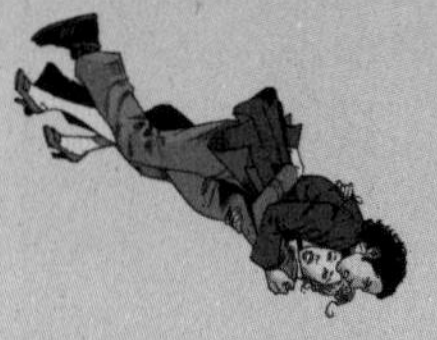

THE PICTURE OF ZAYN AL HARRANI

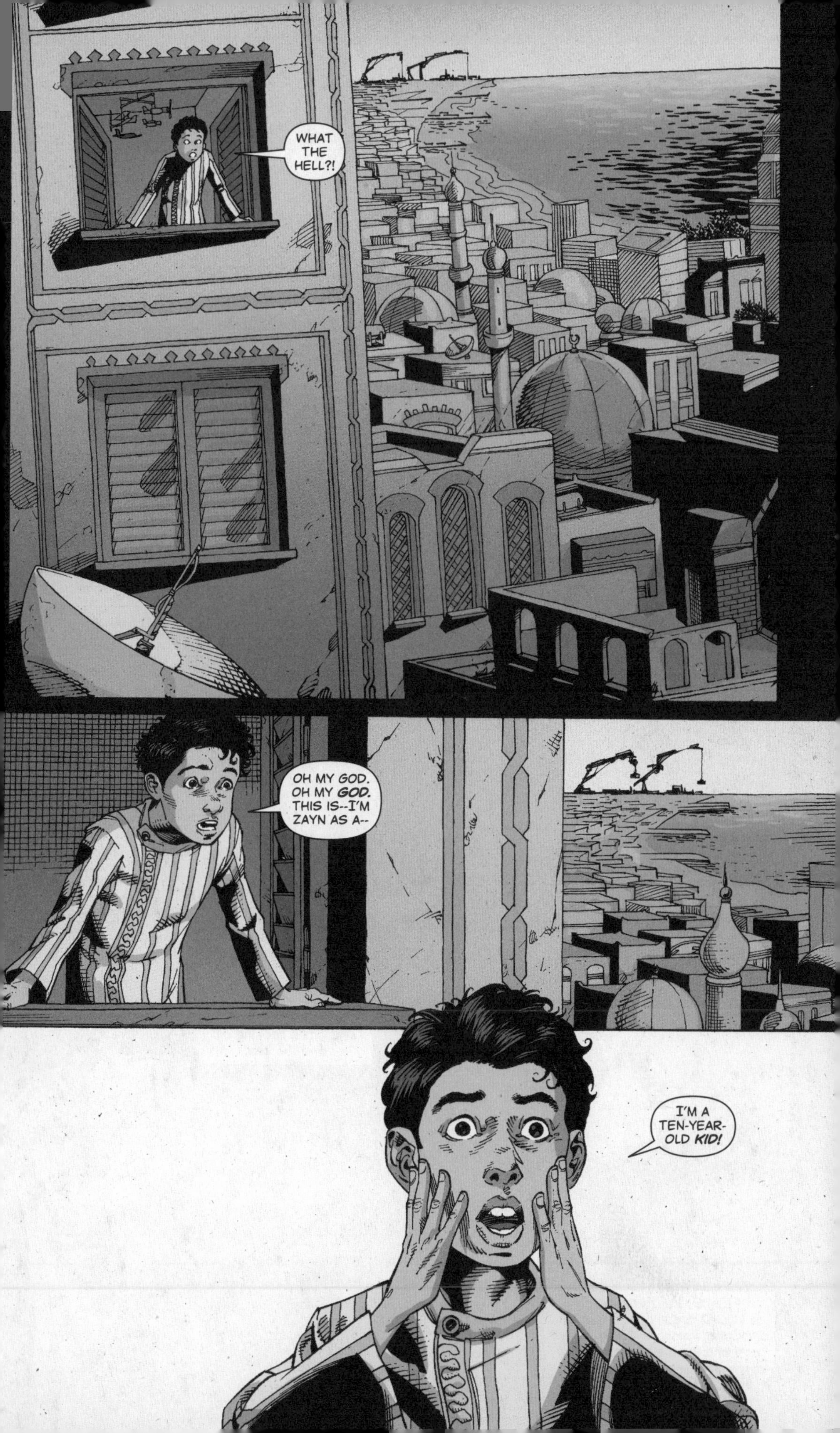
WHAT THE HELL?!
OH MY GOD. OH MY **GOD.** THIS IS--I'M ZAYN AS A--
I'M A TEN-YEAR-OLD **KID!**

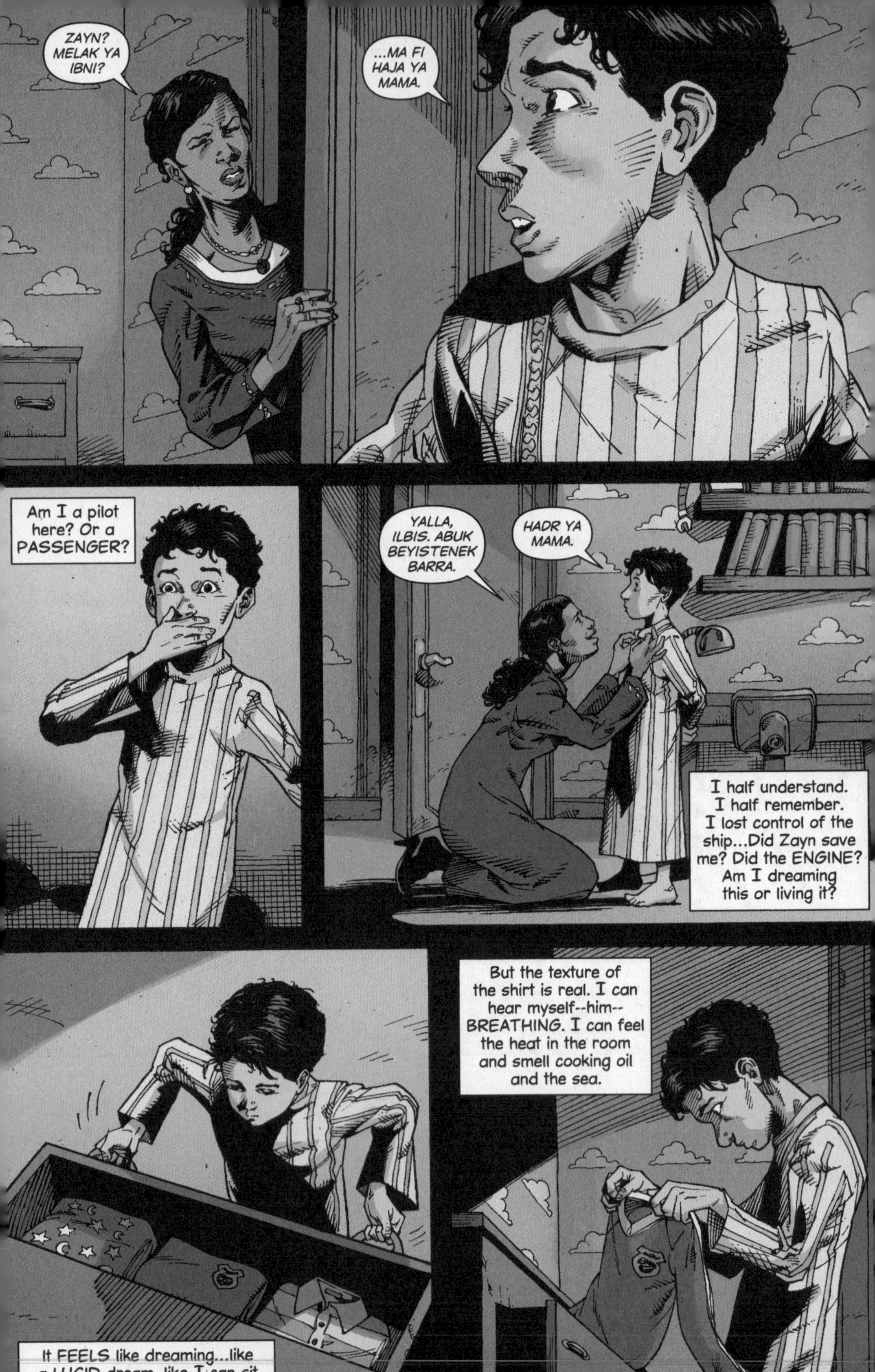
ZAYN? MELAK YA IBNI?
...MA FI HAJA YA MAMA.
Am I a pilot here? Or a PASSENGER?
YALLA, ILBIS. ABUK BEYISTENEK BARRA.
HADR YA MAMA.
I half understand. I half remember. I lost control of the ship...Did Zayn save me? Did the ENGINE? Am I dreaming this or living it?
It FEELS like dreaming...like a LUCID dream, like I can sit back and watch, or lift my finger and change the whole scene...
But the texture of the shirt is real. I can hear myself--him--BREATHING. I can feel the heat in the room and smell cooking oil and the sea.

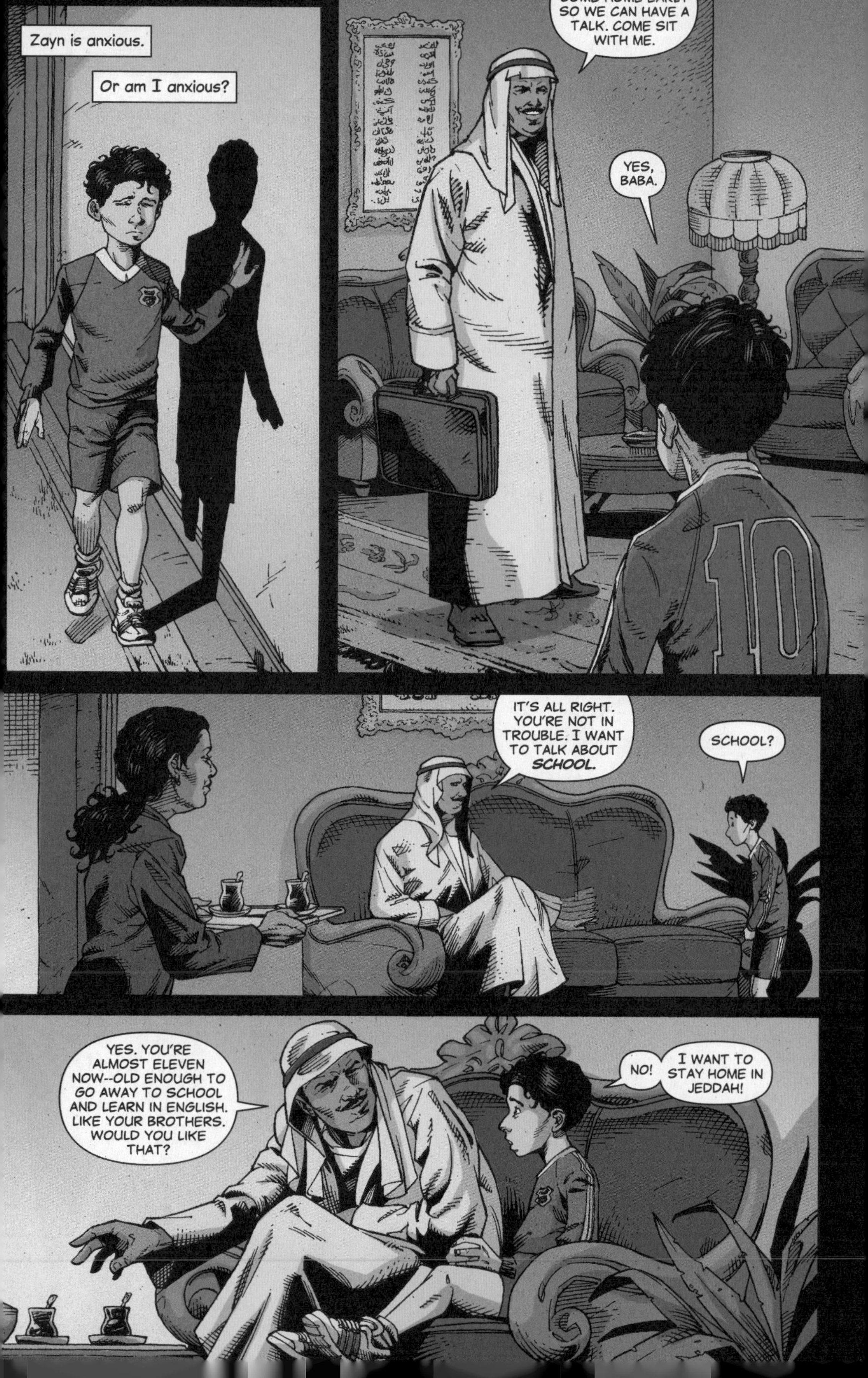
Zayn is anxious.
Or am I anxious?
ZAYN, MY SON. I'VE COME HOME EARLY SO WE CAN HAVE A TALK. COME SIT WITH ME.
YES, BABA.
IT'S ALL RIGHT. YOU'RE NOT IN TROUBLE. I WANT TO TALK ABOUT SCHOOL.
SCHOOL?
YES. YOU'RE ALMOST ELEVEN NOW--OLD ENOUGH TO GO AWAY TO SCHOOL AND LEARN IN ENGLISH. LIKE YOUR BROTHERS. WOULD YOU LIKE THAT?
NO!
I WANT TO STAY HOME IN JEDDAH!

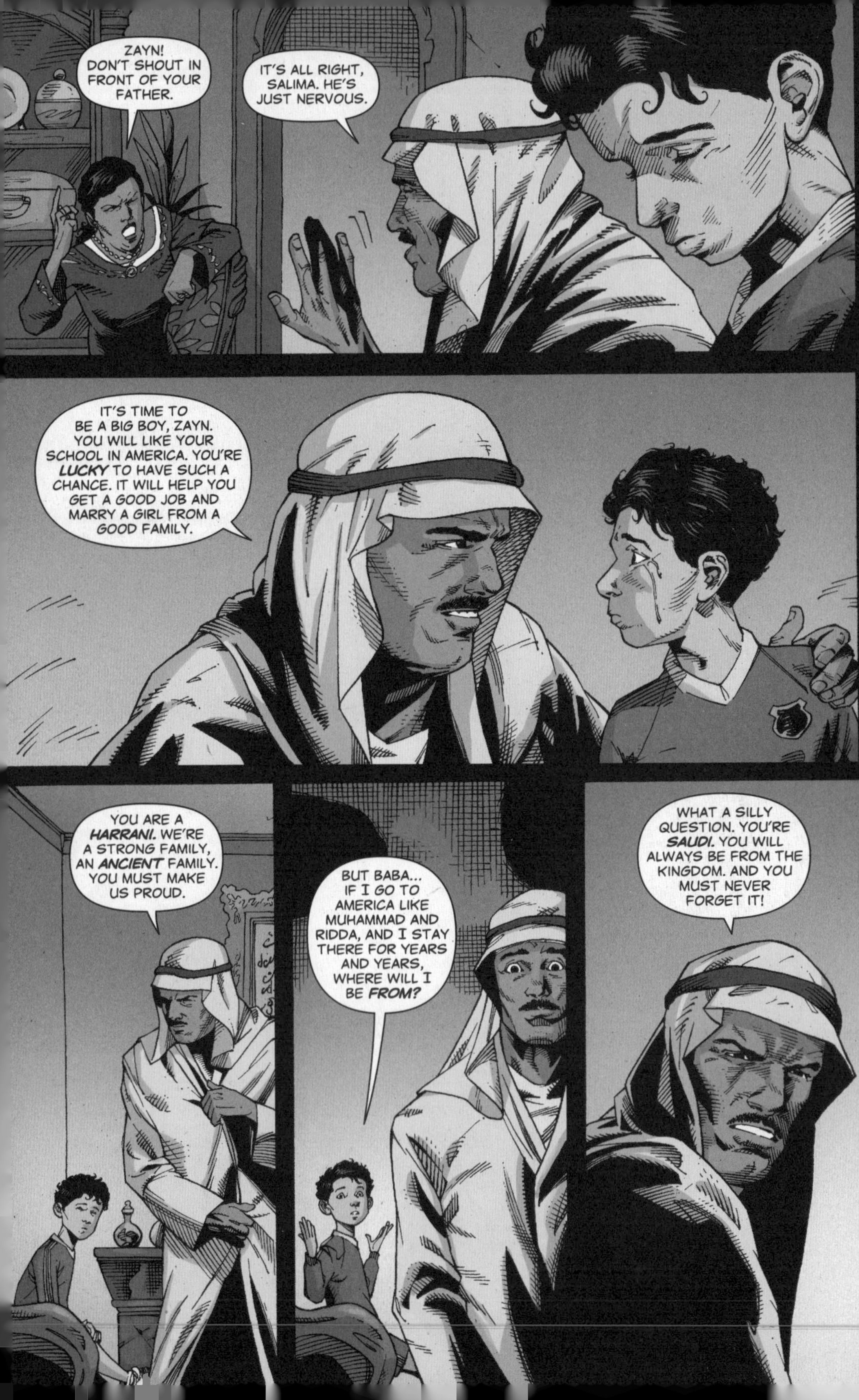
ZAYN! DON'T SHOUT IN FRONT OF YOUR FATHER.
IT'S ALL RIGHT, SALIMA. HE'S JUST NERVOUS.
IT'S TIME TO BE A BIG BOY, ZAYN. YOU WILL LIKE YOUR SCHOOL IN AMERICA. YOU'RE LUCKY TO HAVE SUCH A CHANCE. IT WILL HELP YOU GET A GOOD JOB AND MARRY A GIRL FROM A GOOD FAMILY.
YOU ARE A HARRANI. WE'RE A STRONG FAMILY, AN ANCIENT FAMILY. YOU MUST MAKE US PROUD.
BUT BABA... IF I GO TO AMERICA LIKE MUHAMMAD AND RIDDA, AND I STAY THERE FOR YEARS AND YEARS, WHERE WILL I BE FROM?
WHAT A SILLY QUESTION. YOU'RE SAUDI. YOU WILL ALWAYS BE FROM THE KINGDOM. AND YOU MUST NEVER FORGET IT!

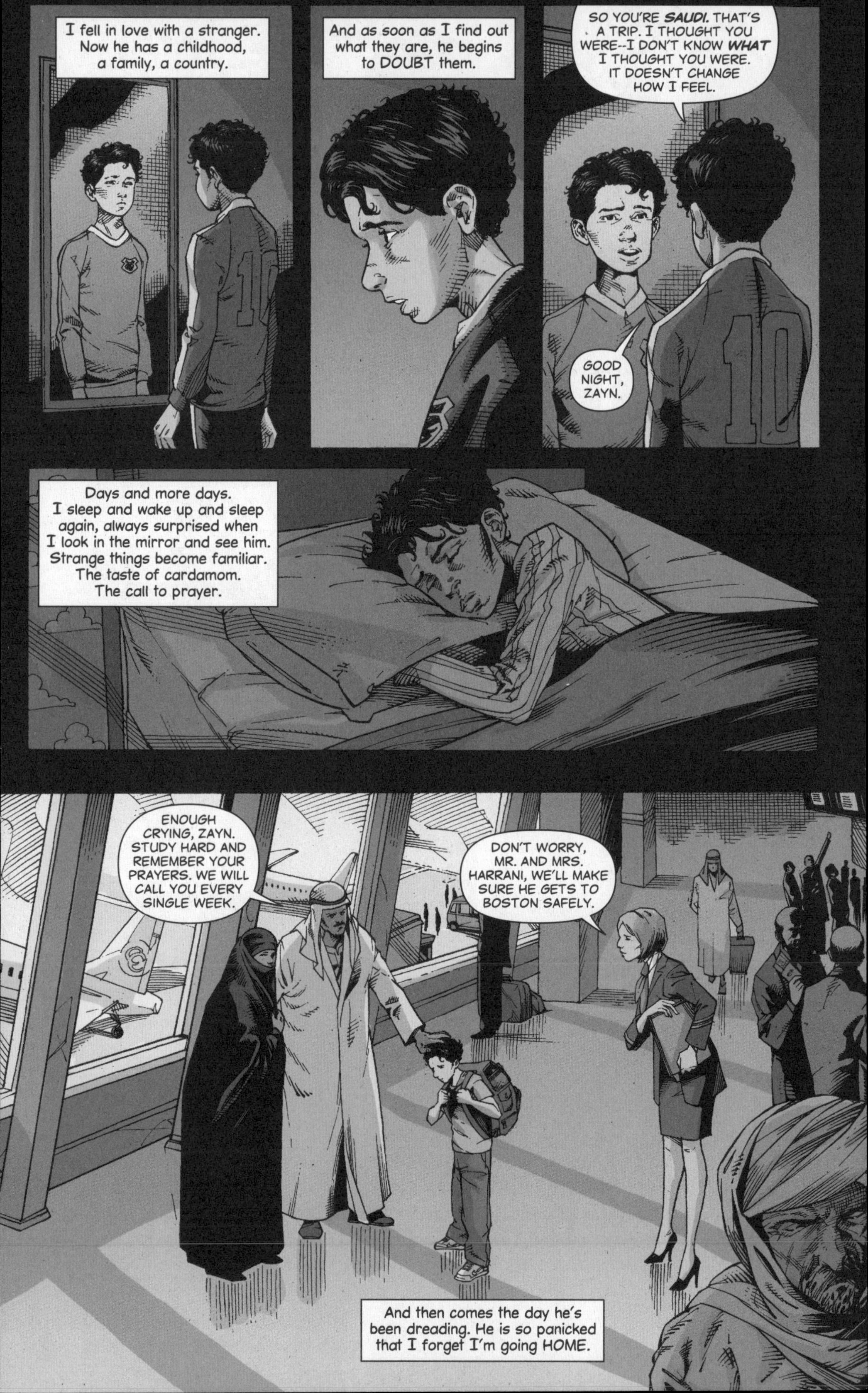
I fell in love with a stranger. Now he has a childhood, a family, a country.
And as soon as I find out what they are, he begins to DOUBT them.
SO YOU'RE SAUDI. THAT'S A TRIP. I THOUGHT YOU WERE--I DON'T KNOW WHAT I THOUGHT YOU WERE. IT DOESN'T CHANGE HOW I FEEL.
GOOD NIGHT, ZAYN.
Days and more days. I sleep and wake up and sleep again, always surprised when I look in the mirror and see him. Strange things become familiar. The taste of cardamom. The call to prayer.
ENOUGH CRYING, ZAYN. STUDY HARD AND REMEMBER YOUR PRAYERS. WE WILL CALL YOU EVERY SINGLE WEEK.
DON'T WORRY, MR. AND MRS. HARRANI, WE'LL MAKE SURE HE GETS TO BOSTON SAFELY.
And then comes the day he's been dreading. He is so panicked that I forget I'm going HOME.

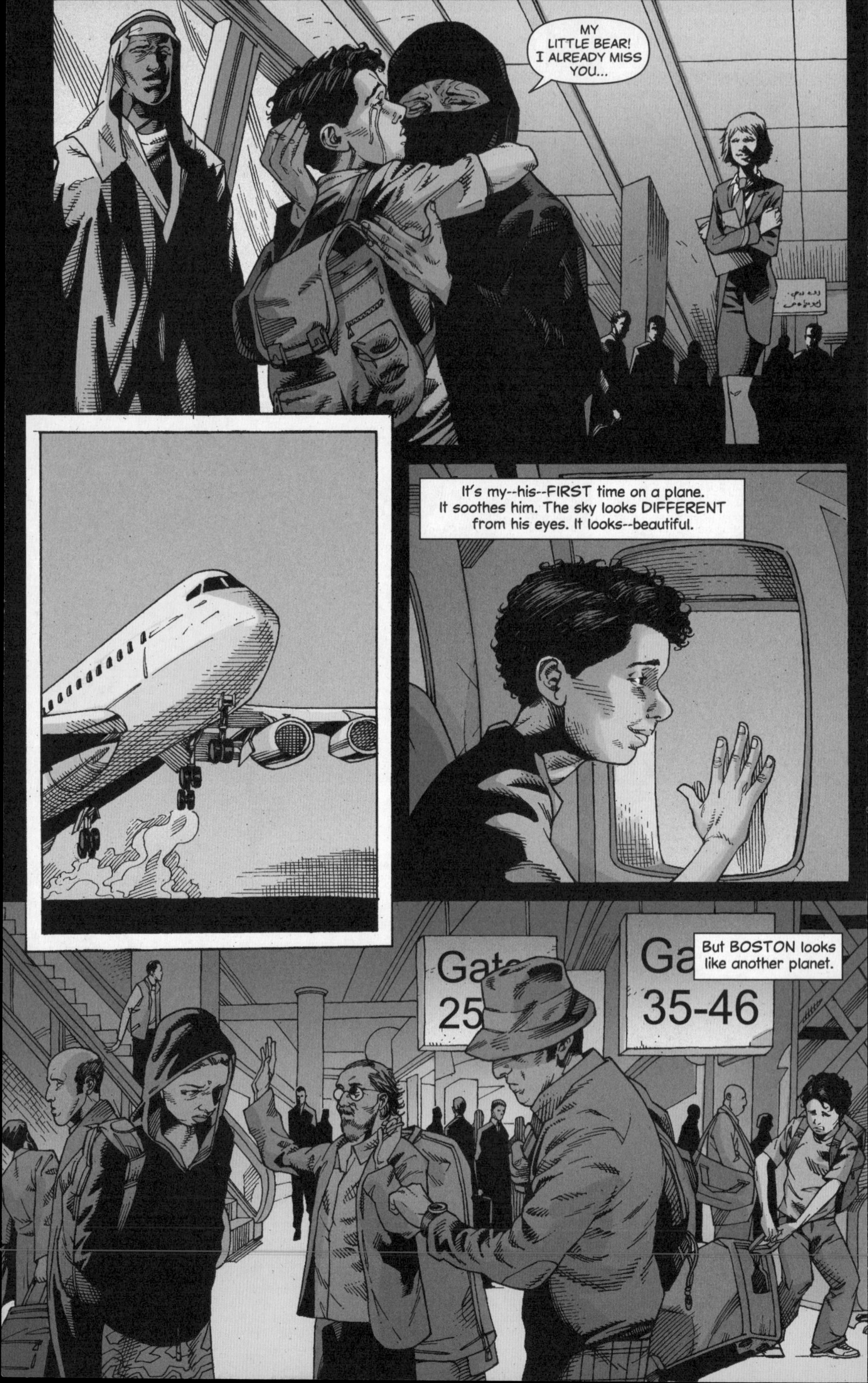
MY LITTLE BEAR! I ALREADY MISS YOU...
It's my--his--FIRST time on a plane. It soothes him. The sky looks DIFFERENT from his eyes. It looks--beautiful.
But BOSTON looks like another planet.
Ga
35-46

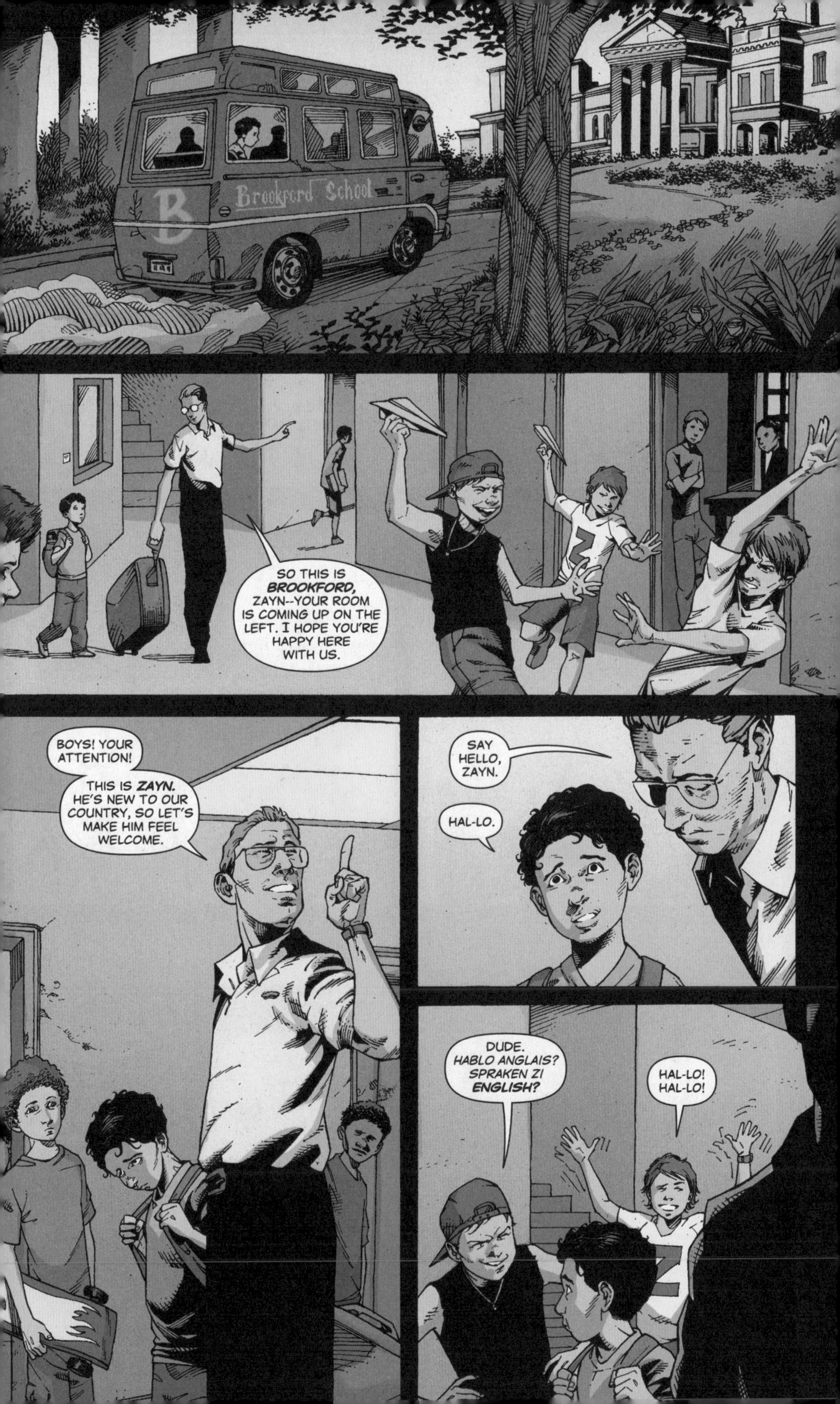
Brookford School
SO THIS IS BROOKFORD, ZAYN--YOUR ROOM IS COMING UP ON THE LEFT. I HOPE YOU'RE HAPPY HERE WITH US.
BOYS! YOUR ATTENTION!
THIS IS ZAYN. HE'S NEW TO OUR COUNTRY, SO LET'S MAKE HIM FEEL WELCOME.
SAY HELLO, ZAYN.
HAL-LO.
DUDE. HABLO ANGLAIS? SPRAKEN ZI ENGLISH?
HAL-LO! HAL-LO!

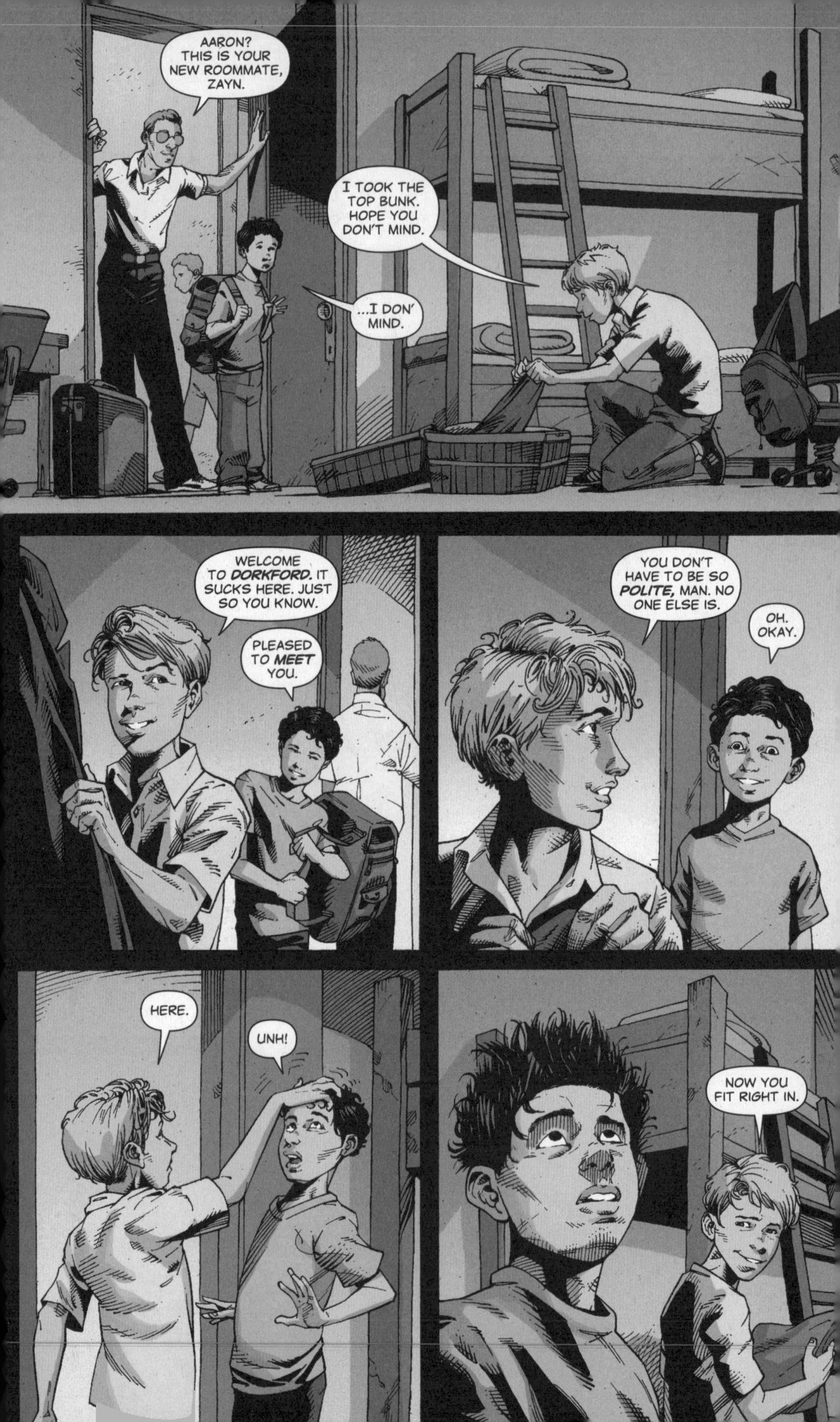

AARON? THIS IS YOUR NEW ROOMMATE, ZAYN.
I TOOK THE TOP BUNK. HOPE YOU DON'T MIND.
...I DON' MIND.
WELCOME TO DORKFORD. IT SUCKS HERE. JUST SO YOU KNOW.
PLEASED TO MEET YOU.
YOU DON'T HAVE TO BE SO POLITE, MAN. NO ONE ELSE IS.
OH. OKAY.
HERE.
UNH!
NOW YOU FIT RIGHT IN.

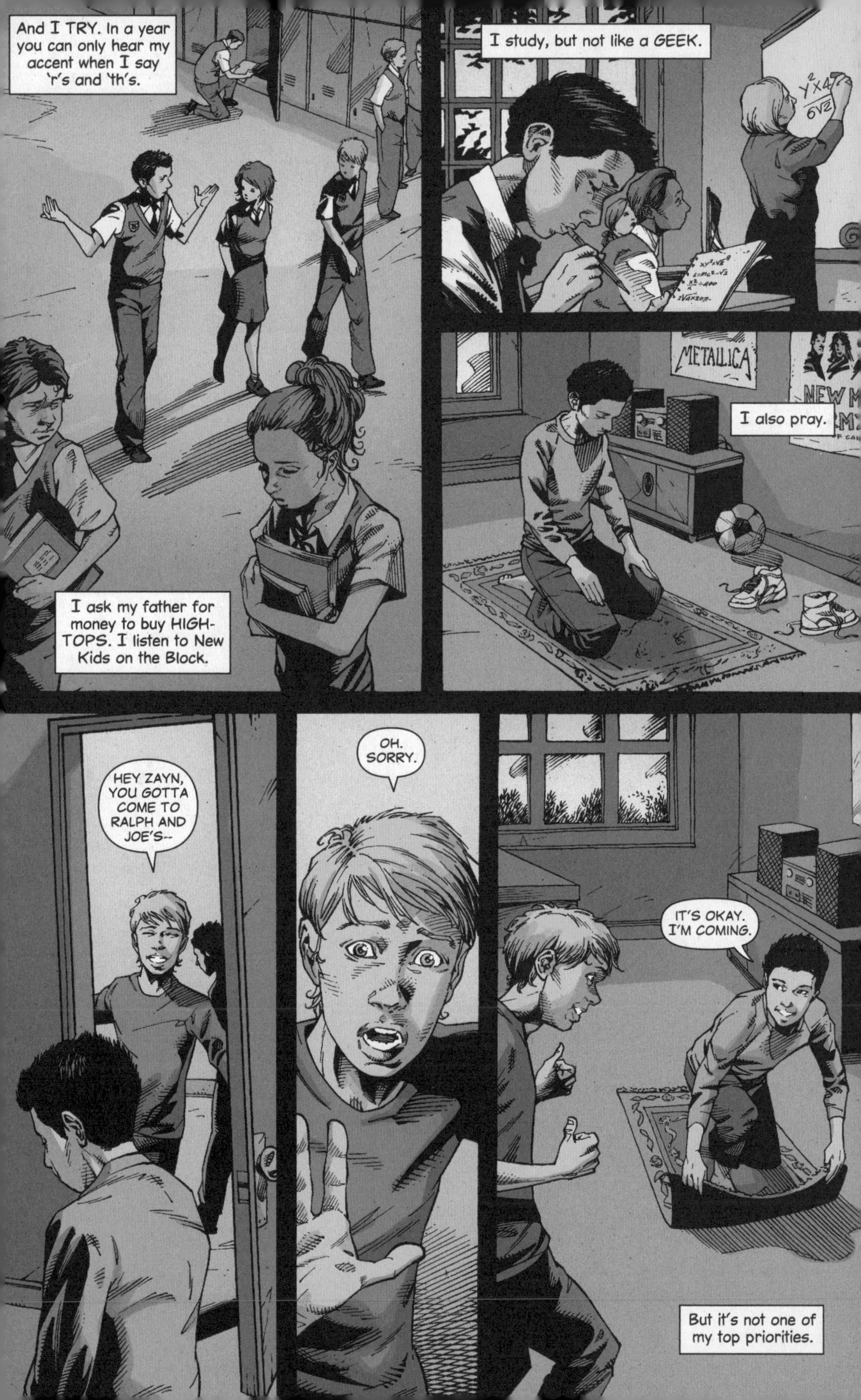
And I TRY. In a year you can only hear my accent when I say 'r's and 'th's.
I ask my father for money to buy HIGH-TOPS. I listen to New Kids on the Block.
I study, but not like a GEEK.
METALLICA
I also pray.
HEY ZAYN, YOU GOTTA COME TO RALPH AND JOE'S--
OH. SORRY.
IT'S OKAY. I'M COMING.
But it's not one of my top priorities.

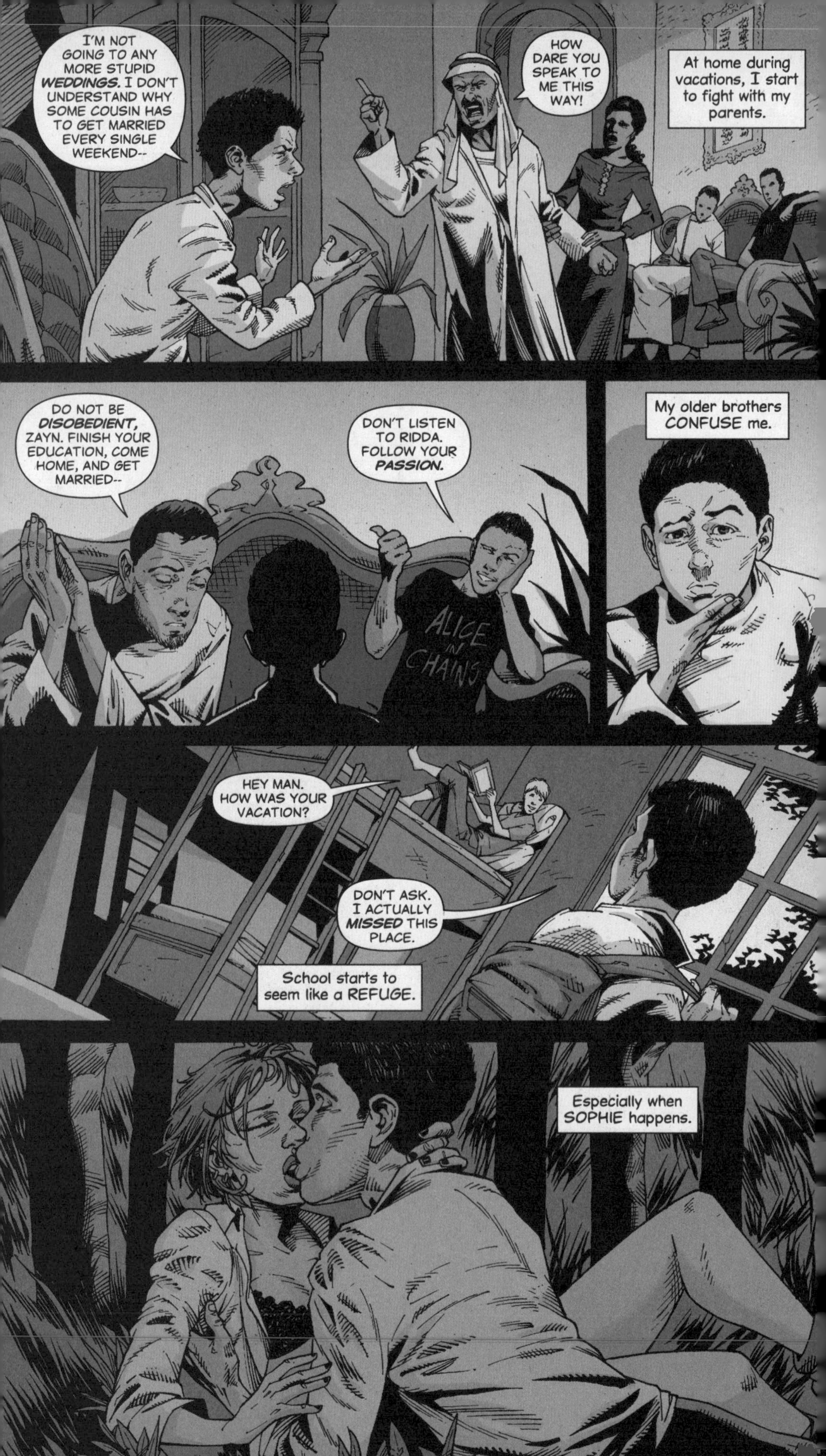
I'M NOT GOING TO ANY MORE STUPID WEDDINGS. I DON'T UNDERSTAND WHY SOME COUSIN HAS TO GET MARRIED EVERY SINGLE WEEKEND--
HOW DARE YOU SPEAK TO ME THIS WAY!
At home during vacations, I start to fight with my parents.
DO NOT BE DISOBEDIENT, ZAYN. FINISH YOUR EDUCATION, COME HOME, AND GET MARRIED--
DON'T LISTEN TO RIDDA. FOLLOW YOUR PASSION.
ALICE IN CHAINS
My older brothers CONFUSE me.
HEY MAN. HOW WAS YOUR VACATION?
DON'T ASK. I ACTUALLY MISSED THIS PLACE.
School starts to seem like a REFUGE.
Especially when SOPHIE happens.

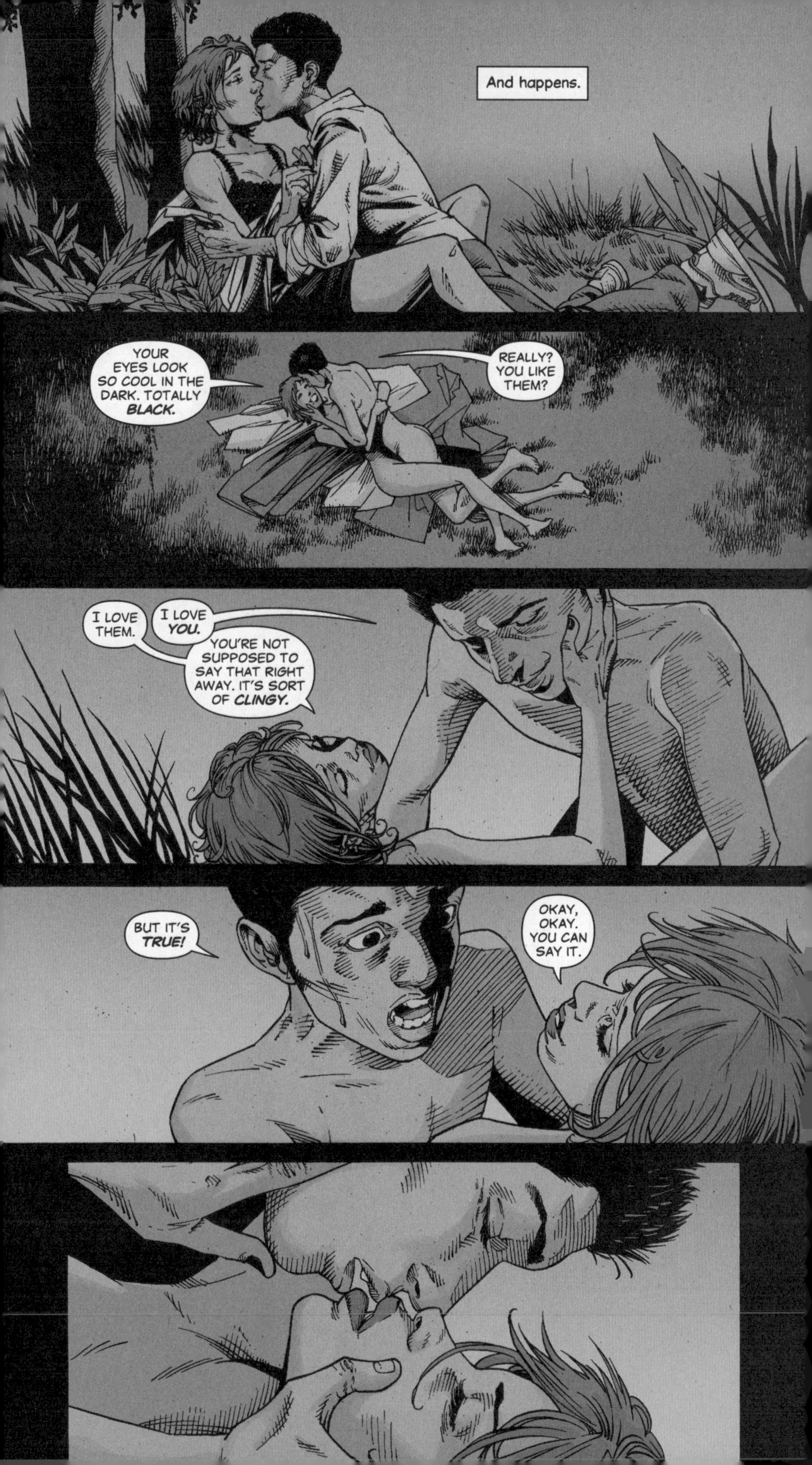

And happens.
YOUR EYES LOOK SO COOL IN THE DARK. TOTALLY BLACK.
REALLY? YOU LIKE THEM?
I LOVE THEM.
I LOVE YOU.
YOU'RE NOT SUPPOSED TO SAY THAT RIGHT AWAY. IT'S SORT OF CLINGY.
BUT IT'S TRUE!
OKAY, OKAY. YOU CAN SAY IT.

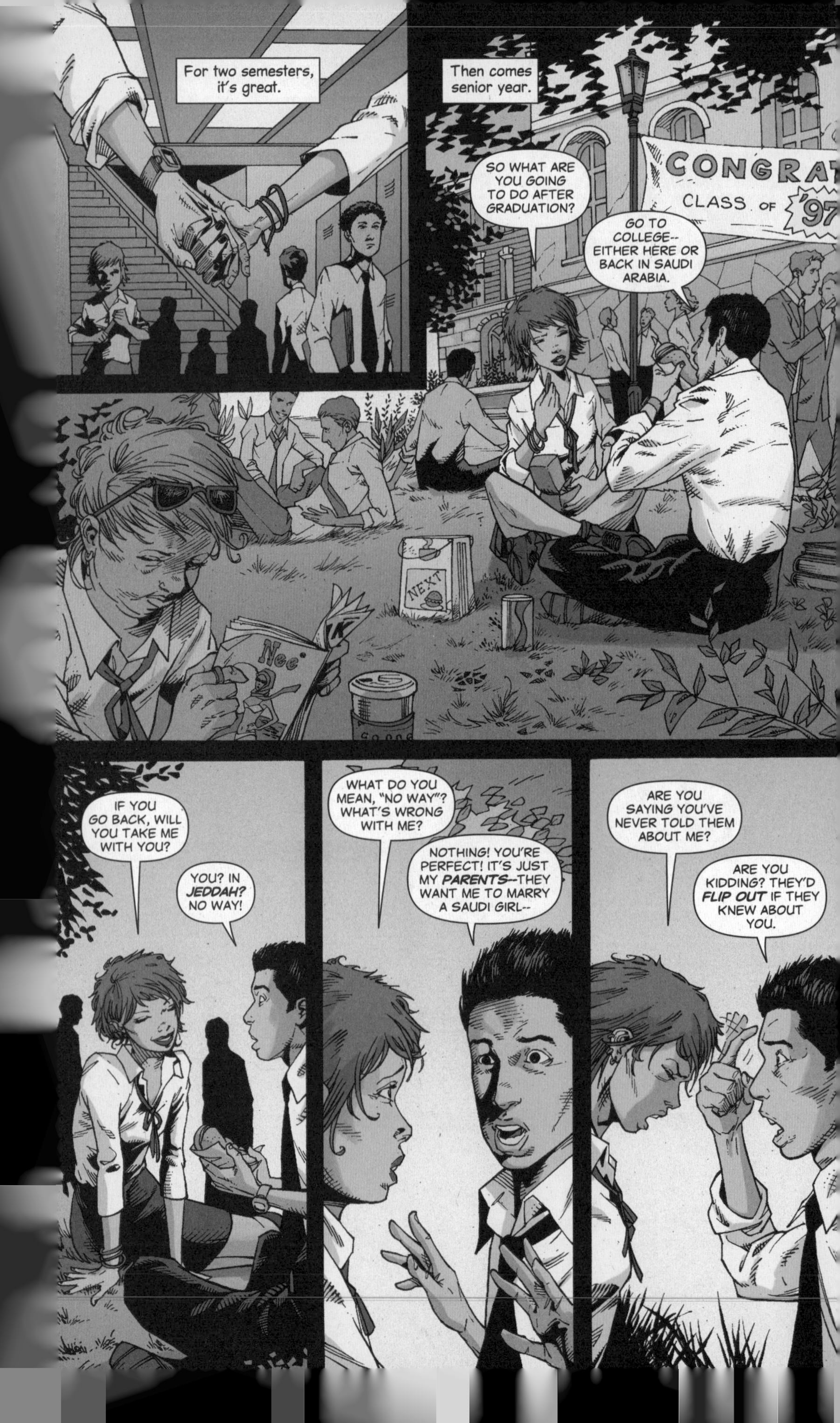
For two semesters, it's great.
Then comes senior year.
CONGRAT
CLASS OF '97
SO WHAT ARE YOU GOING TO DO AFTER GRADUATION?
GO TO COLLEGE-- EITHER HERE OR BACK IN SAUDI ARABIA.
NEXT
IF YOU GO BACK, WILL YOU TAKE ME WITH YOU?
YOU? IN *JEDDAH?* NO WAY!
WHAT DO YOU MEAN, "NO WAY"? WHAT'S WRONG WITH ME?
NOTHING! YOU'RE PERFECT! IT'S JUST MY *PARENTS*--THEY WANT ME TO MARRY A SAUDI GIRL--
ARE YOU SAYING YOU'VE NEVER TOLD THEM ABOUT ME?
ARE YOU KIDDING? THEY'D *FLIP OUT* IF THEY KNEW ABOUT YOU.

SO WHAT, I'M JUST SOME WHITE GIRL YOU'RE *SCREWING* UNTIL MOMMY AND DADDY SET YOU UP WITH A NICE *VIRGIN*?

IT'S NOT LIKE THAT. I LOVE YOU, SOPH--HOME IS JUST SO *DIFFERENT*--

IF YOU LOVE ME, WHY DON'T YOU *STICK UP* FOR ME TO YOUR PARENTS?

I *CAN'T.* THEY WOULDN'T UNDERSTAND. DON'T YOU GET IT?

I GUESS NOT, ZAYN. I GUESS I DON'T FUCKING GET IT AT ALL.

SOPH! *SOPHIE!*

After that, it's back to square one.

LOOK AT IT THIS WAY, MAN: AT LEAST YOU DON'T HAVE A B.O. PROBLEM LIKE THAT KID BRIAN.

I HAVE *SOCIAL* B.O. EVERYBODY FUCKING HATES ME.

NO THEY DON'T. THEY JUST DON'T UNDERSTAND WHERE YOU COME FROM.

45

SCREW THEM, THEN.

SATAN HAS TURNED THEM AWAY FROM THE PATH, SO THEY DO NOT FIND THE WAY TO WORSHIP GOD, WHO BRINGS TO LIGHT WHAT IS HIDDEN...

When I tell my parents I've decided to go to a MADRASSA instead of college, my father refuses to speak to me for weeks.

My mother just cries.

I WANT TO LEARN *MORE,* SHEIKH HAZIM. THERE IS SO MUCH I DON'T KNOW--

DO NOT BE *GREEDY* FOR KNOWLEDGE, ZAYN. ALL UNDERSTANDING COMES FROM GOD, AND HIS FAVOR REQUIRES *HUMILITY.*

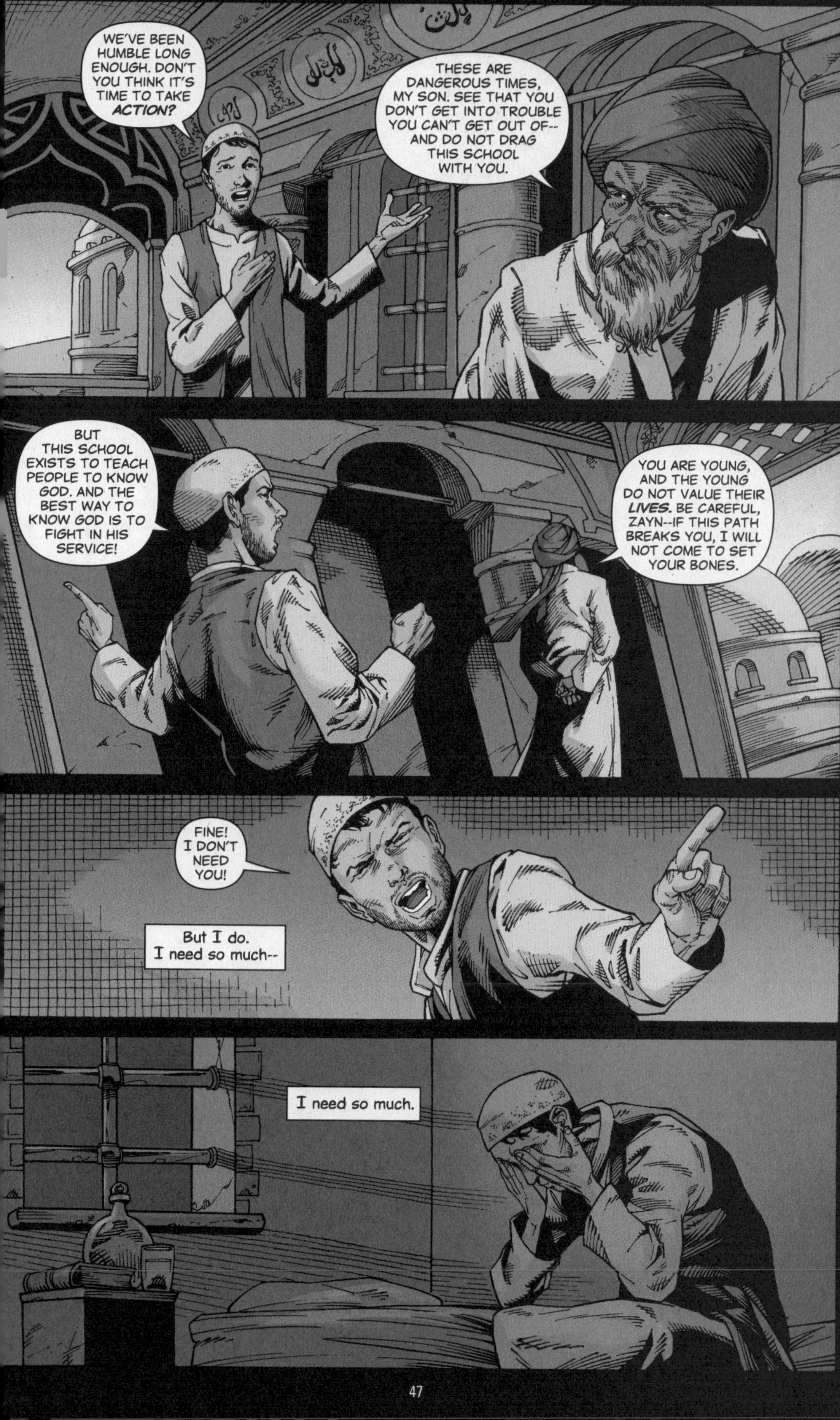
WE'VE BEEN HUMBLE LONG ENOUGH. DON'T YOU THINK IT'S TIME TO TAKE ***ACTION?***
THESE ARE DANGEROUS TIMES, MY SON. SEE THAT YOU DON'T GET INTO TROUBLE YOU CAN'T GET OUT OF-- AND DO NOT DRAG THIS SCHOOL WITH YOU.
BUT THIS SCHOOL EXISTS TO TEACH PEOPLE TO KNOW GOD. AND THE BEST WAY TO KNOW GOD IS TO FIGHT IN HIS SERVICE!
YOU ARE YOUNG, AND THE YOUNG DO NOT VALUE THEIR ***LIVES.*** BE CAREFUL, ZAYN--IF THIS PATH BREAKS YOU, I WILL NOT COME TO SET YOUR BONES.
FINE! I DON'T NEED YOU!
But I do. I need so much--
I need so much.

NNGH!

AS SALAAMU ALAYKUM, ZAYN.

WHAT IS THIS? WHO ARE YOU?

WE REPRESENT AN ORGANIZATION DEDICATED TO BRINGING *TRUE* JUSTICE TO AN UNJUST WORLD.

AN ORGANIZATION THAT HAS BEEN *WATCHING* YOU FOR QUITE AWHILE. YOU FEEL ISOLATED. YOU WANT TO TAKE ACTION. AND YOU *CAN*.

THE TIME HAS COME FOR YOU TO *JOIN* US, ZAYN. TO TAKE YOUR PLACE IN THE INTERNATIONAL CRI--

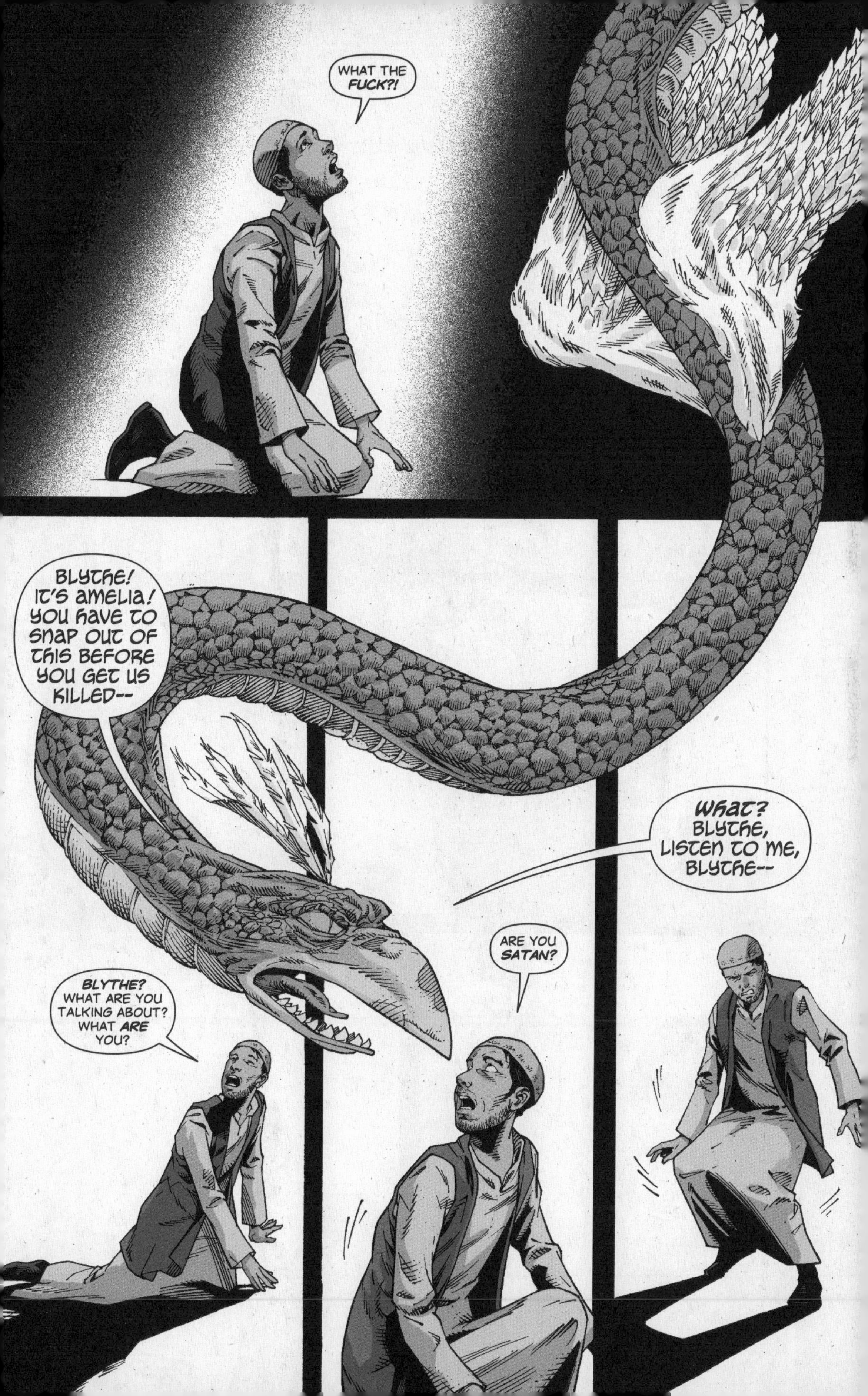
WHAT THE *FUCK?!*
BLYTHE! IT'S AMELIA! YOU HAVE TO SNAP OUT OF THIS BEFORE YOU GET US KILLED--
BLYTHE? WHAT ARE YOU TALKING ABOUT? WHAT *ARE* YOU?
ARE YOU *SATAN?*
WHAT? BLYTHE, LISTEN TO ME, BLYTHE--

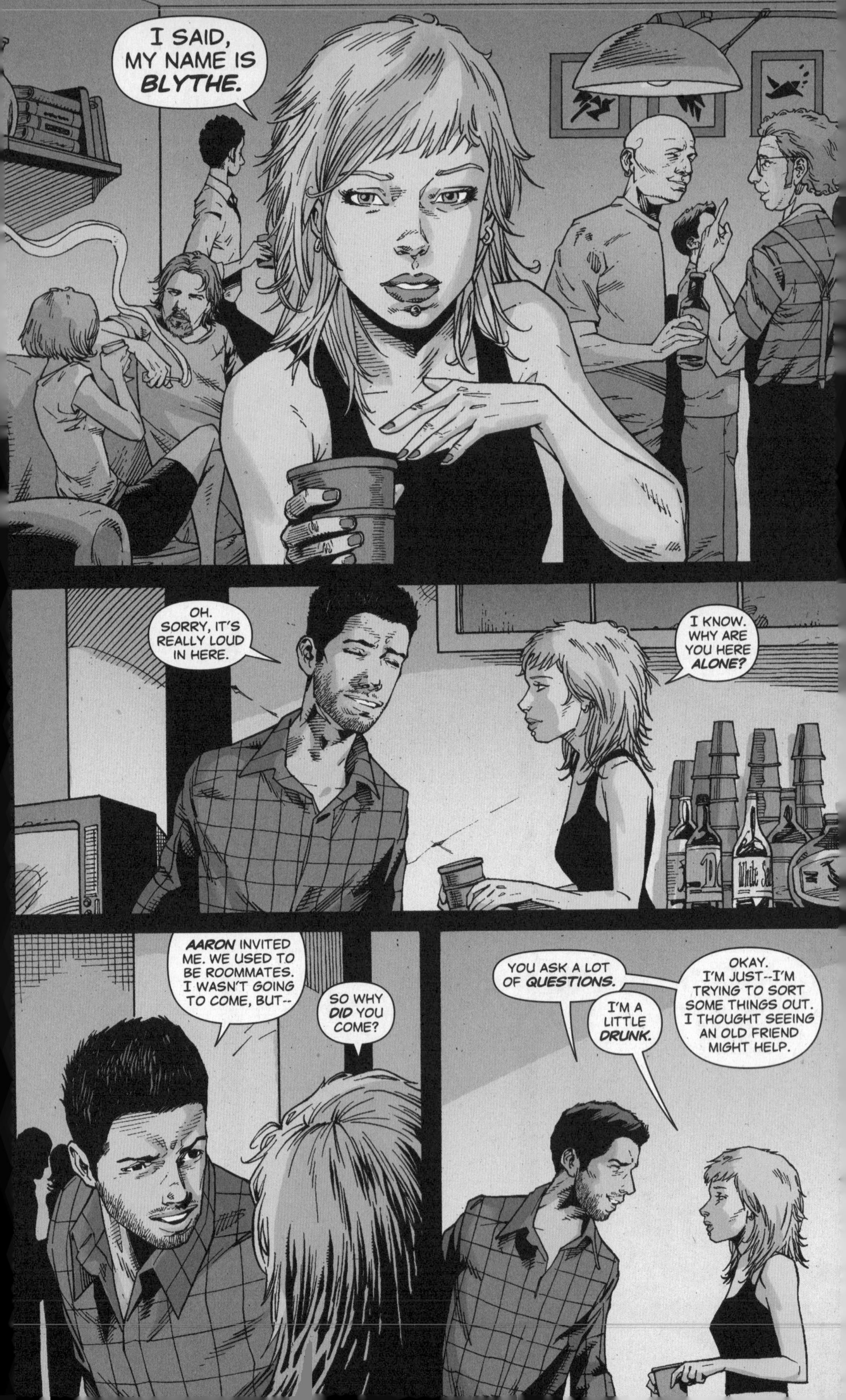
I SAID, MY NAME IS BLYTHE.
OH. SORRY, IT'S REALLY LOUD IN HERE.
I KNOW. WHY ARE YOU HERE ALONE?
AARON INVITED ME. WE USED TO BE ROOMMATES. I WASN'T GOING TO COME, BUT--
SO WHY DID YOU COME?
YOU ASK A LOT OF QUESTIONS.
I'M A LITTLE DRUNK.
OKAY. I'M JUST--I'M TRYING TO SORT SOME THINGS OUT. I THOUGHT SEEING AN OLD FRIEND MIGHT HELP.

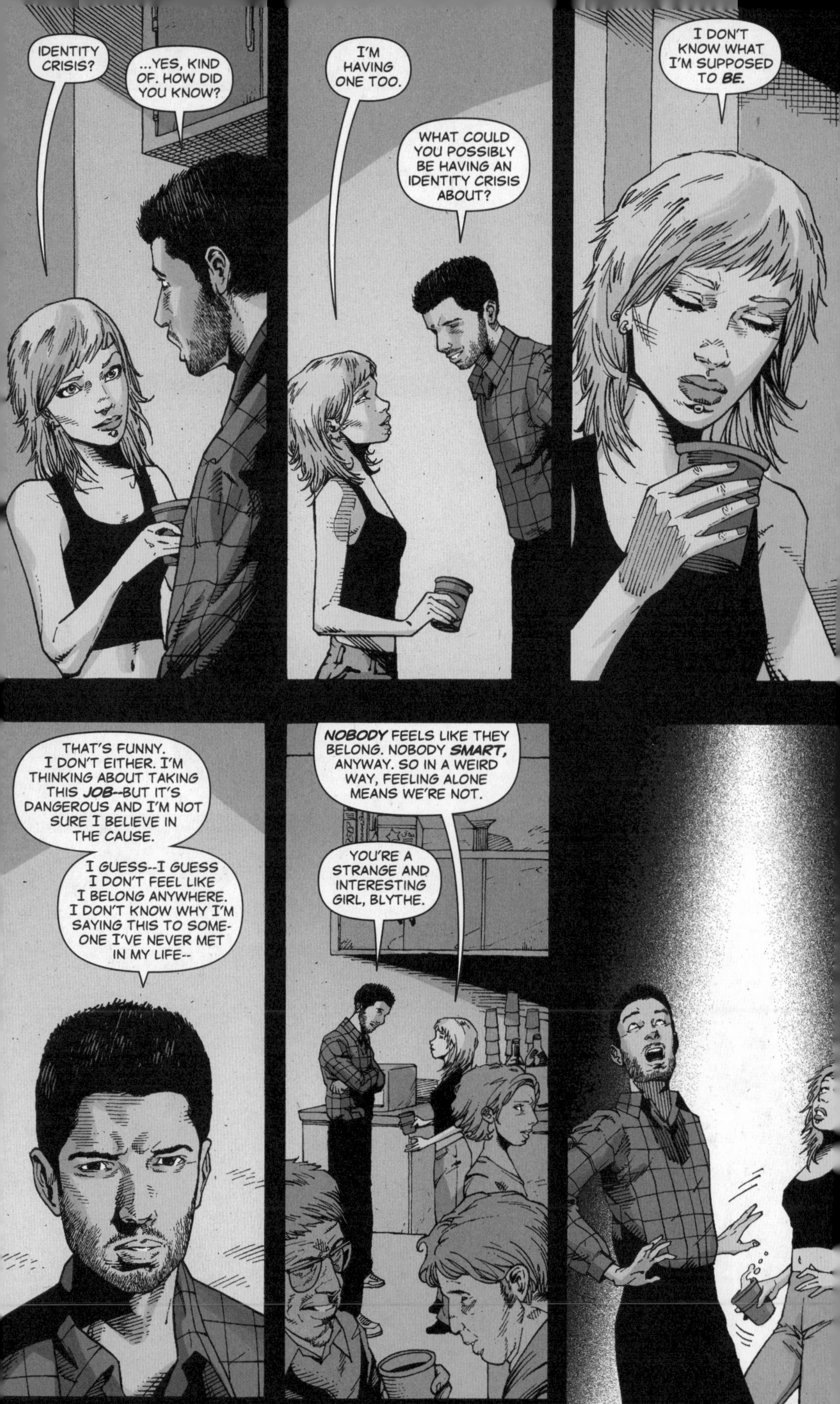
IDENTITY CRISIS?
...YES, KIND OF. HOW DID YOU KNOW?
I'M HAVING ONE TOO.
WHAT COULD YOU POSSIBLY BE HAVING AN IDENTITY CRISIS ABOUT?
I DON'T KNOW WHAT I'M SUPPOSED TO BE.
THAT'S FUNNY. I DON'T EITHER. I'M THINKING ABOUT TAKING THIS JOB--BUT IT'S DANGEROUS AND I'M NOT SURE I BELIEVE IN THE CAUSE.
I GUESS--I GUESS I DON'T FEEL LIKE I BELONG ANYWHERE. I DON'T KNOW WHY I'M SAYING THIS TO SOME-ONE I'VE NEVER MET IN MY LIFE--
NOBODY FEELS LIKE THEY BELONG. NOBODY SMART, ANYWAY. SO IN A WEIRD WAY, FEELING ALONE MEANS WE'RE NOT.
YOU'RE A STRANGE AND INTERESTING GIRL, BLYTHE.

NOW, BLYTHE, NOW!

She tasted like the sky.

AREN'T YOU GLAD THIS ISN'T A SALMAN RUSHDIE NOVEL?

WH-WHY?

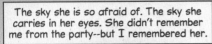

The sky she is so afraid of. The sky she carries in her eyes. She didn't remember me from the party--but I remembered her.

F-FALLING--

YES, WE'RE FALLING, YOU NEED TO COME BACK--

THIS DAMN BOAT IS COMING APART!

What don't I remember? Why aren't we going to DIE?

Look at her. She TRUSTS me. Even though she doesn't know who I am. Even though *I* don't know who I am. She believes I can stop our fall.

Because I don't need to know who I am to know you are worth saving.

BECAUSE WE HAVE A *PARACHUTE.*

...That's it.

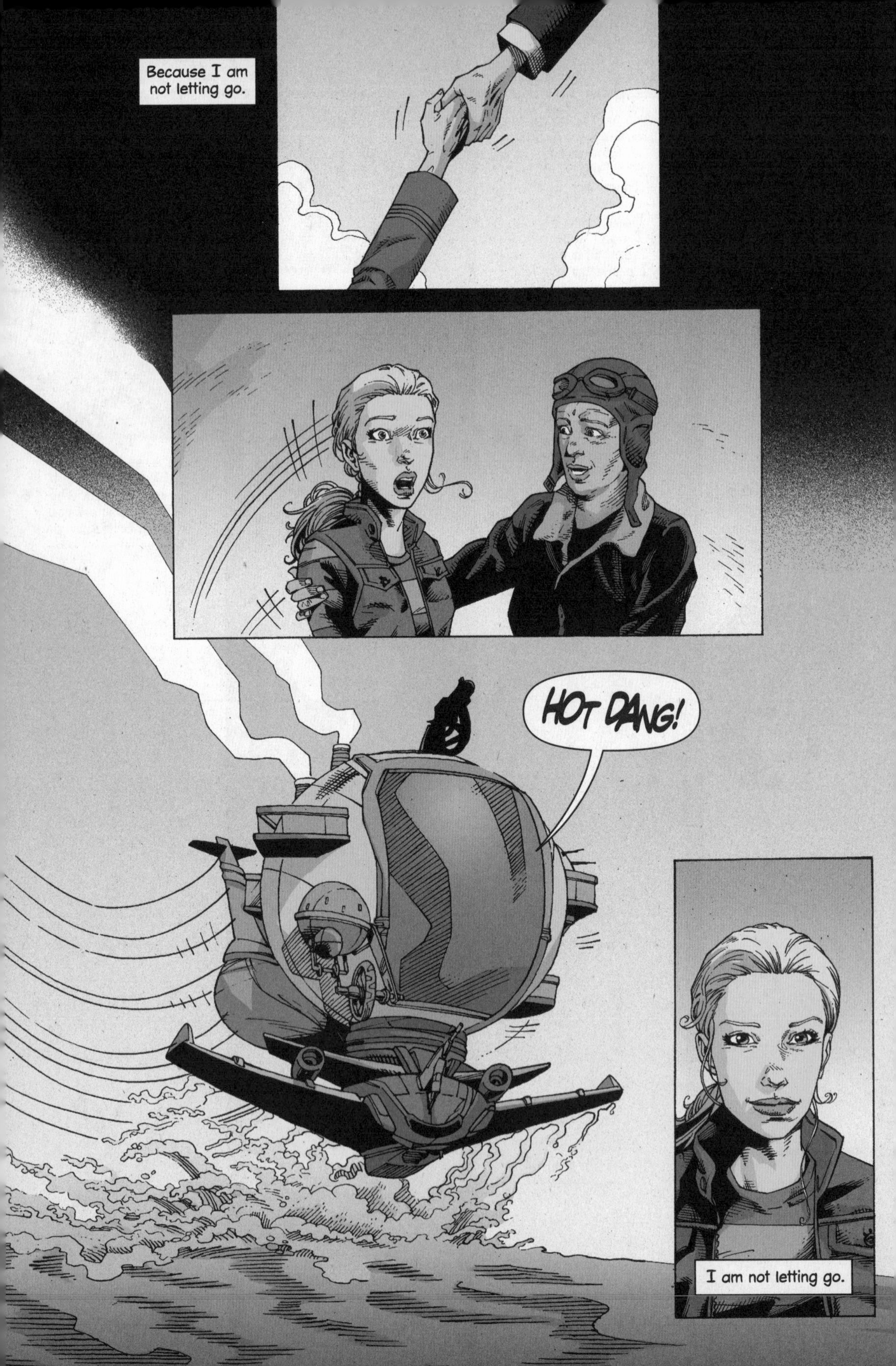
Because I am not letting go.
HOT DANG!
I am not letting go.

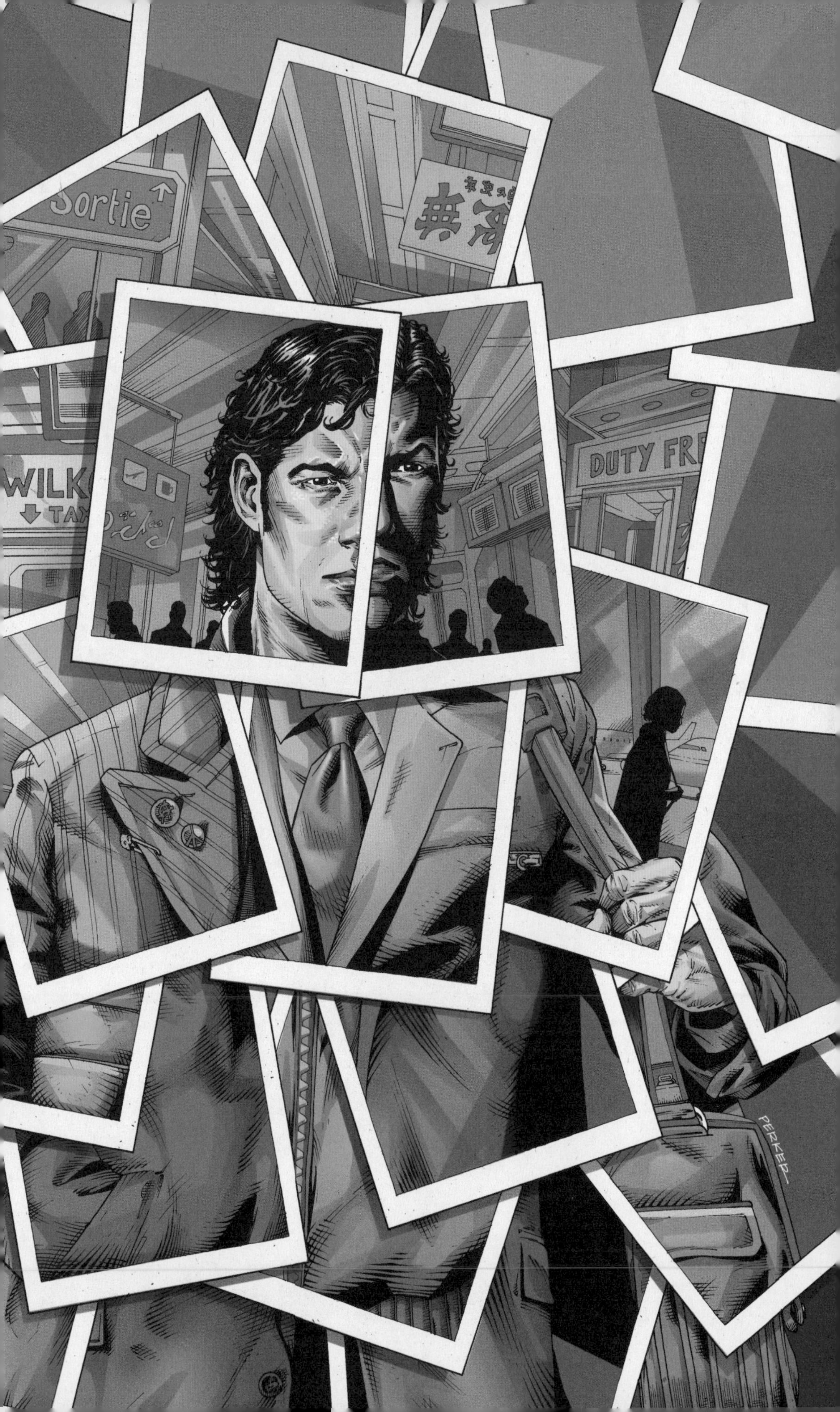
Sortie
PERKER

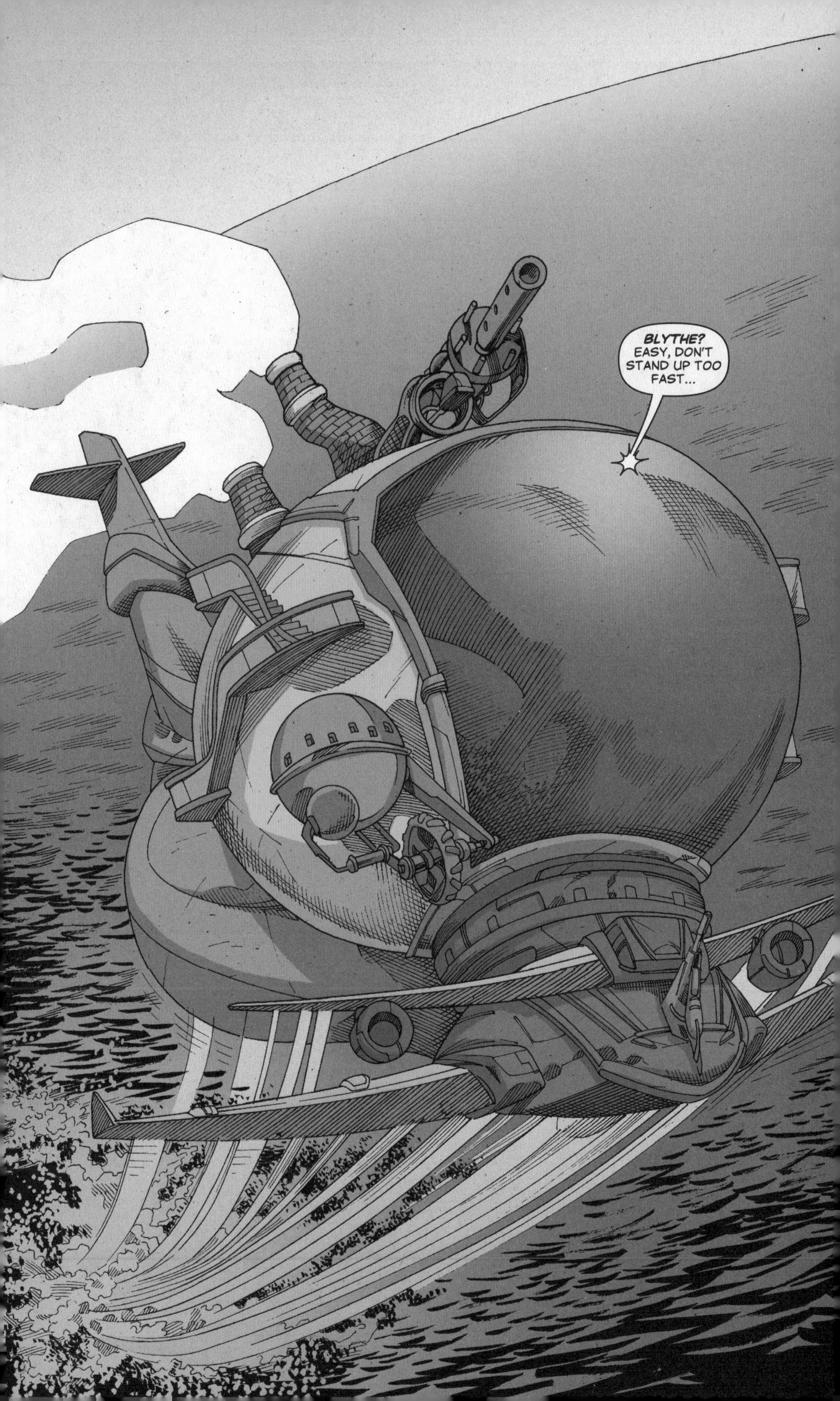
BLYTHE? EASY, DON'T STAND UP TOO FAST...

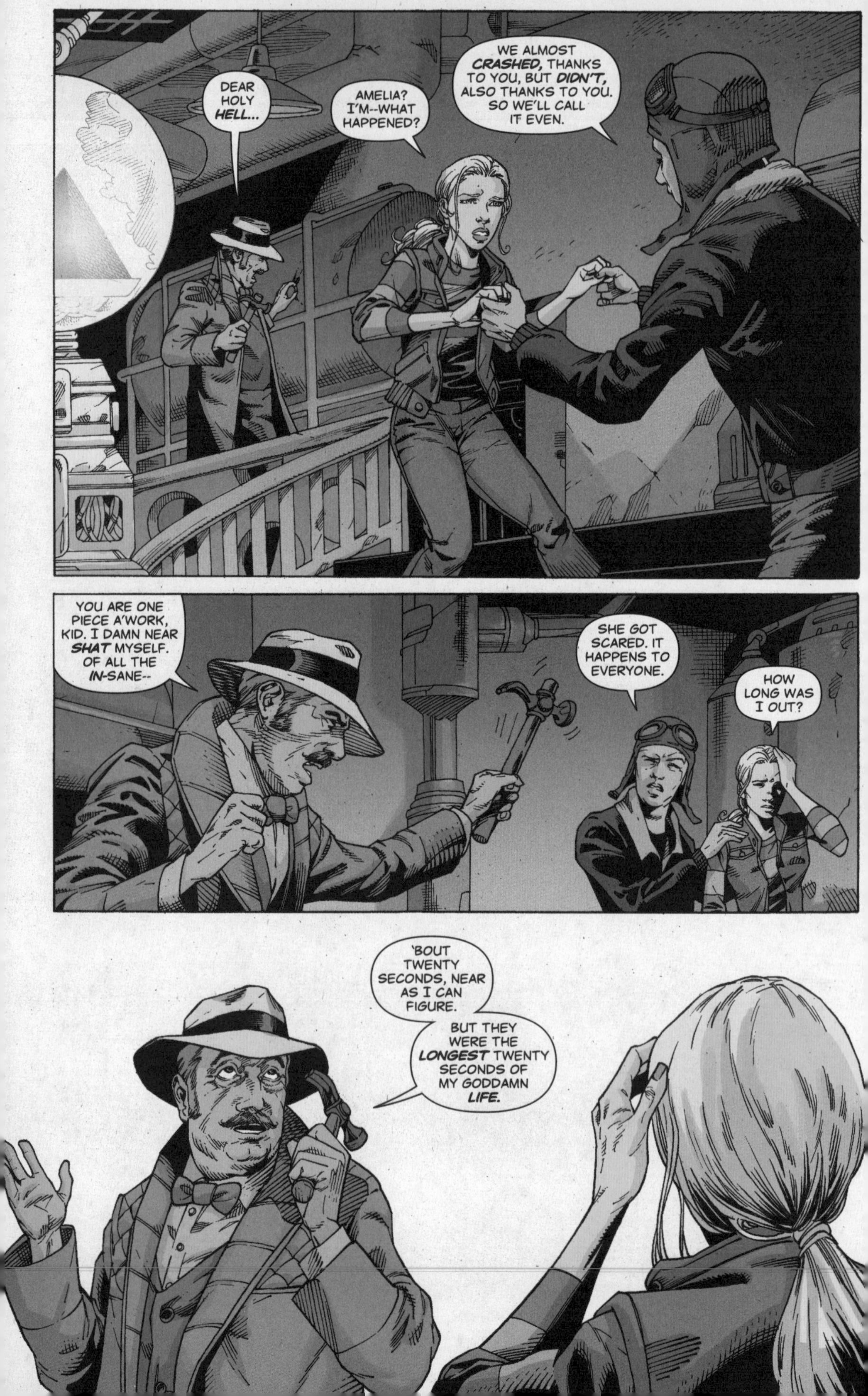
DEAR HOLY HELL...
AMELIA? I'M--WHAT HAPPENED?
WE ALMOST CRASHED, THANKS TO YOU, BUT DIDN'T, ALSO THANKS TO YOU. SO WE'LL CALL IT EVEN.
YOU ARE ONE PIECE A'WORK, KID. I DAMN NEAR SHAT MYSELF. OF ALL THE IN-SANE--
SHE GOT SCARED. IT HAPPENS TO EVERYONE.
HOW LONG WAS I OUT?
'BOUT TWENTY SECONDS, NEAR AS I CAN FIGURE.
BUT THEY WERE THE LONGEST TWENTY SECONDS OF MY GODDAMN LIFE.

FUCK ME... **TWENTY SECONDS?**

I LIVED HIS **WHOLE LIFE.** ZAYN'S. IT WAS LIKE I SLIPPED AND FELL AND LANDED IN HIS **BRAIN,** FOR YEARS AND YEARS--

ZAYN? THIS IS THE ONE WHO LAST HAD THE **DEVICE?**

YEAH, HIM. I--HE--WE'RE IN **LOVE.** I DIDN'T REALIZE--HE REALLY **DOES** LOVE ME. FOR AWHILE I WAS AFRAID HE DIDN'T--

BLYTHE, HONEY, LISTEN TO ME. I KNOW YOU FEEL LIKE A **MENTAL PATIENT** RIGHT NOW, BUT YOU HAVE TO **FOCUS.**

YOU HAVE TO TAKE US **BACK.**

WHAT?! NO WAY!

YOU DON'T UNDERSTAND HOW **WEIRD** THIS IS. IT TOOK ME **TWENTY YEARS** TO GET OUT OF ZAYN'S HEAD--

I KNOW **EXACTLY** HOW WEIRD THIS IS. BUT YOU'VE GOT TO BEAR UP.

RIGHT NOW, THERE ARE HALF A DOZEN OTHER GROUPS WORKING TO FIND THE DEVICE. BUT ONLY **YOU** KNOW WHERE IT IS. IF YOU DON'T GET IT BACK, SOMEONE **NASTY** WILL.

OKAY.

WE ARE *BACK* IN BUSINESS, OLD SAW.

YOU'RE NOT AFRAID SHE'LL CRASH FOR REAL THIS TIME?

IF SHE DOES, I'M BILLIN' *YOU* FOR THE REPAIRS, BOTH BODILY AN' AUTOBODILY.

Symbolism as technology.

Technology as symbolism.

It's easier this time.

GOD, BLYTHE, I--

STAY SAFE, HABIBTI.

ZAYN.

I THOUGHT WE WERE MEETING AT THE HELIPAD.

WE WERE. CENTRALE DECIDED THAT LOCATION WAS NOT SECURE, SO THEY SENT ME TO INTERCEPT YOU.

HERE.

THE DEVICE?

INSIDE, UNDER A FALSE BOTTOM. CLASSIC AND SIMPLE.

DO *NOT* GET CAUGHT. SEE YOU IN BANGLADESH.

YES, SIR.

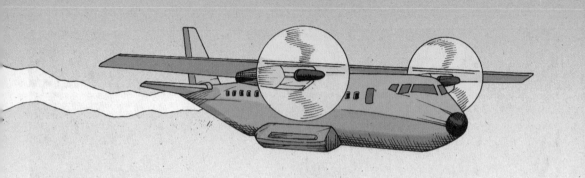

I WIN, YOU BUY ME A PLATE OF SWEET AND SOUR PORK IN DHAKA.

...THEY DON'T EAT PORK IN BANGLADESH, DUDE.

YOU'RE *JAVAD*, RIGHT?

HMM?

OUR TRANSLATOR?

YES, MADAME. I AM FLUENT IN BENGALI, HINDI AND URDU.

THAT'S SO COOL. HOW DID YOU LEARN ENGLISH?

MISSION SCHOOL. ST. FRANCIS ACADEMY, ISLAMABAD.

I'M *SARAH.*

PLEASED TO MEET YOU.

WHY IS IT FLYING SO CLOSE?

CHECK OUT THAT WEIRD *SYMBOL* ON THE WING, DUDE.

...OH *SHIT.*

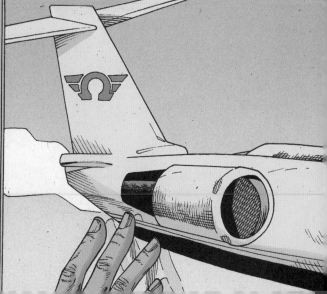

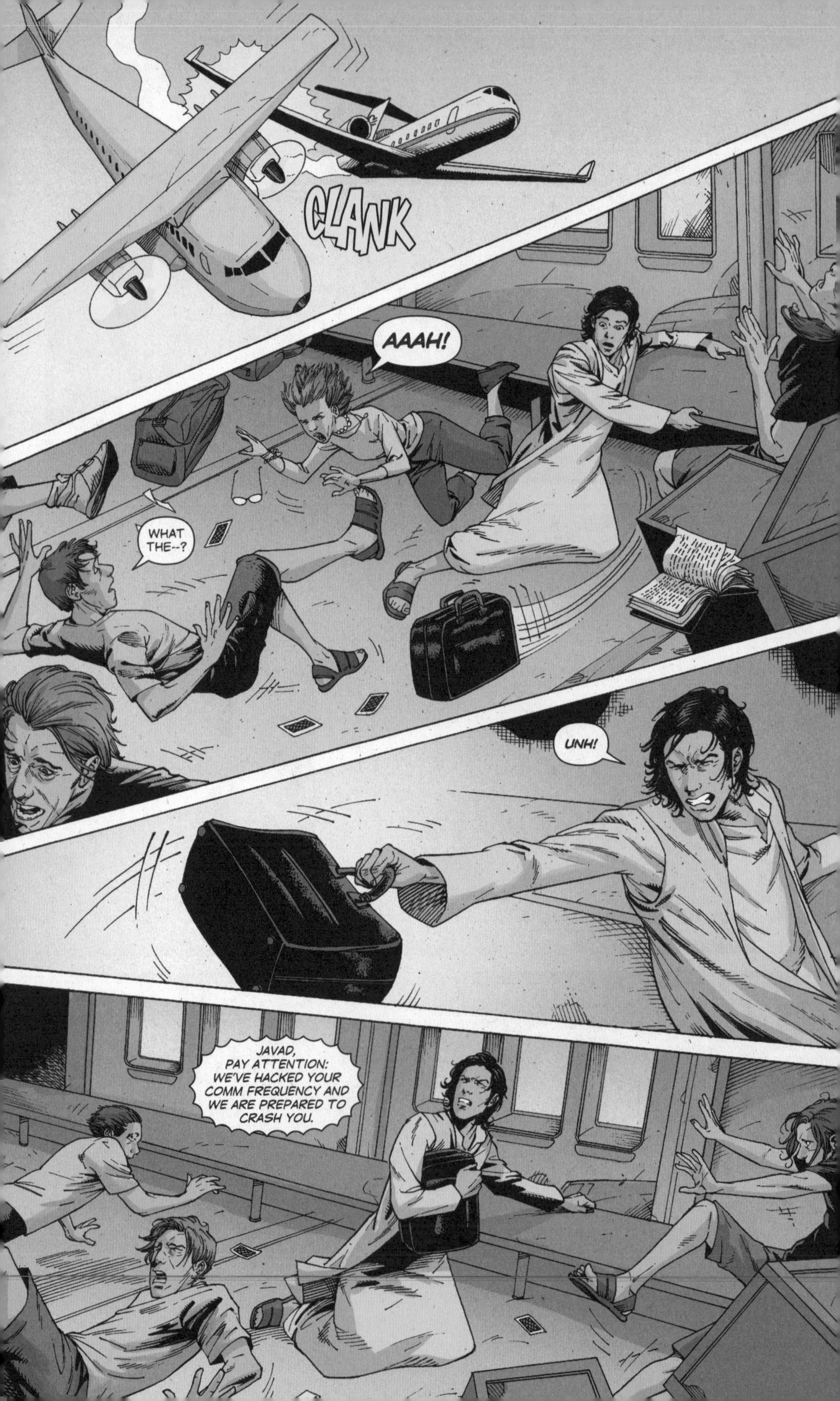
CLANK
AAAH!
WHAT THE--?
UNH!
JAVAD, PAY ATTENTION: WE'VE HACKED YOUR COMM FREQUENCY AND WE ARE PREPARED TO CRASH YOU.

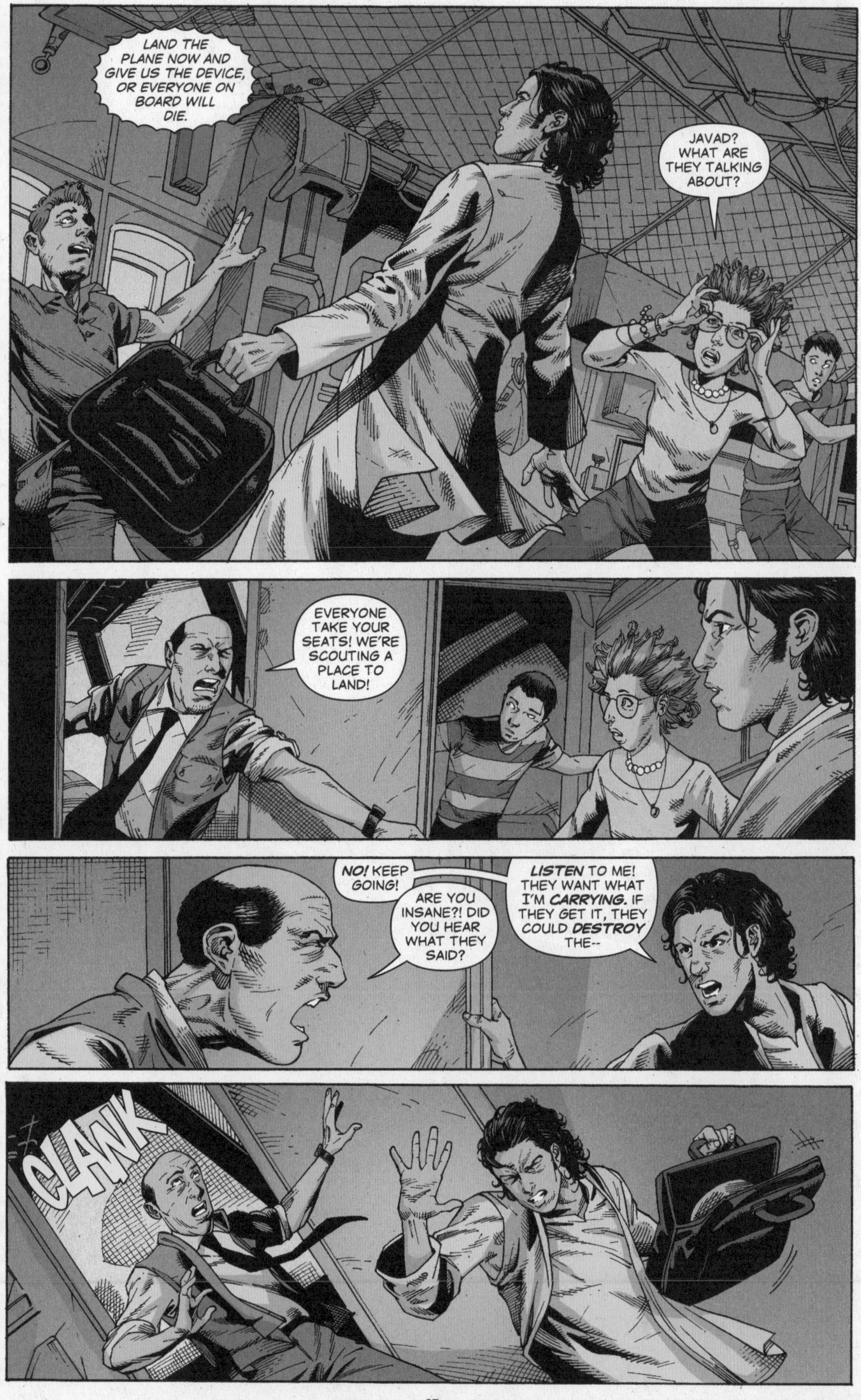

LAND THE PLANE NOW AND GIVE US THE DEVICE, OR EVERYONE ON BOARD WILL DIE.
JAVAD? WHAT ARE THEY TALKING ABOUT?
EVERYONE TAKE YOUR SEATS! WE'RE SCOUTING A PLACE TO LAND!
NO! KEEP GOING!
LISTEN TO ME! THEY WANT WHAT I'M CARRYING. IF THEY GET IT, THEY COULD DESTROY THE--
ARE YOU INSANE?! DID YOU HEAR WHAT THEY SAID?
CLANK

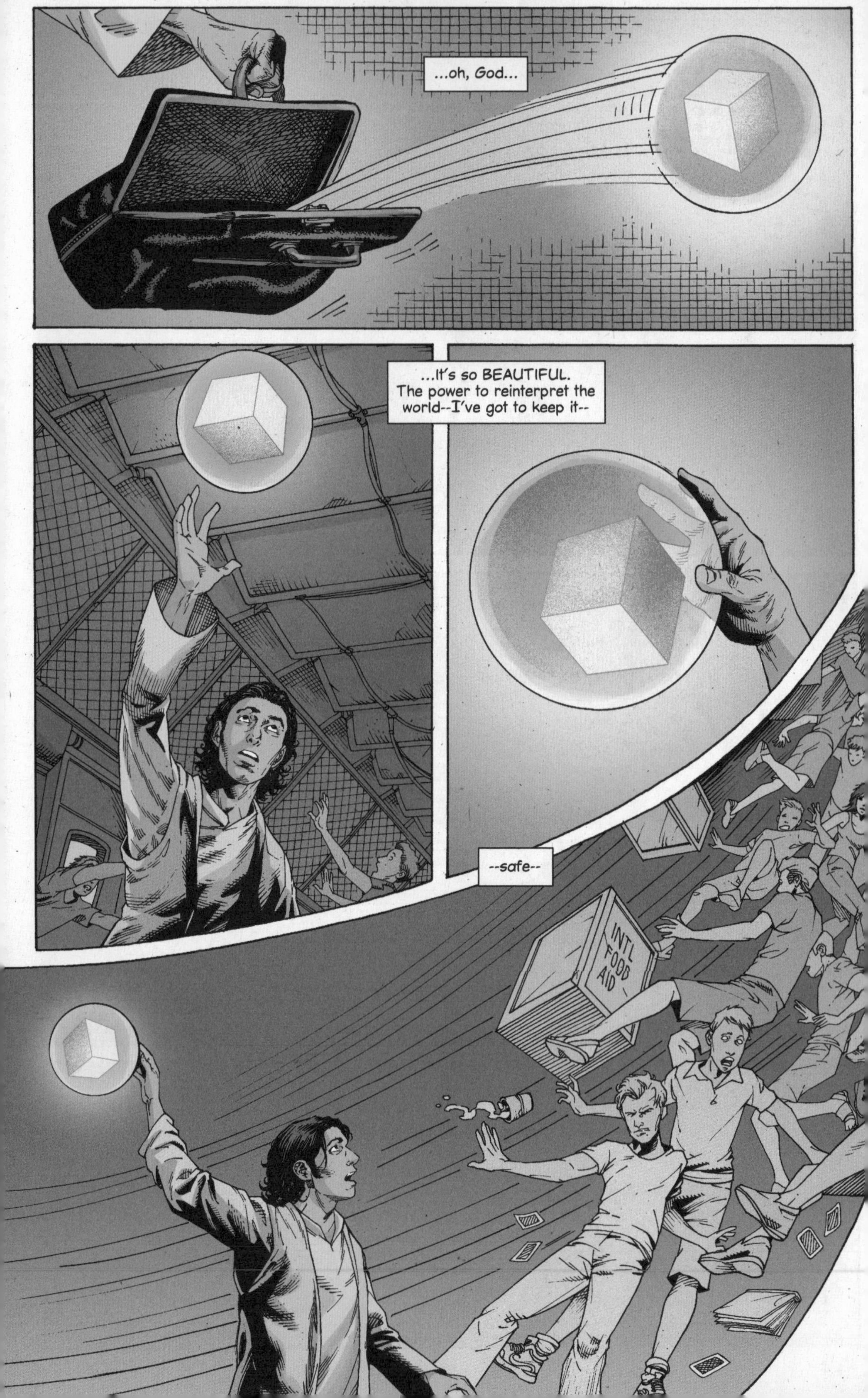

...oh, God...
...It's so BEAUTIFUL.
The power to reinterpret the world--I've got to keep it--
--safe--
INTL FOOD AID

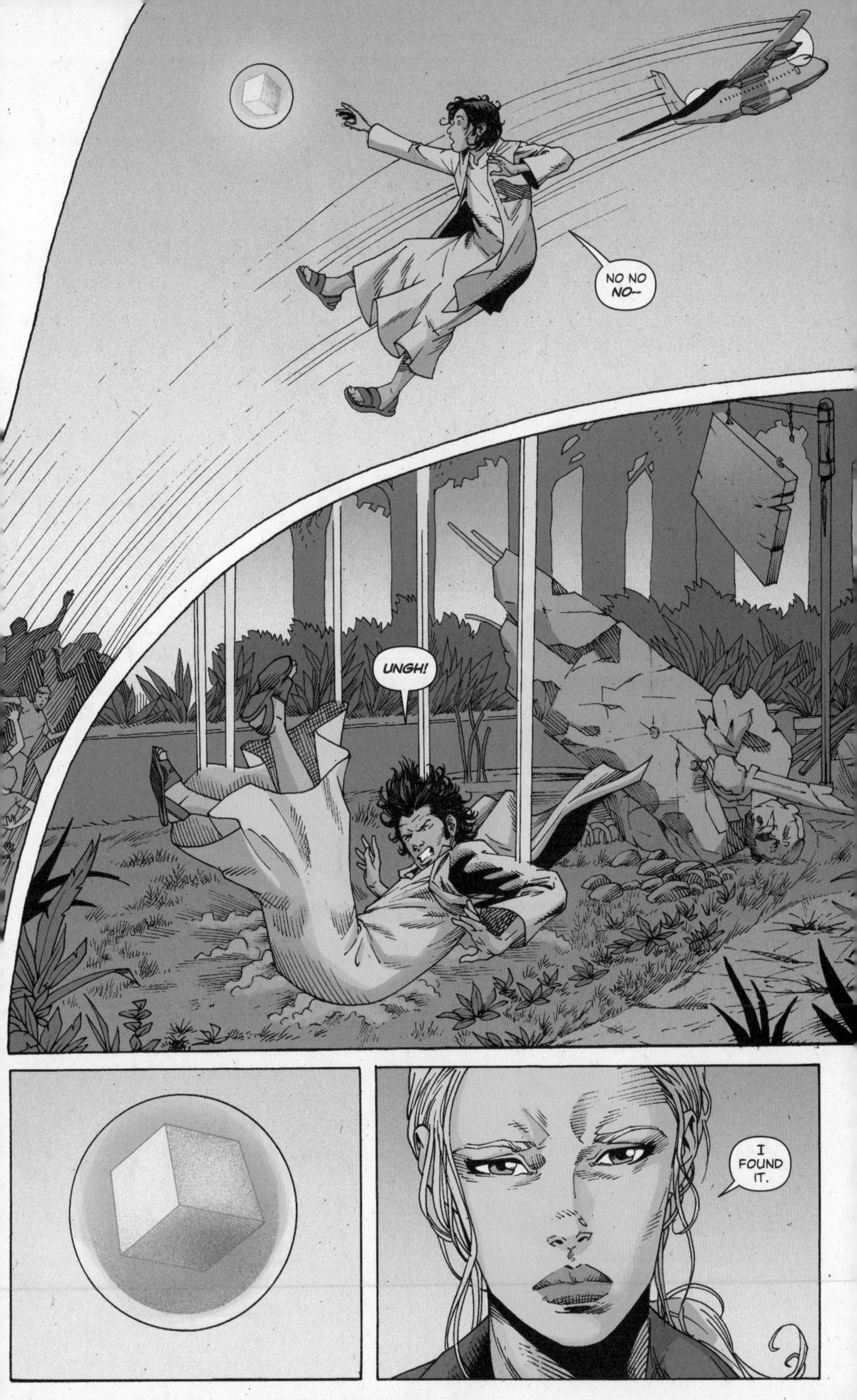
NO NO NO--
UNGH!
I FOUND IT.

GOOD. STAY FOCUSED. DON'T WORRY ABOUT *MOVING* THE SHIP-- JUST *INTERPRET* WHAT YOU SEE AROUND IT.

O-OKAY.

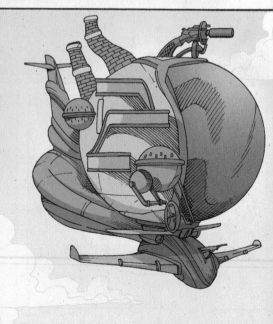

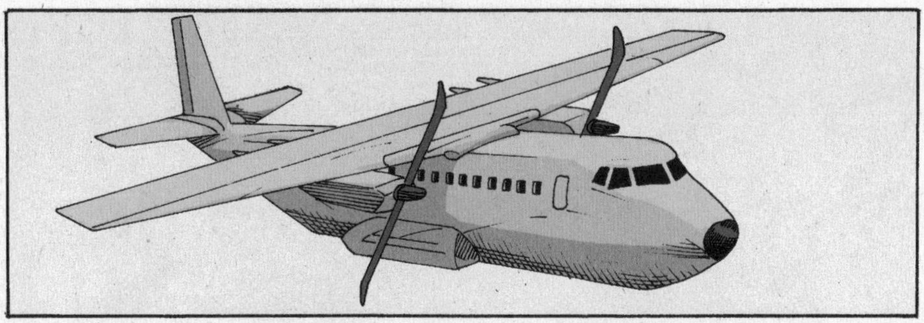

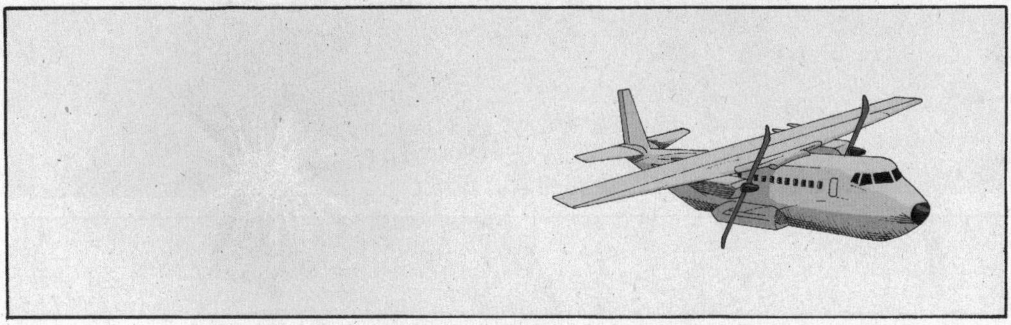

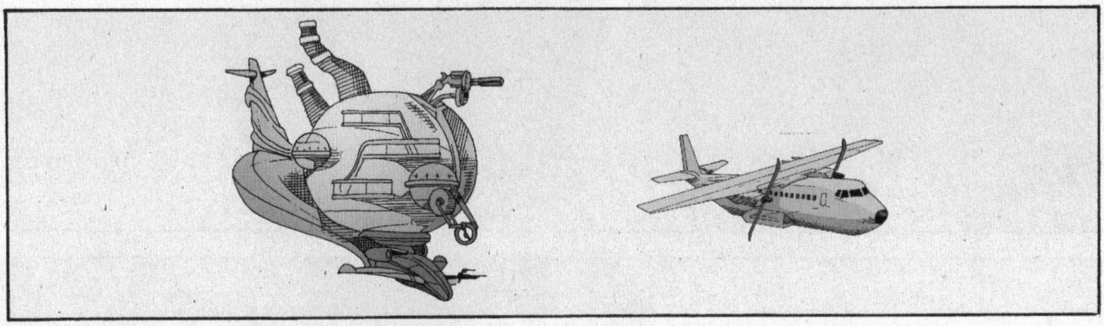

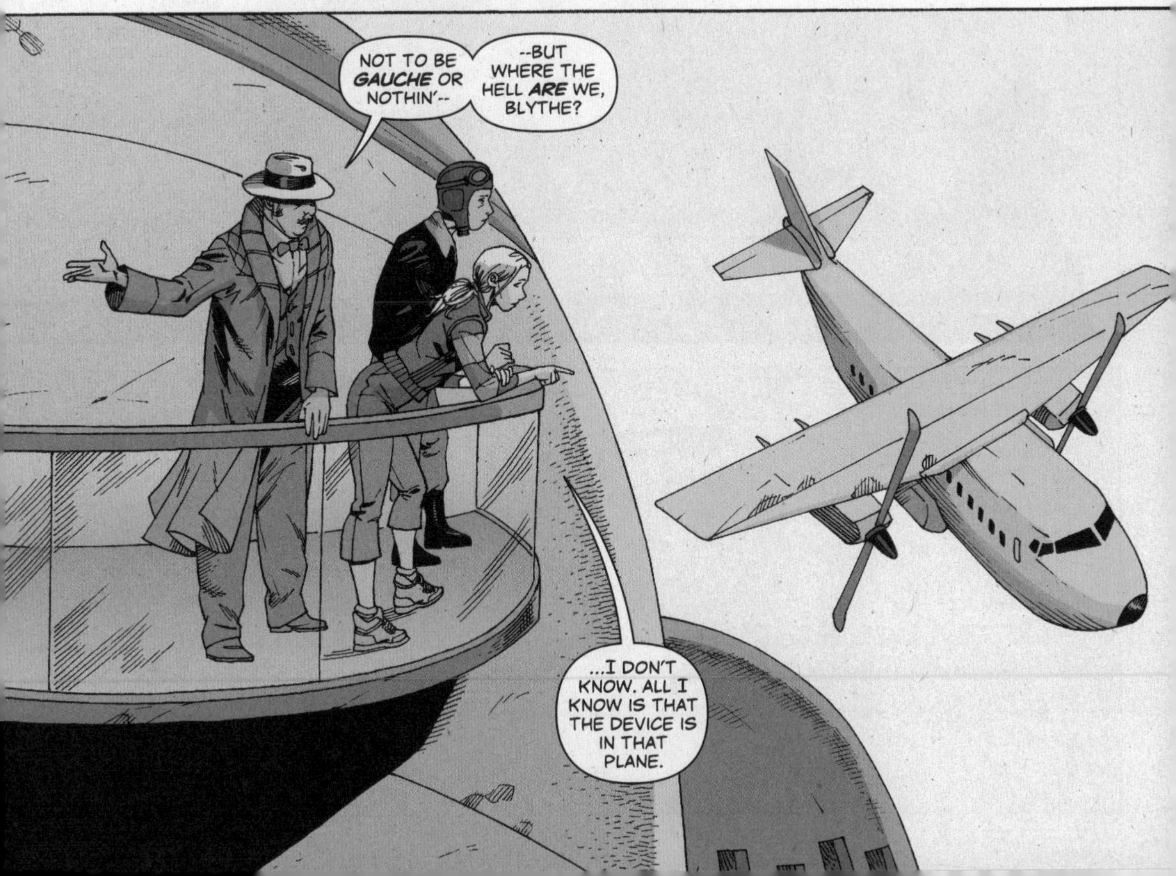
NOT TO BE *GAUCHE* OR NOTHIN'--
--BUT WHERE THE HELL *ARE* WE, BLYTHE?
...I DON'T KNOW. ALL I KNOW IS THAT THE DEVICE IS IN THAT PLANE.

THIS IS WHERE YOU WERE--ISN'T IT? THIS IS WHERE YOU WERE STUCK FOR ALL THOSE YEARS.

...LET'S JUST GET THE *DEVICE* AND GET OUT OF HERE.

AMELIA?

YES, BLYTHE, YES.

THIS IS WHERE--OR SHOULD I SAY *NOWHERE*--

CHARMING.

ON MY FIRST HYPERPRAX TEST FLIGHT, I ALMOST LOST MY *NUTS*--THE FRONT HALF OF THE PLANE *DISAPPEARED*, RIGHT UP TO THE TOES OF MY BOOTS. BUT THIS'S *WORSE*.

YOU'RE NOT *HELPING*, NORTHFIELD.

ALL RIGHT, ALL RIGHT. PULL IT TOGETHER. LET'S GET INSIDE THAT PLANE AND SEE WHAT'S WHAT. *THEN* WE CAN WORRY ABOUT LEAVING.

EVEN THE *AIR* IS WEIRD--IT DOESN'T *SMELL* LIKE ANYTHING.

IT *ISN'T* ANYTHING.

THIS PLANE WAS FULL OF *PEOPLE* WHEN I SAW IT--AID WORKERS. BUT THERE AREN'T EVEN ANY *BODIES* HERE...

NO...I NEVER FOUND MY *CO-PILOT'S* BODY EITHER.

NORTHFIELD! YOU'RE *SEE-THROUGH!*

WHAT IN TARNATION ARE YOU *TALKIN'* AB--

SO ARE *YOU!*

GET IT OFF ME! MAKE IT *STOP!*

WE SHOULDN'A COME HERE WITHOUT A *PLAN,* DAMMIT!

THIS...DIDN'T HAPPEN THE LAST TIME...

WE'RE GOING TO *DIE--*

WE'RE *NOT* GOING TO DIE. TAKE A DEEP BREATH AND FINISH WHAT YOU STARTED. FIND THE DEVICE.

FIND THE DEVICE FIND THE DEVICE FIND THE--

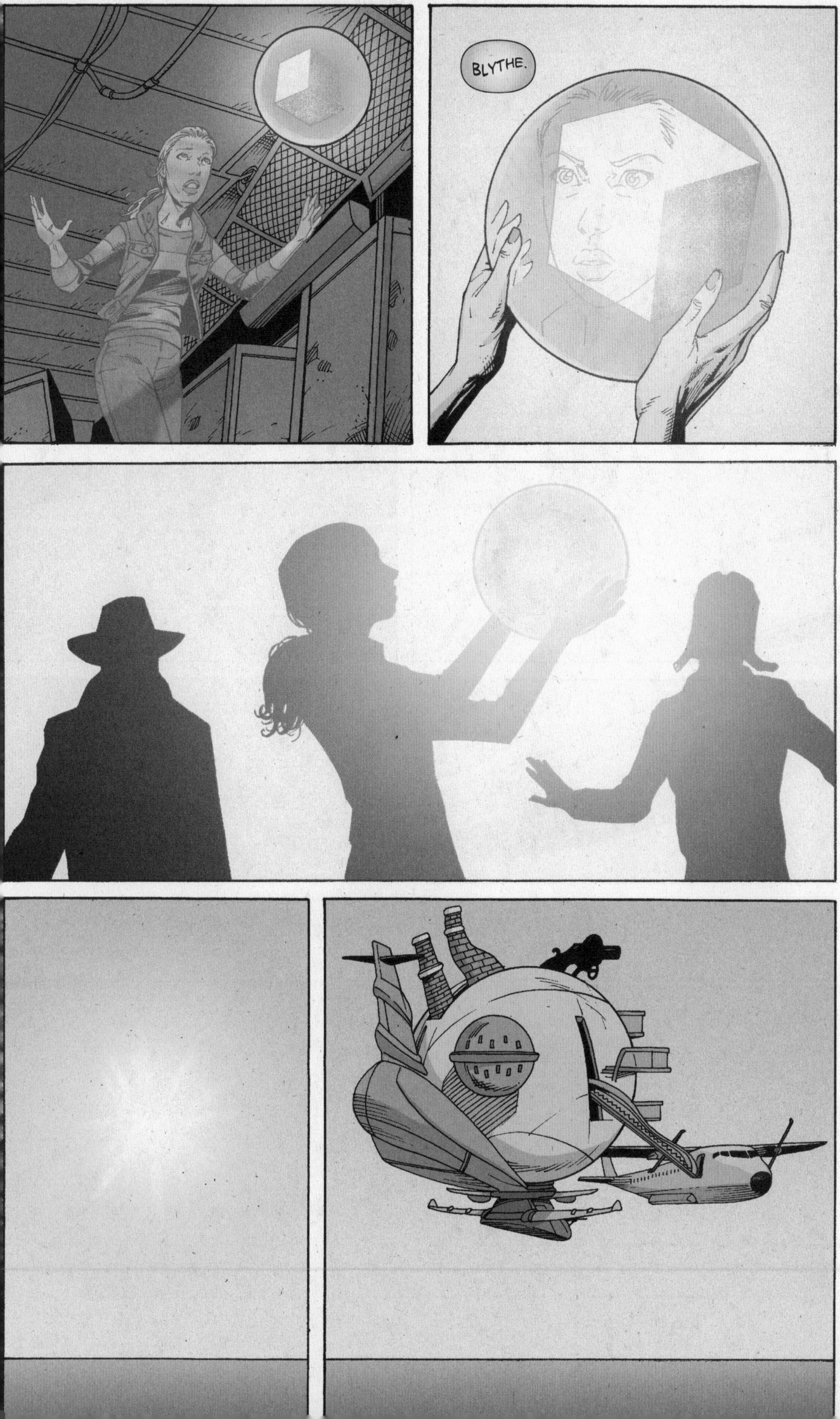
BLYTHE.

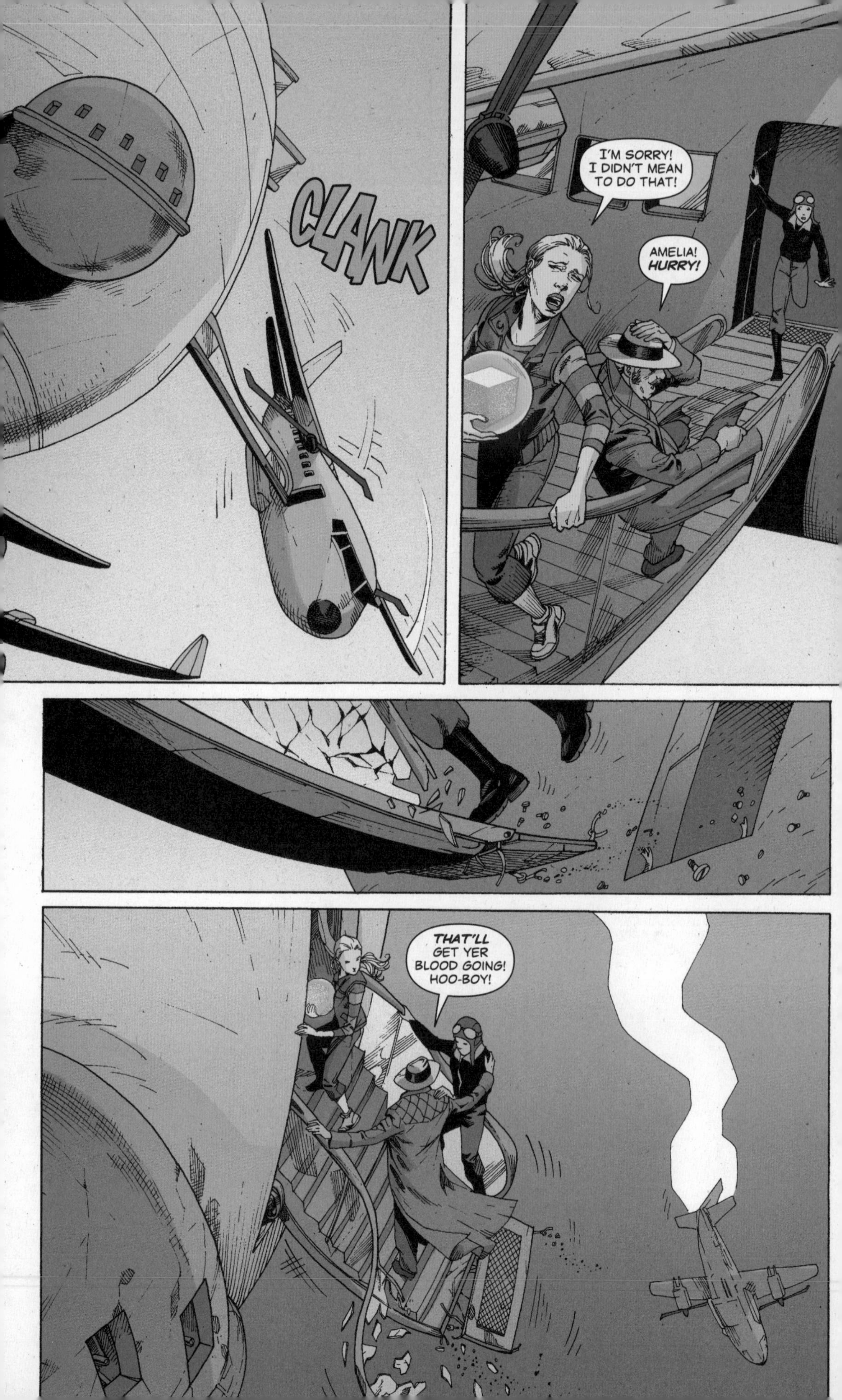
CLANK
I'M SORRY! I DIDN'T MEAN TO DO THAT!
AMELIA! HURRY!
THAT'LL GET YER BLOOD GOING! HOO-BOY!

WELL KNOCK ME OVER--I KNOW I SAID I HOPED YOU HAD A *PLAN,* BUT *JESUS.*

IT SORT OF *HAPPENED.* I REALLY WANTED TO GET OUT OF THERE, AND WHEN I TOUCHED THE DEVICE, I JUST--DID.

I KNOW WE'RE ALL *TIRED,* BUT THIS IS ACTUALLY THE *HARD PART.*

THE MOST VALUABLE ARCHAEOLOGICAL ARTIFACT EVER DISCOVERED IS SITTING IN FRONT OF US. WE'VE GOT TO DECIDE WHAT *HAPPENS* TO IT.

WELL, BLYTHE? TELL US WHAT YOU PLAN TO DO.

ME?!

HER?!

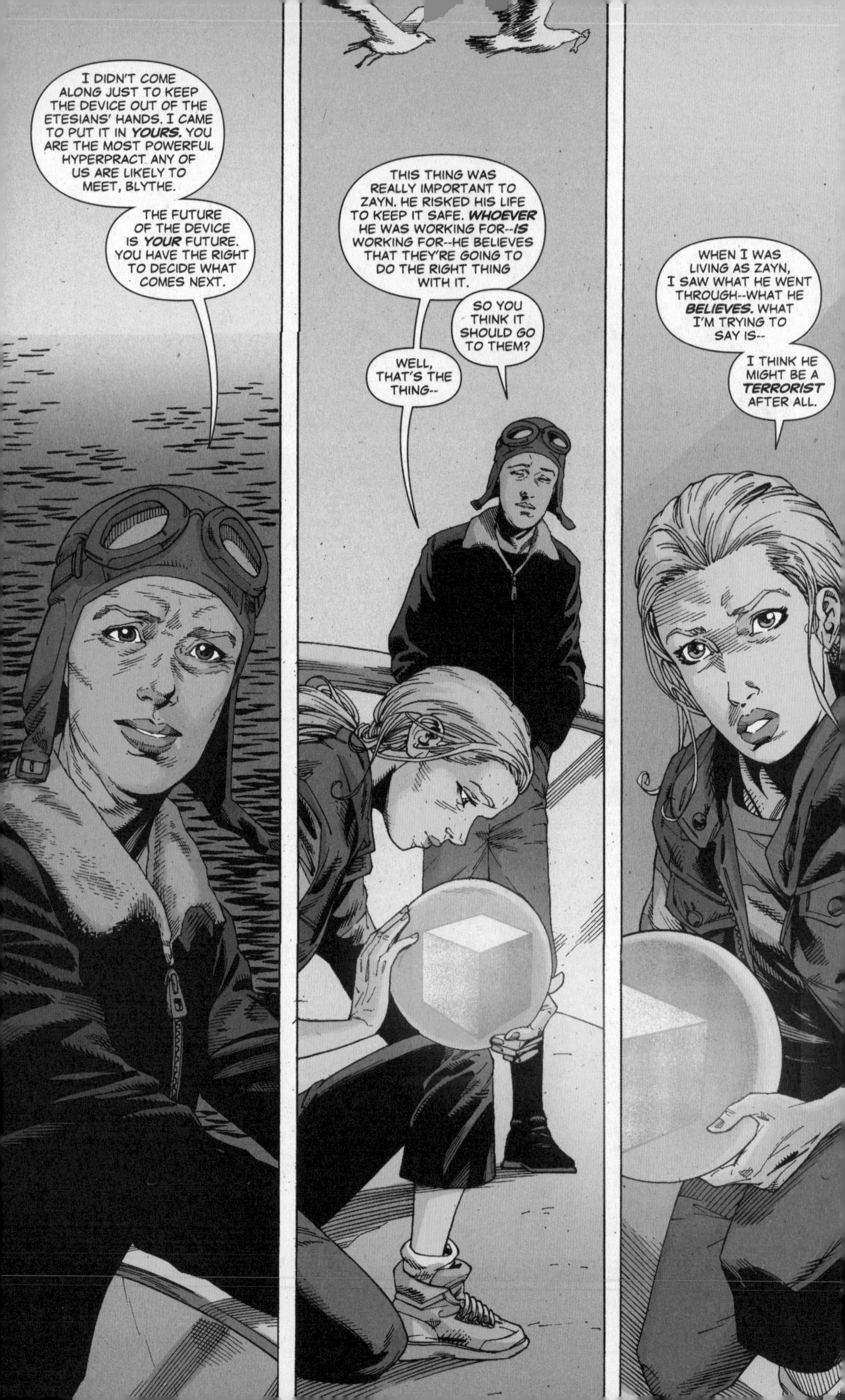
I DIDN'T COME ALONG JUST TO KEEP THE DEVICE OUT OF THE ETESIANS' HANDS. I CAME TO PUT IT IN YOURS. YOU ARE THE MOST POWERFUL HYPERPRACT ANY OF US ARE LIKELY TO MEET, BLYTHE.
THE FUTURE OF THE DEVICE IS YOUR FUTURE. YOU HAVE THE RIGHT TO DECIDE WHAT COMES NEXT.
THIS THING WAS REALLY IMPORTANT TO ZAYN. HE RISKED HIS LIFE TO KEEP IT SAFE. WHOEVER HE WAS WORKING FOR--IS WORKING FOR--HE BELIEVES THAT THEY'RE GOING TO DO THE RIGHT THING WITH IT.
SO YOU THINK IT SHOULD GO TO THEM?
WELL, THAT'S THE THING--
WHEN I WAS LIVING AS ZAYN, I SAW WHAT HE WENT THROUGH--WHAT HE BELIEVES. WHAT I'M TRYING TO SAY IS--
I THINK HE MIGHT BE A TERRORIST AFTER ALL.

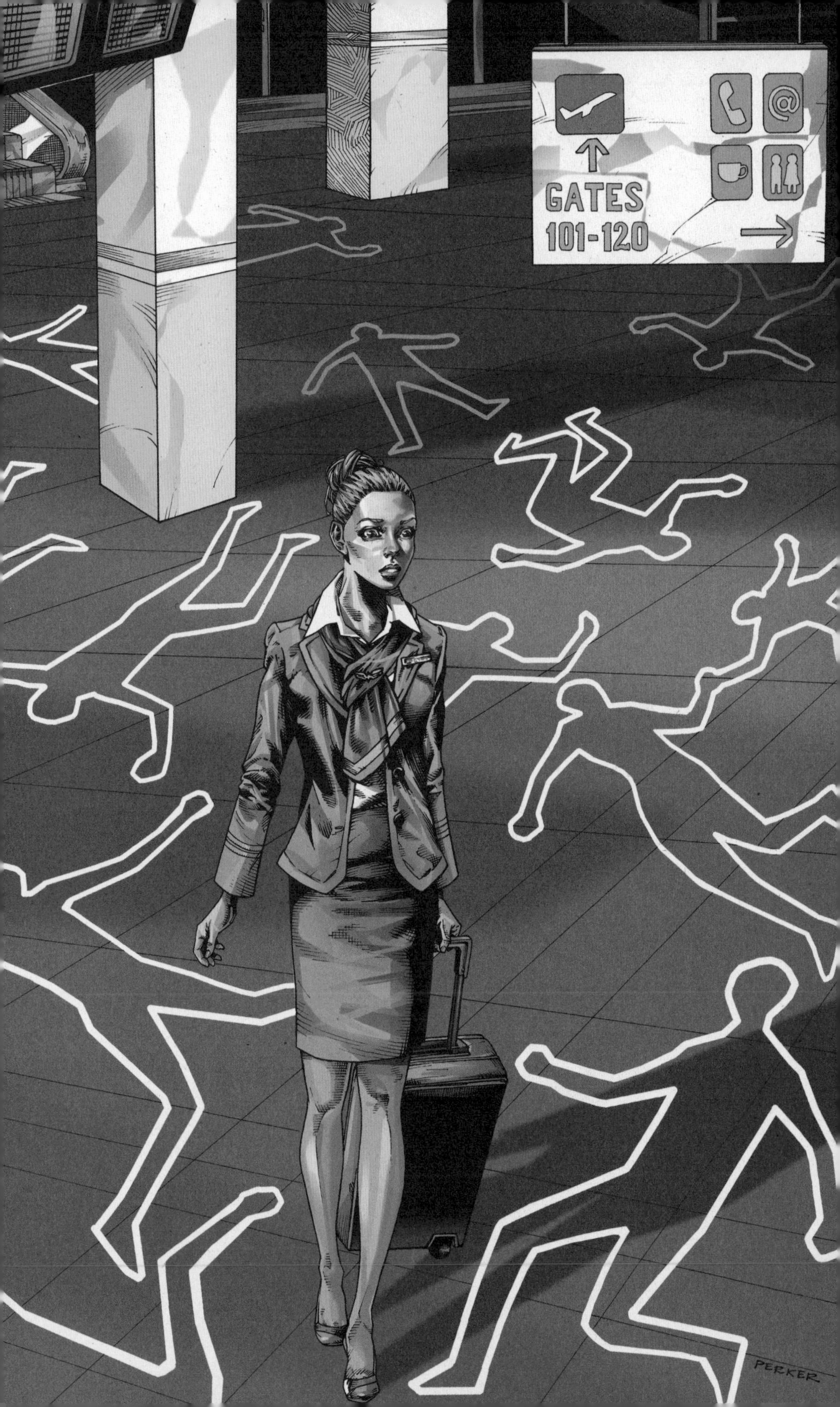
GATES
101-120
PERKER

I wrote to Zayn at this *poste restante* address in France. He once told me I could reach him there in an *emergency.*

Schiphol

Not an email address, not a cell phone number. I don't even know if he *has* those things. But he has this.

I told him I had the *device.* And that I knew about his mission to *protect* it. And that I would give it to him.

I didn't expect him to respond.

But he *did.*

I think I might have agreed to this just to see him again.

...Which, considering the fact that he could be a *criminal,* is incredibly stupid.

I trust Zayn. I know he wouldn't hurt me. And if he wouldn't hurt me, he wouldn't *work* for people who would hurt me.

I think.

The Device gives off a little bit of heat, like a warm body. I have this paranoid idea that people *know* what I'm carrying.

Jesus.

I try to look like a normal flight attendant on her way to serve peanuts and coffee.

I want that to be true. For the first time in my life, I just want to get on a plane.

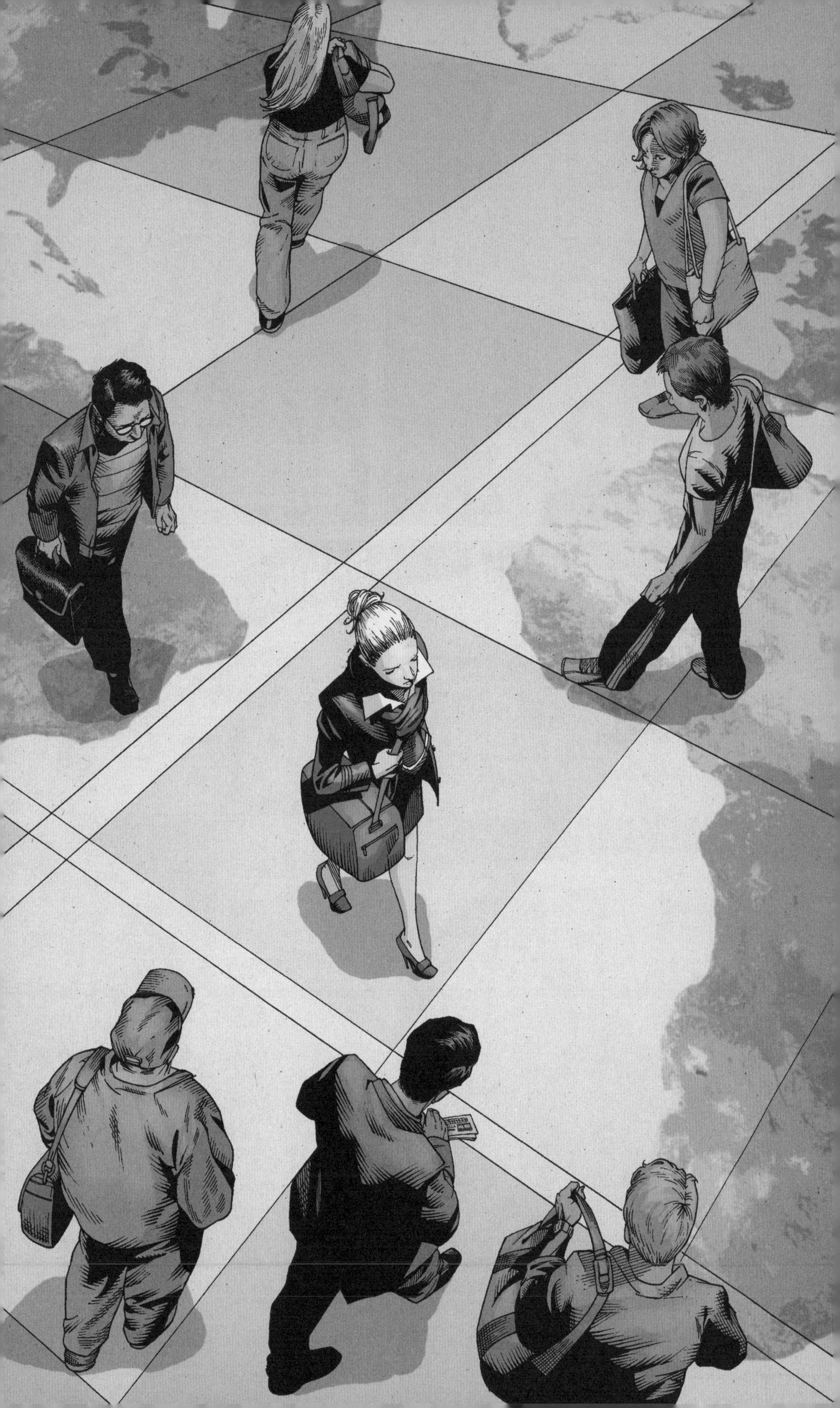

YOU CAN'T **SMOKE** IN HERE, SIR.

WA BA'DAYN, YANNI? THIS IS HASHISH CAPITAL OF EUROPE, AND I CAN'T SMOKE **CIGARETTE**?

NO, SIR.

THIS IS VIOLATION OF MY HUMAN RIGHTS--

TAKE IT UP WITH THE HAGUE, SIR.

I'm starting to remember why I love *airports.*

CHANNEL

All the bright, generic duty-free shops and over-oxygenated air--

They do something to you. In here, your life is *on hold.*

You can put off saying goodbye until the last minute.

Or, if you need to, just put off saying goodbye.

It's not *real*, this place. It's just the blank space between an origin and a destination.

But real things happen here, to real people.

EXCUSE ME, MISS--ARE YOU WORKING HERE?

SORT OF. I WORK FOR CLEARFL--

THANK GOD. I NEED HELP.

I'M NOT SURE I'M THE BEST PERSON TO--

MY NAME IS *RUFAD SALIHOVIC.* I AM LOOKING FOR MY WIFE.

OH. UMN, OKAY.

DID YOU GET *SEPARATED?* IF YOU GO TO THE INFORMATION DESK, THEY CAN PAGE HER--

YES, YES, SEPARATED. BUT NOT *HERE.* I AM WAITING FOURTEEN YEARS--

FOURTEEN *YEARS?*

SINCE 1994. IN ZVORNIK-- IN *BOSNIA.* WE WERE BORN THERE, LIVED THERE--UNTIL THE *WAR.*

What happened?

It was February--snow everywhere. I saw their *footprints* at our door. And *blood.* The neighbor's wife *crying,* saying they take her away--

Who's "they"?

Jugoslavenska Narodna Armija--JNA. Serb *militia.*

I search, I bribe.

I go to UN, they say it's almost *impossible* to know where she is, if she is alive or dead. They are doing DNA testing on *bodies.*

After three years, I los hope. I got work visa in UK--I cannot stay in Bosnia, not after that.

Then, two years ago, I got *letter*.

A *miracle*--she is alive, she escaped. She went first to Croatia, secretly over the border, and now she is living in Turkey.

HOW CAN I DESCRIBE? IT IS LIKE MY SOUL IS BACK IN MY BODY.

FOR TWO YEARS I WORK, TRYING TO GET HER VISA. FINALLY, EVERYTHING IS READY. I SENT HER *TICKET*, I FLEW HERE TO MEET HER HALFWAY.

SHE WAS SUPPOSED TO BE ON MORNING FLIGHT. BUT SHE NEVER ARRIVE. *PLEASE*, HELP ME FIND OUT WHERE SHE IS.

...OF COURSE I WILL.

ANDRIES?

HEY!

INFORMATION

BLYTHE, MY FAVORITE *STEWARDESS.* GOEDEMORGAN.

I NEED YOU TO LOOK UP A PASSENGER WHO MAY HAVE MISSED A CONNECTION.

DAT HANGT ER VAN AF...

WHAT DO YOU MEAN, "THAT DEPENDS"? IT'S A SIMPLE REQUEST.

WELL, MISS PRISS, I HAVE A SIMPLE REQUEST FOR *YOU.* THERE'S A RUSSIAN *BALLET DANCER* WHO NEEDS TO GET TO MOSCOW, AND EVERYTHING IS BOOKED.

GET HIM ON A CLEARFLEET FLIGHT.

HIM?

YES, *HIM,* YOU PHILISTINE.

WHAT'S HE TO YOU?

A SUPPLY OF UNFILTERED *CLOVE* CIGARETTES.

WHERE IS THIS MANOREXIC BOY WONDER?

SITTING AT GATE 37.

INF

I HAVE TO GO DO THIS. I'LL MEET YOU BACK HERE IN HALF AN HOUR.

DON'T WORRY, OKAY? WE'RE GOING TO FIND YOUR WIFE.

VALENTIN CHERNOFF?

THAT IS ME!

ARE YOU SERIOUSLY WEARING *TIGHTS*?

I HAVE *PERFORMANCE* TONIGHT. IN MOSCOW. SINCE I MISSED EARLY FLIGHT, I MUST GO STRAIGHT TO *THEATER*.

WELL, HERE'S YOUR *TICKET*. THANK ANDRIES.

THANK *YOU*.

DON'T MENTION IT.

YOU HAVE REALLY SAVED MY BUTT!

I CHANGED MY MIND. WALK WITH ME.

WHAT? WHY?

PLEASE.

HEY-- YOU ARE OKAY?

THIS IS IT, ISN'T IT? THIS IS WHAT IT'S ALWAYS GOING TO BE LIKE. I'M NEVER GETTING MY LIFE BACK.

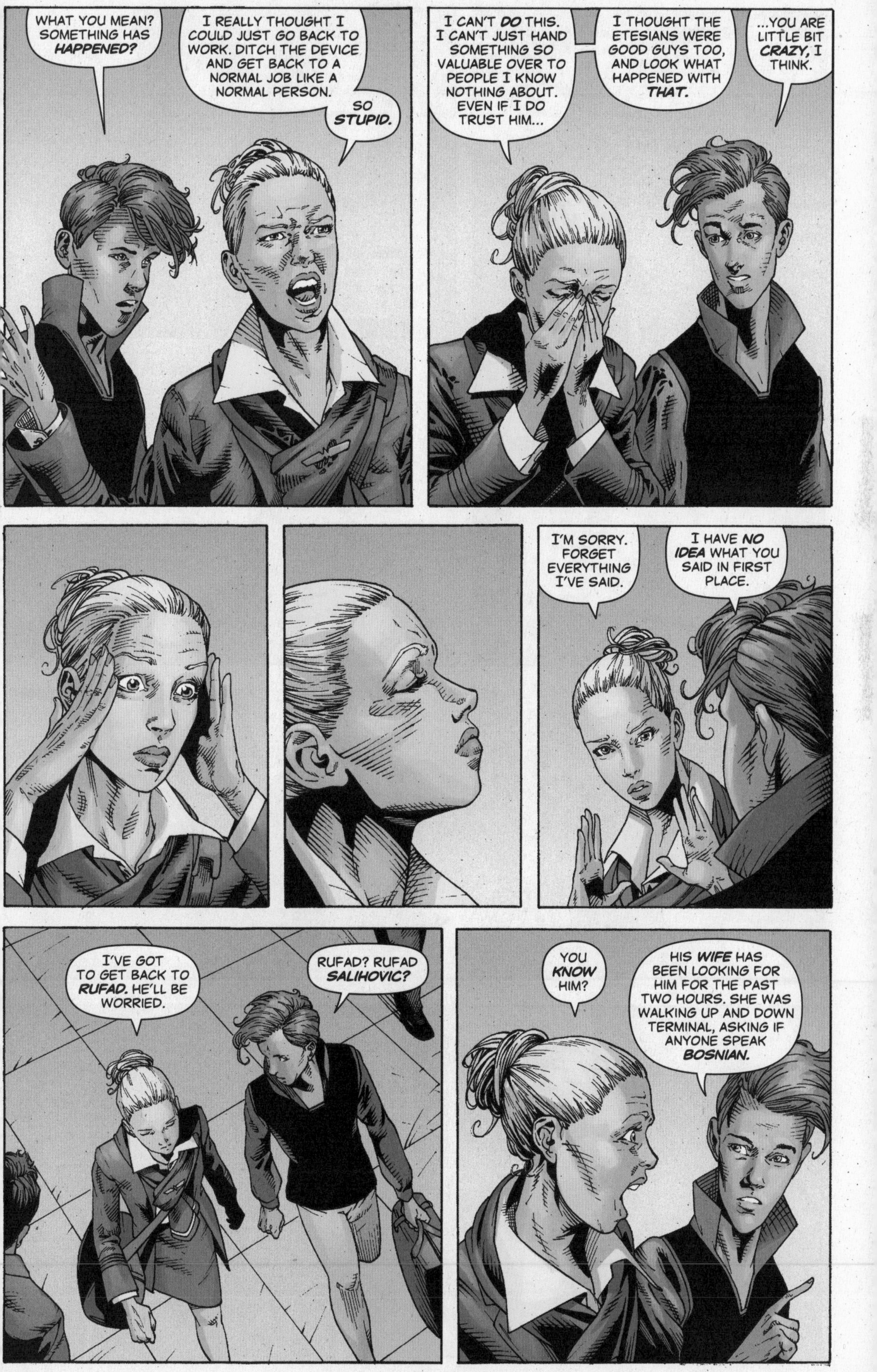
WHAT YOU MEAN? SOMETHING HAS HAPPENED?
I REALLY THOUGHT I COULD JUST GO BACK TO WORK. DITCH THE DEVICE AND GET BACK TO A NORMAL JOB LIKE A NORMAL PERSON.
SO STUPID.
I CAN'T DO THIS. I CAN'T JUST HAND SOMETHING SO VALUABLE OVER TO PEOPLE I KNOW NOTHING ABOUT. EVEN IF I DO TRUST HIM...
I THOUGHT THE ETESIANS WERE GOOD GUYS TOO, AND LOOK WHAT HAPPENED WITH THAT.
...YOU ARE LITTLE BIT CRAZY, I THINK.
I'M SORRY. FORGET EVERYTHING I'VE SAID.
I HAVE NO IDEA WHAT YOU SAID IN FIRST PLACE.
I'VE GOT TO GET BACK TO RUFAD. HE'LL BE WORRIED.
RUFAD? RUFAD SALIHOVIC?
YOU KNOW HIM?
HIS WIFE HAS BEEN LOOKING FOR HIM FOR THE PAST TWO HOURS. SHE WAS WALKING UP AND DOWN TERMINAL, ASKING IF ANYONE SPEAK BOSNIAN.

YOU'VE SEEN HER? YOU *SPOKE* TO HER?

YES, YES! I SPEAK LITTLE BOSNIAN BECAUSE I HAVE BOSNIAN *GRANDMOTHER--*

WHERE IS SHE NOW?

IN *CAFE.*

I can either hide from this guy, or I can help Rufad and his wife.

And I'm done hiding.

GO GET HER AND MEET ME AT THE INFORMATION DESK WHERE ANDRIES WORKS. I'VE GOT HER *HUSBAND.*

OKAY, FINE.

GATES
101 -120
←

Fuck normal life.

92

EVERYTHING IS OKAY? THIS MAN WILL HELP YOU FIND MY WIFE NOW?

ANDRIES' RUSSIAN FRIEND ALREADY *FOUND* HER. HE'S BRINGING HER HERE NOW.

THANK GOD, THANK GOD!

YOU HAVE NO IDEA WHAT THIS MEAN TO ME. TO *US.*

I REALLY DIDN'T DO ANYTHING.

YOU *LISTENED.* THANK YOU.

CAN I ASK YOU SOME-THING?

YES, WHATEVER YOU WANT.

HOW DO YOU KNOW IT'S GOING TO BE OKAY? AFTER ALL THESE YEARS AND EVERYTHING THAT'S HAPPENED?

SOME PEOPLE, THEY ARE **CONNECTED**. NOT JUST BY LOVE. BY SOMETHING ELSE. IF THIS IS TRUE, IT DOESN'T MATTER WHAT *HAPPEN*. YOU WILL FIGHT FOR THAT PERSON EVEN IF YOU DON'T UNDERSTAND WHY.

I *TRUST* THIS FEELING. I KNOW SHE DOES ALSO.

...WOW.

...RUFAD? RUFAD!

AIDA!

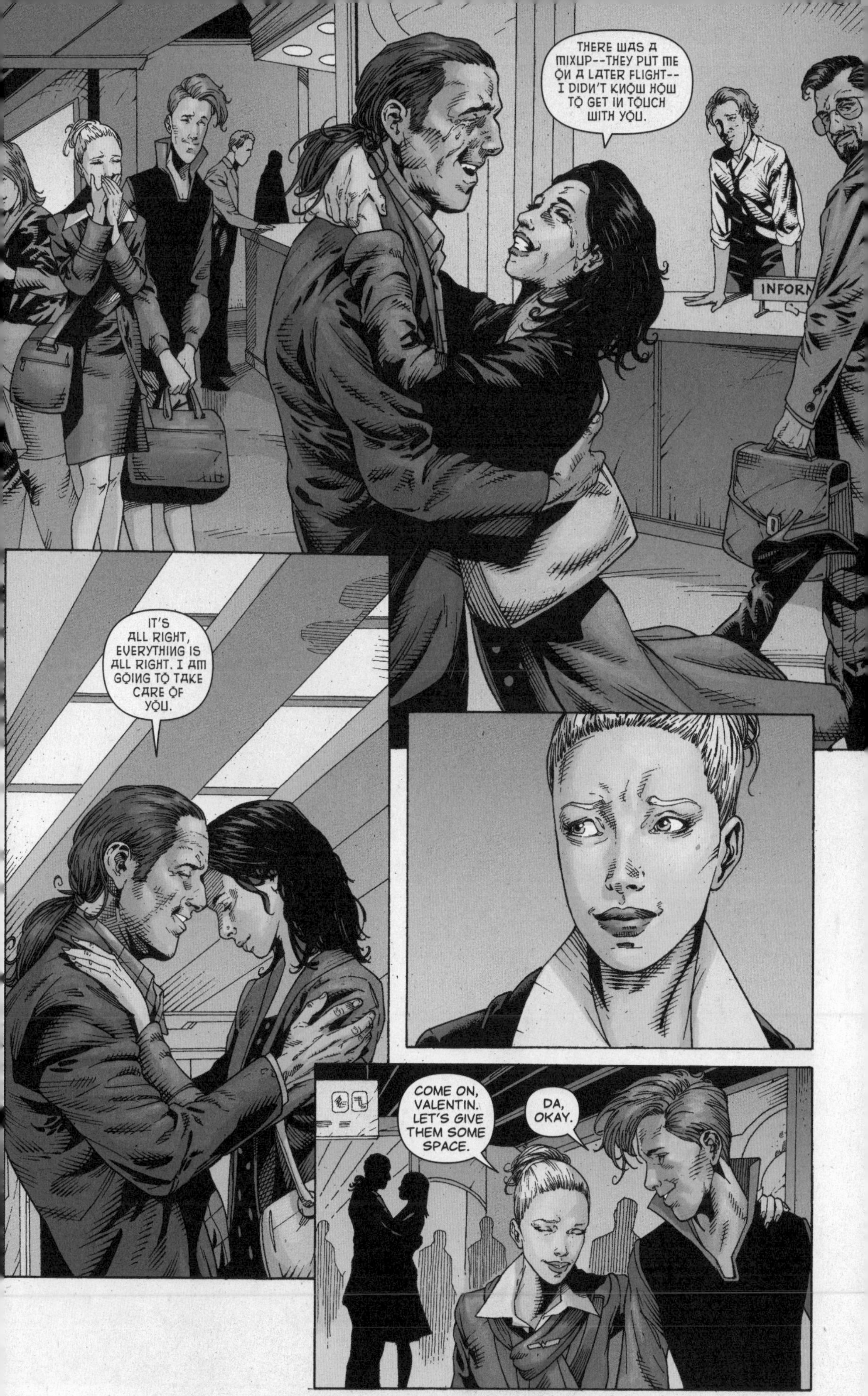

THERE WAS A MIXUP--THEY PUT ME ON A LATER FLIGHT--I DIDN'T KNOW HOW TO GET IN TOUCH WITH YOU.
INFORM
IT'S ALL RIGHT, EVERYTHING IS ALL RIGHT. I AM GOING TO TAKE CARE OF YOU.
COME ON, VALENTIN. LET'S GIVE THEM SOME SPACE.
DA, OKAY.

ISN'T IT **WEIRD** THAT I KNEW ANDRIES, AND ANDRIES KNEW YOU, AND YOU SPEAK BOSNIAN?

IS NOT WEIRD. IS **SYNCHRONICITY.** WORLD **RUNS** ON SYNCHRONICITY.

ALL THIS TIME I THOUGHT THE WORLD HAD **CHANGED** WHEN I WASN'T LOOKING-- BUT MAYBE THIS IS THE WAY IT'S BEEN ALL ALONG. MAYBE I WAS JUST TOO DISTRACTED TO **NOTICE.**

WHAT TIME IS IT?

ALMOST **NOON.**

I HAVE TO GO DROP SOMETHING OFF. BUT IT WAS NICE MEETING YOU. I HOPE YOU GET BACK TO MOSCOW IN TIME FOR YOUR SHOW.

IF NOT, NO BIG DEAL. I PLAY ONLY THIRD SERVANT FROM LEFT.

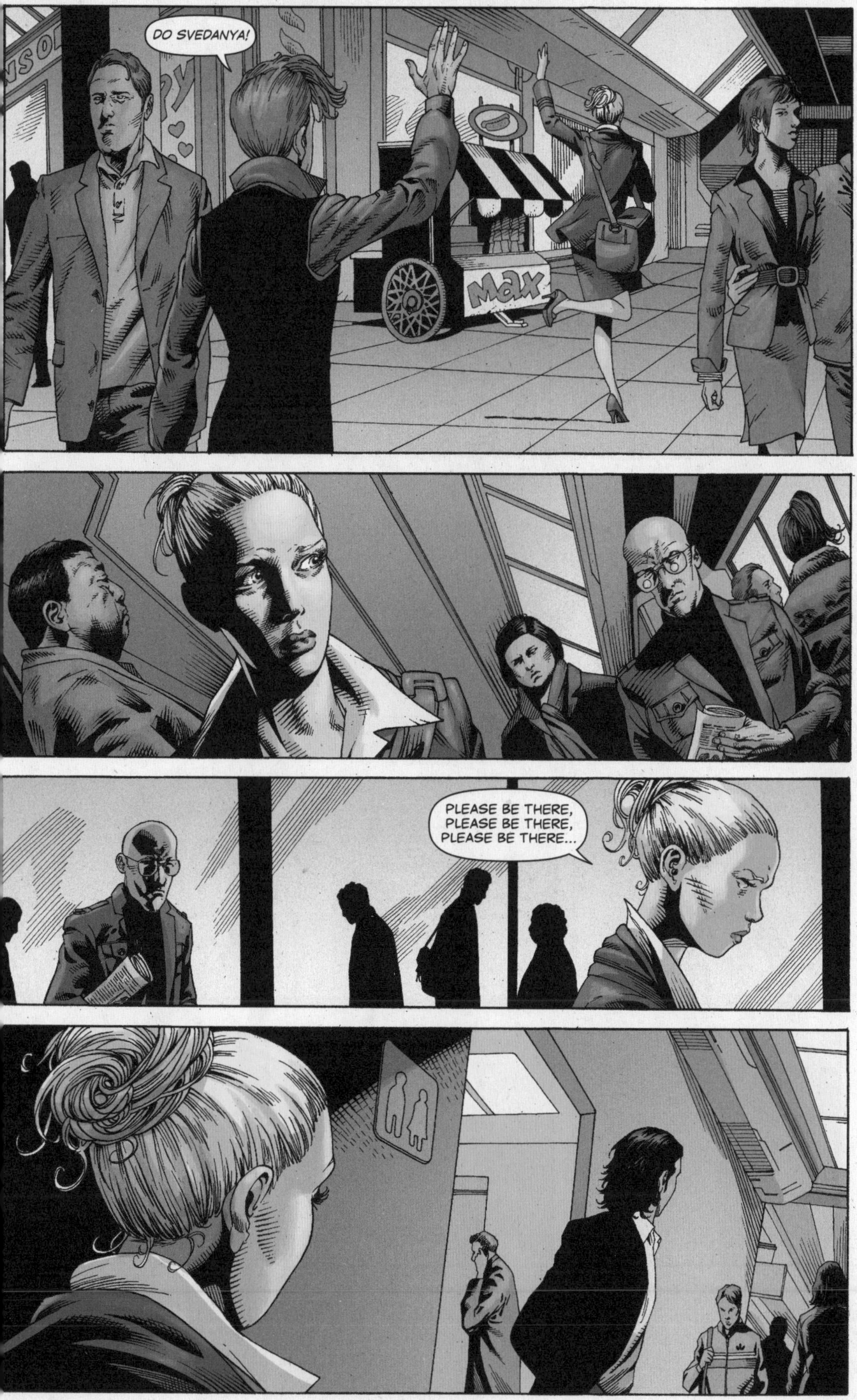
DO SVEDANYA!
MAX
PLEASE BE THERE, PLEASE BE THERE, PLEASE BE THERE...

ZAYN...

ZAYN! YOU DID COME--

BLYTHE CAMERON, I PRESUME.

NOT ZAYN.

NO. MY NAME IS *SHUN MU.* I WORK WITH ZAYN. WHEN WE RECEIVED YOUR LETTER, OUR SUPERVISOR SENT ME TO COLLECT THE DEVICE.

...OH.

DON'T LOOK SO UPSET. ZAYN DID SEND A MESSAGE.

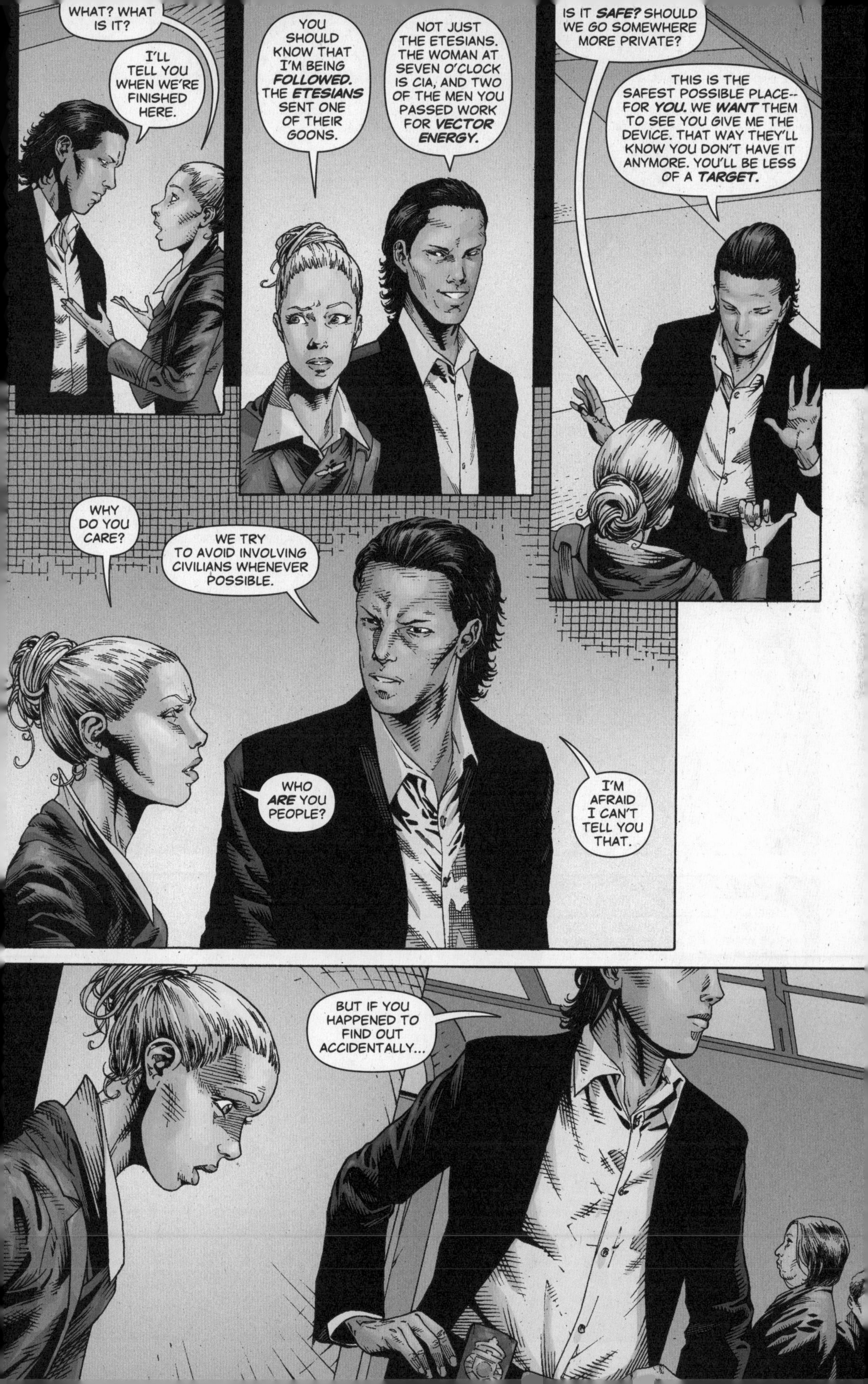
WHAT? WHAT IS IT?
I'LL TELL YOU WHEN WE'RE FINISHED HERE.
YOU SHOULD KNOW THAT I'M BEING *FOLLOWED.* THE *ETESIANS* SENT ONE OF THEIR GOONS.
NOT JUST THE ETESIANS. THE WOMAN AT SEVEN O'CLOCK IS CIA, AND TWO OF THE MEN YOU PASSED WORK FOR *VECTOR ENERGY.*
IS IT *SAFE?* SHOULD WE GO SOMEWHERE MORE PRIVATE?
THIS IS THE SAFEST POSSIBLE PLACE-- FOR *YOU.* WE *WANT* THEM TO SEE YOU GIVE ME THE DEVICE. THAT WAY THEY'LL KNOW YOU DON'T HAVE IT ANYMORE. YOU'LL BE LESS OF A *TARGET.*
WHY DO YOU CARE?
WE TRY TO AVOID INVOLVING CIVILIANS WHENEVER POSSIBLE.
WHO *ARE* YOU PEOPLE?
I'M AFRAID I CAN'T TELL YOU THAT.
BUT IF YOU HAPPENED TO FIND OUT ACCIDENTALLY...

"...NO HARM,
NO FOUL."

...INTERPOL.

WHEN I FOUND OUT WHERE ZAYN WAS FROM-- WHAT HE *WENT* THROUGH-- I WAS AFRAID HE REALLY *WAS* A TERRORIST--

FAR FROM IT.

SO WHAT HAPPENS NOW? WHAT ARE YOU GOING TO DO WITH THE DEVICE?

IT WILL BE STUDIED UNDER GUARD AT ONE OF OUR LABS IN ASIA. INFORMATION WILL BE MADE AVAILABLE TO THE INTERNATIONAL COMMUNITY IN AS UNBIASED A WAY AS POSSIBLE.

AND WE WILL BE IN TOUCH WITH YOU AGAIN VERY SOON. CLEARFLEET IS ABOUT TO *PROMOTE* YOU-- A HYPERPRACT WITH YOUR SKILLS BELONGS IN A COCKPIT, NOT BEHIND A BEVERAGE CART.

WE'LL BE WATCHING.

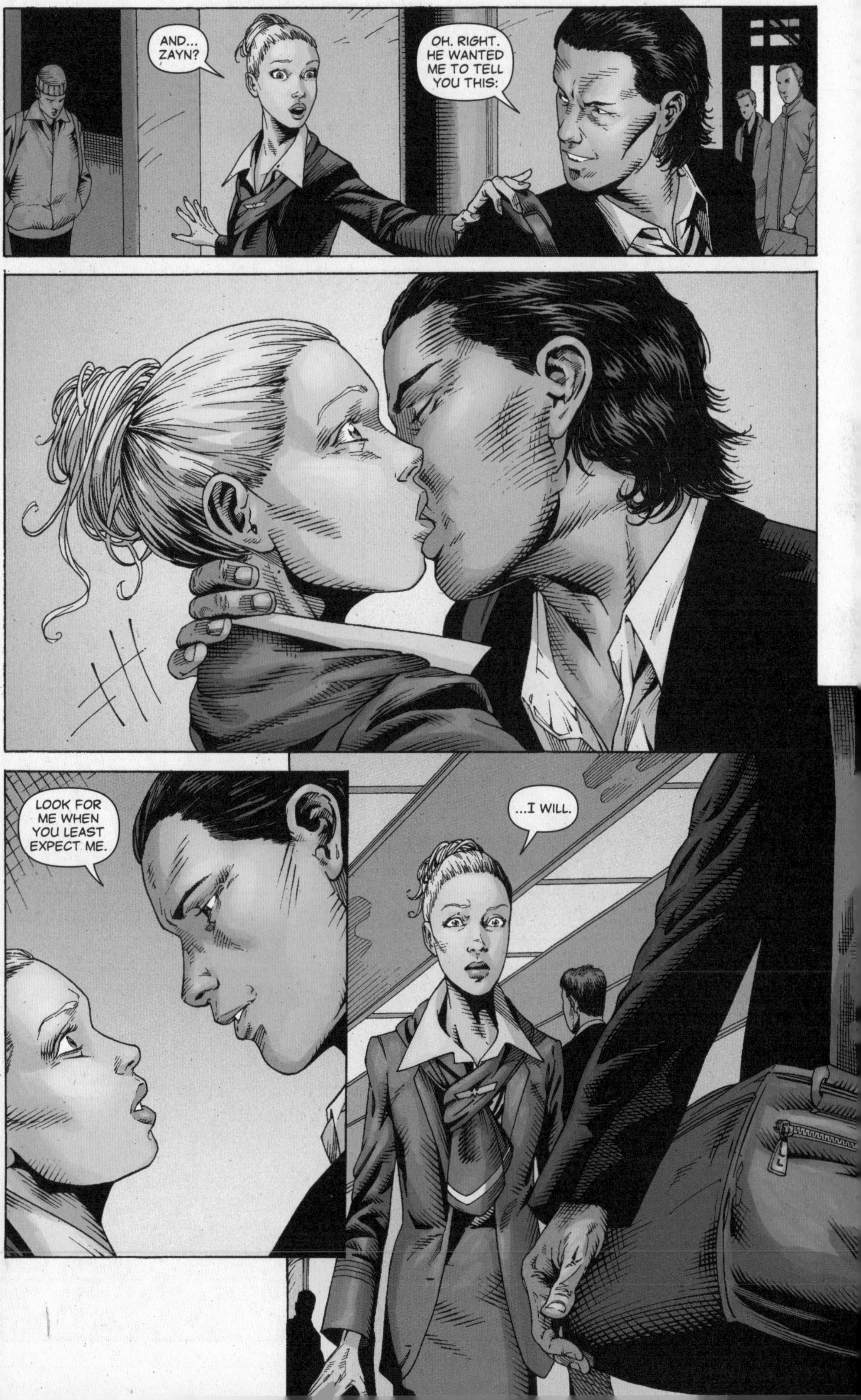
AND... ZAYN?
OH. RIGHT. HE WANTED ME TO TELL YOU THIS:
LOOK FOR ME WHEN YOU LEAST EXPECT ME.
...I WILL.

MIND IF I JOIN YOU?

WHERE DID YOU COME FROM? HOW DID YOU *FIND* ME?

THIS IS WHERE I WOULD COME IF I WANTED TO THINK.

YOU ALL RIGHT?

I FEEL...LIKE I CAN'T KEEP UP WITH EVERY-THING EVERYONE EXPECTS FROM ME.

I WANT SOME *STABILITY*. SOMETHING I CAN COUNT ON.

YOU HAVE THE AIR UP THERE, KID.

YOU HAVE THE AIR UP THERE.

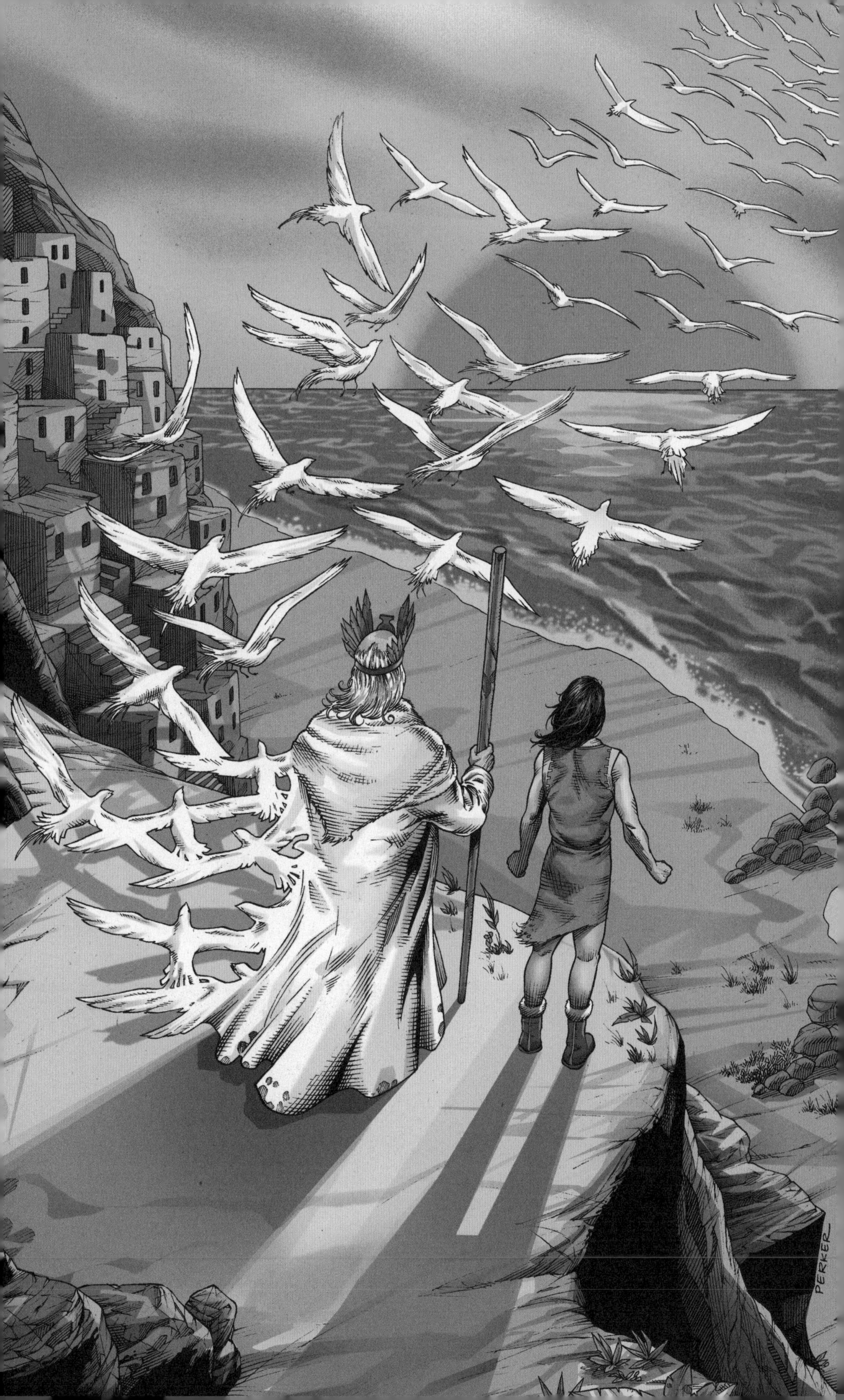
PERKER

PLACE OF THE EGRETS

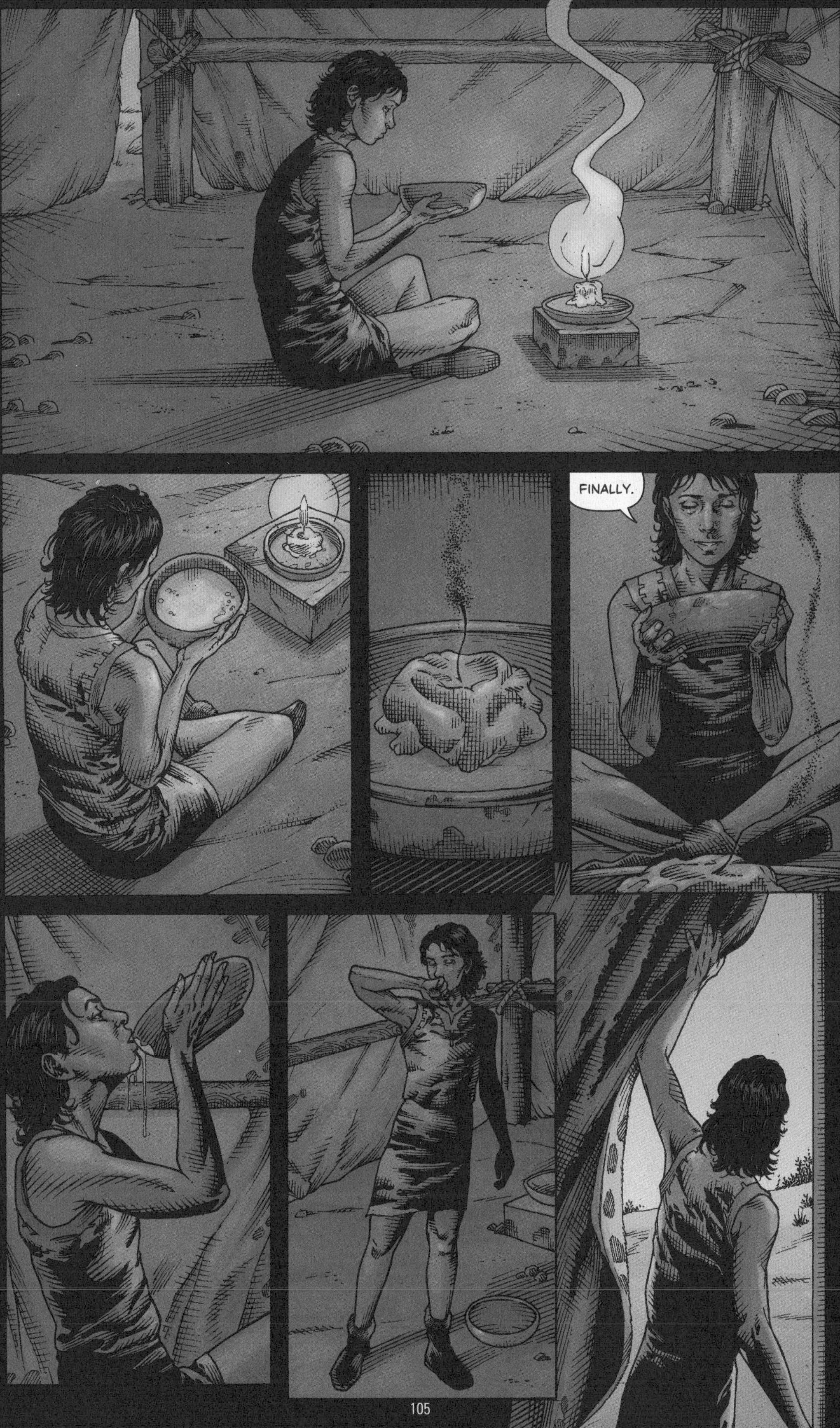
FINALLY.

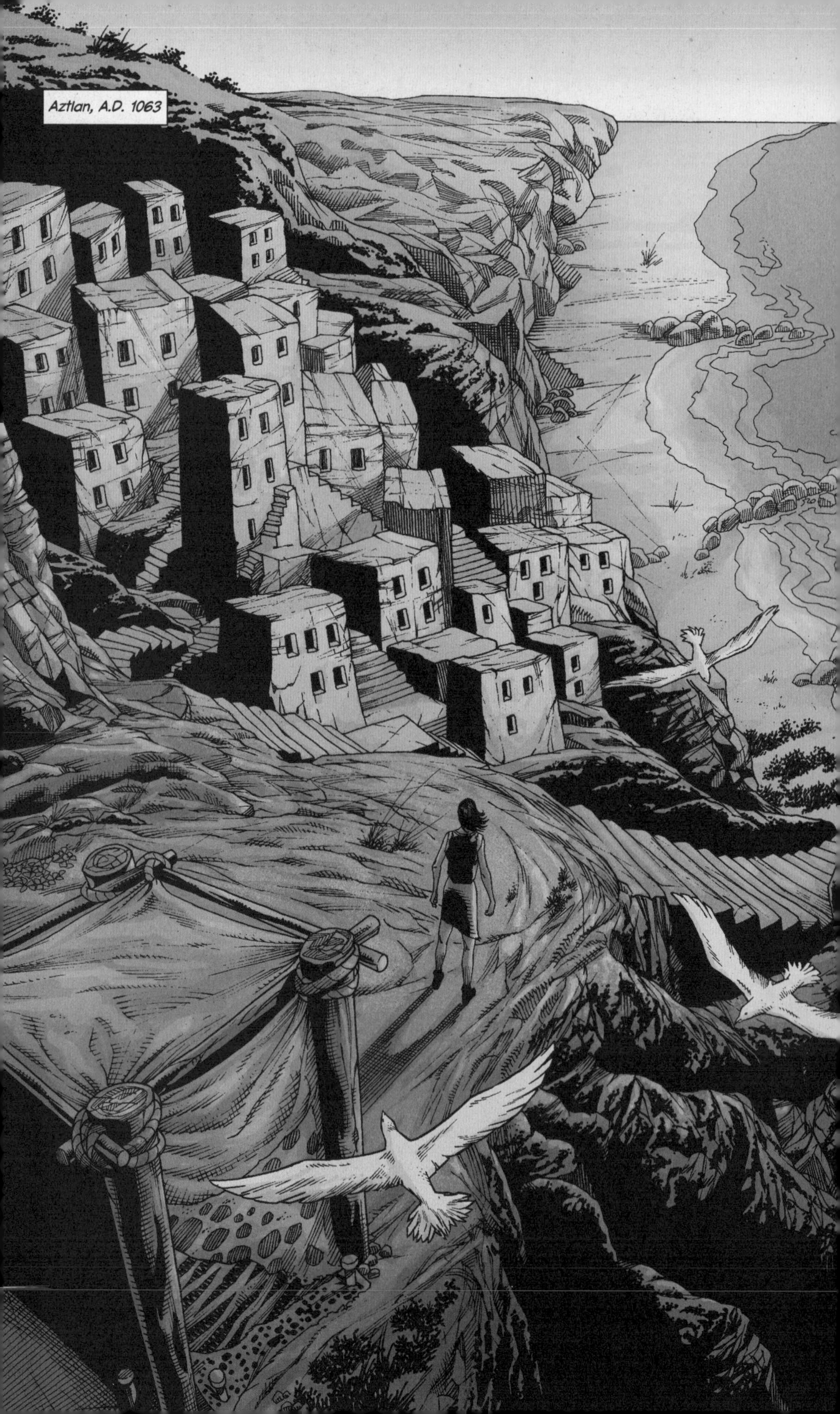
Aztlan, A.D. 1063

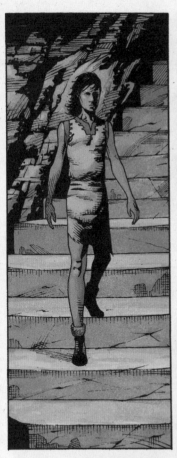

HELLO, LUC. HAVE YOU BROKEN YOUR FAST?

YES, YAOTL.

GOOD. THERE IS SOMETHING I WANT TO SHOW YOU.

ANOTHER *TEST?*

NO. THE TIME OF TESTING IS OVER. YOU ARE NEARLY READY TO BECOME A PRIEST.

WHAT, THEN?

SOMETHING *SECRET.*

WHEN YOU ARE INITIATED, WE WILL BE *BRETHREN.* THAT IS WHY I SHOW YOU THIS NOW. I TRUST YOU-- I *MUST* TRUST YOU.

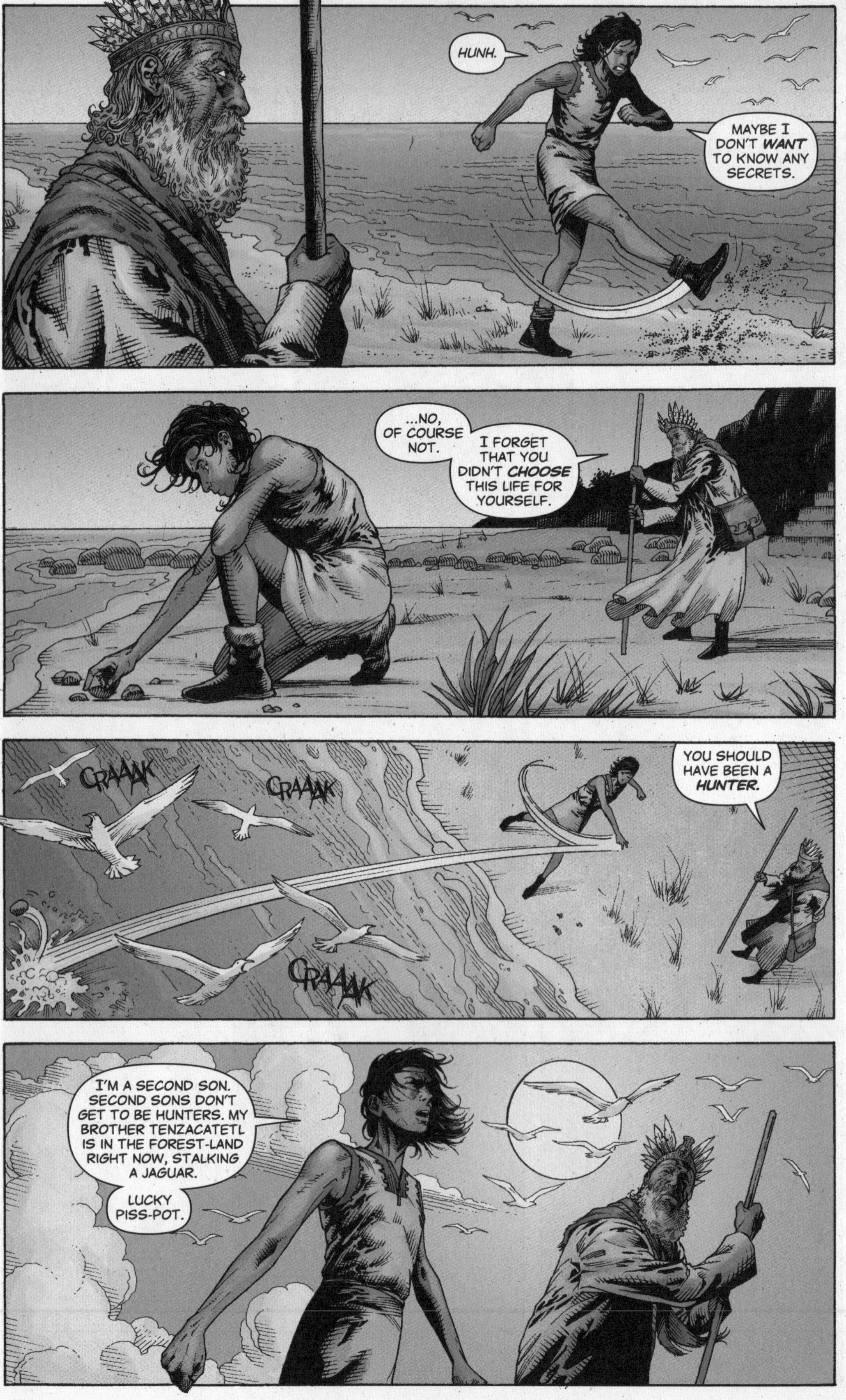
HUNH.
MAYBE I DON'T WANT TO KNOW ANY SECRETS.
...NO, OF COURSE NOT.
I FORGET THAT YOU DIDN'T CHOOSE THIS LIFE FOR YOURSELF.
CRAAAK
CRAAAK
YOU SHOULD HAVE BEEN A HUNTER.
CRAAAK
I'M A SECOND SON. SECOND SONS DON'T GET TO BE HUNTERS. MY BROTHER TENZACATETL IS IN THE FOREST-LAND RIGHT NOW, STALKING A JAGUAR.
LUCKY PISS-POT.

LOOK.

"PLACE OF THE EGRETS." THAT'S WHAT AZTLAN MEANS. A SACRED WORD FOR A SACRED CITY.

SOMEDAY, IT WILL BE YOUR RESPONSIBILITY. YOUR INHERITANCE WILL BE **GREATER** THAN YOUR BROTHER'S, LUC.

WHAT'S WRONG, YAOTL? WHY ARE WE TALKING ABOUT SUCH SERIOUS THINGS?

...I HAVE **SEEN** SOMETHING THAT KEEPS ME FROM MY REST. IT'S PART OF THE REASON I HAVE BROUGHT YOU HERE.

AAH.

HERE-- LET ME HELP YOU WITH THAT.

THANK YOU, MY BOY. THERE'S A *NIGHT-GLASS* INSIDE. TAKE IT OUT AND LOOK THROUGH IT.

ALL RIGHT.

YES. FIFTEEN DEGREES WEST OF THE ZENITH. WHAT DO YOU SEE?

...I SEE THE *CRAB NEBULA.*

SOMETHING'S... SOMETHING'S *WRONG.*

"IT'S...*COLLAPSING.*"

YAOTL... WHAT DOES IT *MEAN*?

WE MUST *LEAVE* AZTLAN.

WE MUST TRAVEL TO A LAND OF LESSER MEN, AND MAKE OUR HOME THERE.

BUT *WHY*?

CHANGE IS COMING.

I DON'T UNDERSTAND.

YOU WILL. PICK UP THE NIGHT-GLASS AND FOLLOW ME.

TELL ME, LUC: WHAT WAS THE FIRST CREATED THING?

A *WORD*. I LEARNED THAT AS A NOVICE.

YES, A WORD. NOT A THING, BUT THE *CODE* FOR A THING. THE *MAP* OF A THING. THE SYMBOLS THAT DESCRIBE THE UNIVERSE ARE *OLDER* THAN THE UNIVERSE ITSELF.

AZTLAN WAS BUILT IN AN AGE WHEN MEN COULD STILL READ THE WORDS WRITTEN ON THE BACK OF THE CREATED WORLD.

AN AGE OF *PROPHECY.*

THAT AGE IS *PASSING.*

LIGHT.

WHAT IS THIS PLACE?

IT IS THE *OLDEST* CAVE IN ALL THE MOUNTAINS. WHEN OUR ANCESTORS ARRIVED HERE, THEY MADE IT A TEMPLE FOR THE *NAHUI*--

THE *FOURTH?*

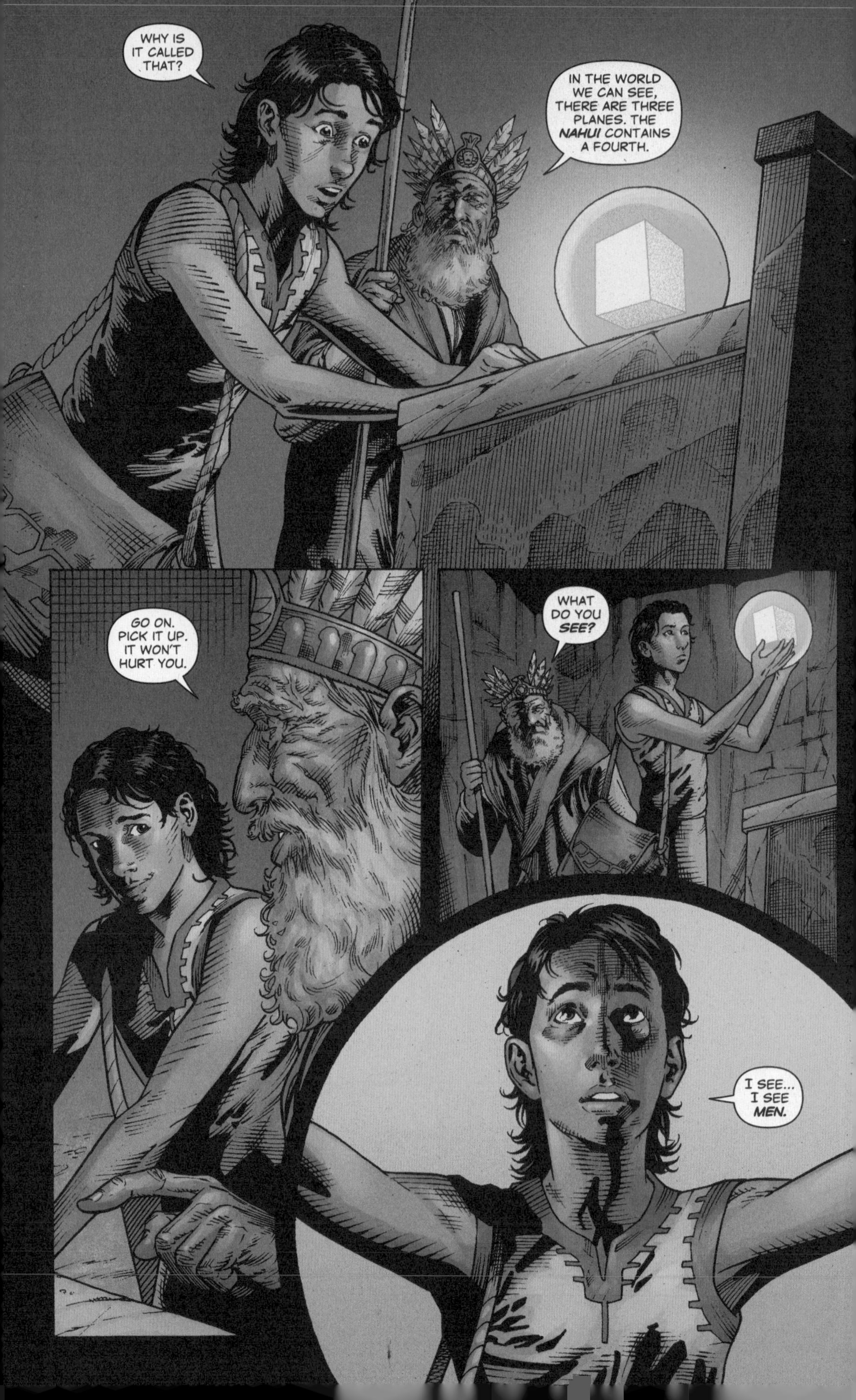
WHY IS IT CALLED THAT?
IN THE WORLD WE CAN SEE, THERE ARE THREE PLANES. THE NAHUI CONTAINS A FOURTH.
GO ON. PICK IT UP. IT WON'T HURT YOU.
WHAT DO YOU SEE?
I SEE... I SEE MEN.

"THEY ARE THIN... SICK FROM... A LONG JOURNEY... THEY LUST FOR SOMETHING..."

AND AZTECS. BUT THEY ARE WEAK...ARMED WITH STICKS. OUR MACHINES... OUR MACHINES ARE GONE. WE CAN'T RESIST THE OUTSIDERS--

THEY WILL SPREAD FAR TO THE NORTH, AS FAR AS THE WINTERLAND. THEY WILL BUILD TOWERS THAT TOUCH THE SUN--

THE TOWERS ARE FALLING-- SO MUCH HURT, YAOTL--THERE WILL BE A WAR IN THE SKY--

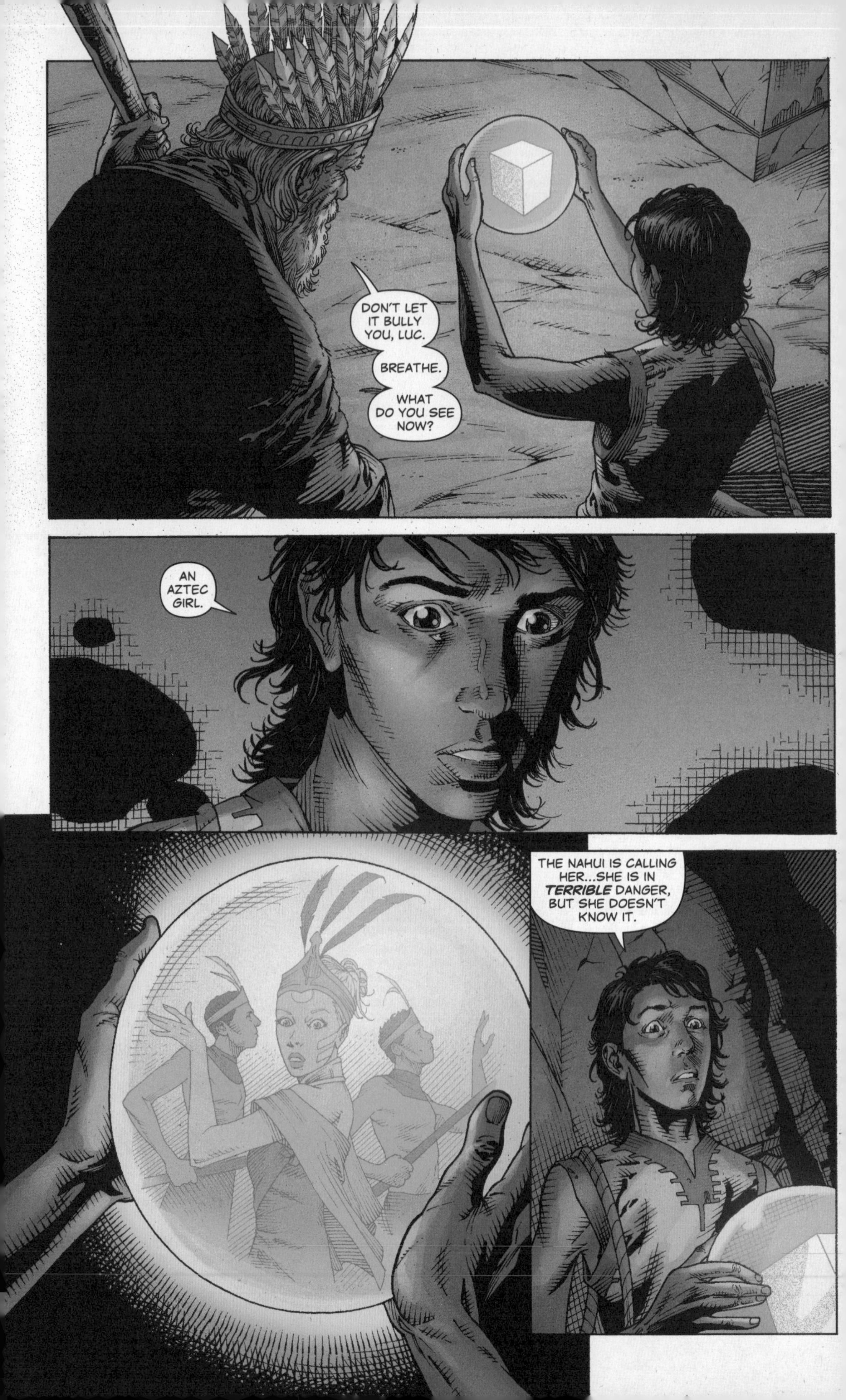
DON'T LET IT BULLY YOU, LUC.
BREATHE.
WHAT DO YOU SEE NOW?
AN AZTEC GIRL.
THE NAHUI IS CALLING HER...SHE IS IN *TERRIBLE* DANGER, BUT SHE DOESN'T KNOW IT.

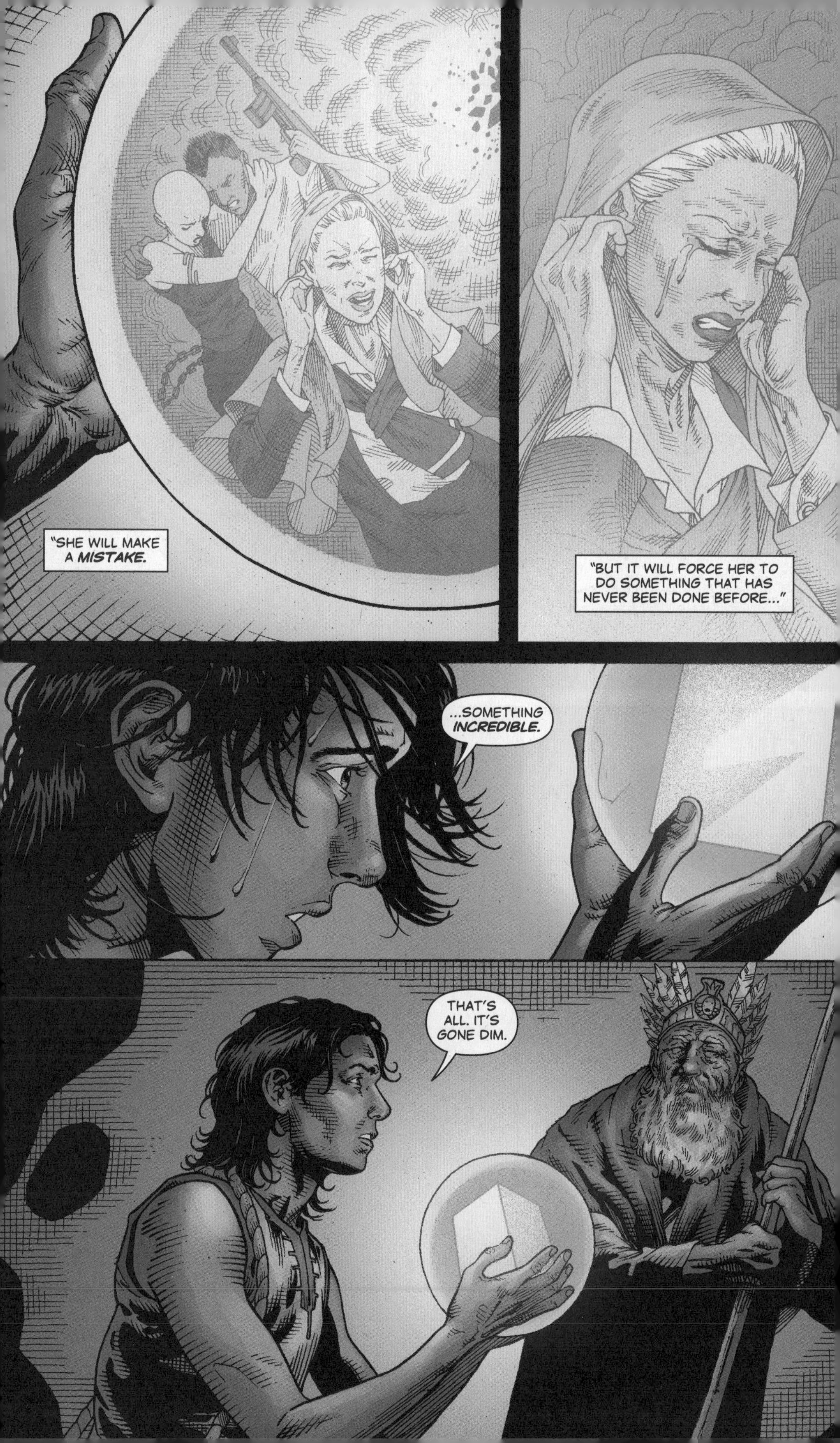
"SHE WILL MAKE A MISTAKE.
"BUT IT WILL FORCE HER TO DO SOMETHING THAT HAS NEVER BEEN DONE BEFORE..."
...SOMETHING INCREDIBLE.
THAT'S ALL. IT'S GONE DIM.

YAOTL...IF WE LEAVE AZTLAN, THERE WILL BE *WAR* FOR A *THOUSAND YEARS.*

YES.

THEN *WHY?* WHY MUST WE LEAVE? WHY TELL ME I WILL INHERIT AZTLAN AND THEN SHOW ME *THIS?*

CONTROL YOURSELF!

THERE ARE SIGNS WITHIN SIGNS, LUC.

ON ONE SIDE OF PROPHECY IS GRAVEN THE IMAGE OF *TRUTH.* ON THE OTHER, THE IMAGE OF *CONQUEST.*

AS LONG AS MAN IS MAN...

...THE TWO WILL BE INSEPARABLE.

MEN *KILL* FOR THE TRUTH BECAUSE THEY DO NOT KNOW HOW TO *LIVE* FOR IT.

IF WE LEAVE AZTLAN AND GO OUT AMONG OTHER MEN, THE KNOWLEDGE WE HAVE GAINED HERE WILL FADE. WE WILL FORGET HOW TO USE OUR MACHINES, AND THEN WE WILL FORGET HOW TO *BUILD* THEM.

WAR WILL ENGULF THE EARTH. BUT *WONDER* WILL NOT GO OUT OF IT.

BECAUSE YOU WILL TAKE THE NAHUI, AND THE STORY OF THIS PLACE, AND HAND THEM DOWN THROUGH THE YEARS. THE *GODS* WILL NOT BE FORGOTTEN.

BUT YAOTL...I AM NOT **WORTHY** OF THIS TASK.

I DON'T EVEN **BELIEVE** IN THE GODS!

BELIEF IS NOT NECESSARY. ONLY **GOODNESS** IS NECESSARY. AND YOU HAVE THAT IN ABUNDANCE.

THE FATE OF THE AZTEC WILL BE THE SAME IN ANY CASE. IF WE STAY, WE WILL DIE-- AZTLAN IS A **HOLY** PLACE, AND THE HOLY PLACES ARE RETREATING FROM THE WORLD OF MEN.

AS THE AGE OF PROPHECY PASSES, SO DO THEY.

"BUT IF WE GO, OUR STORIES WILL **NOT** DIE WITH US."

AND THE KNOWLEDGE OF THE WORDS WRITTEN ON THE BACK OF CREATION WILL NOT PASS FROM THE HEARTS OF MEN.

"ALL OVER THE WORLD, THIS SAME CONVERSATION IS TAKING PLACE... IN MONASTERIES, IN TEMPLES, IN DOMED LIBRARIES ON SANDY PLAINS.

"WHAT DO WE DO WITH THE KNOWLEDGE OF FIRST THINGS? KEEP IT LOCKED UP AND HIDDEN AWAY, WHERE IT HARMS NO ONE?

"OR PROCLAIM IT AND RISK CONFLICT?

"WHY IS IT SO COSTLY TO PRESERVE OUR HISTORY?"

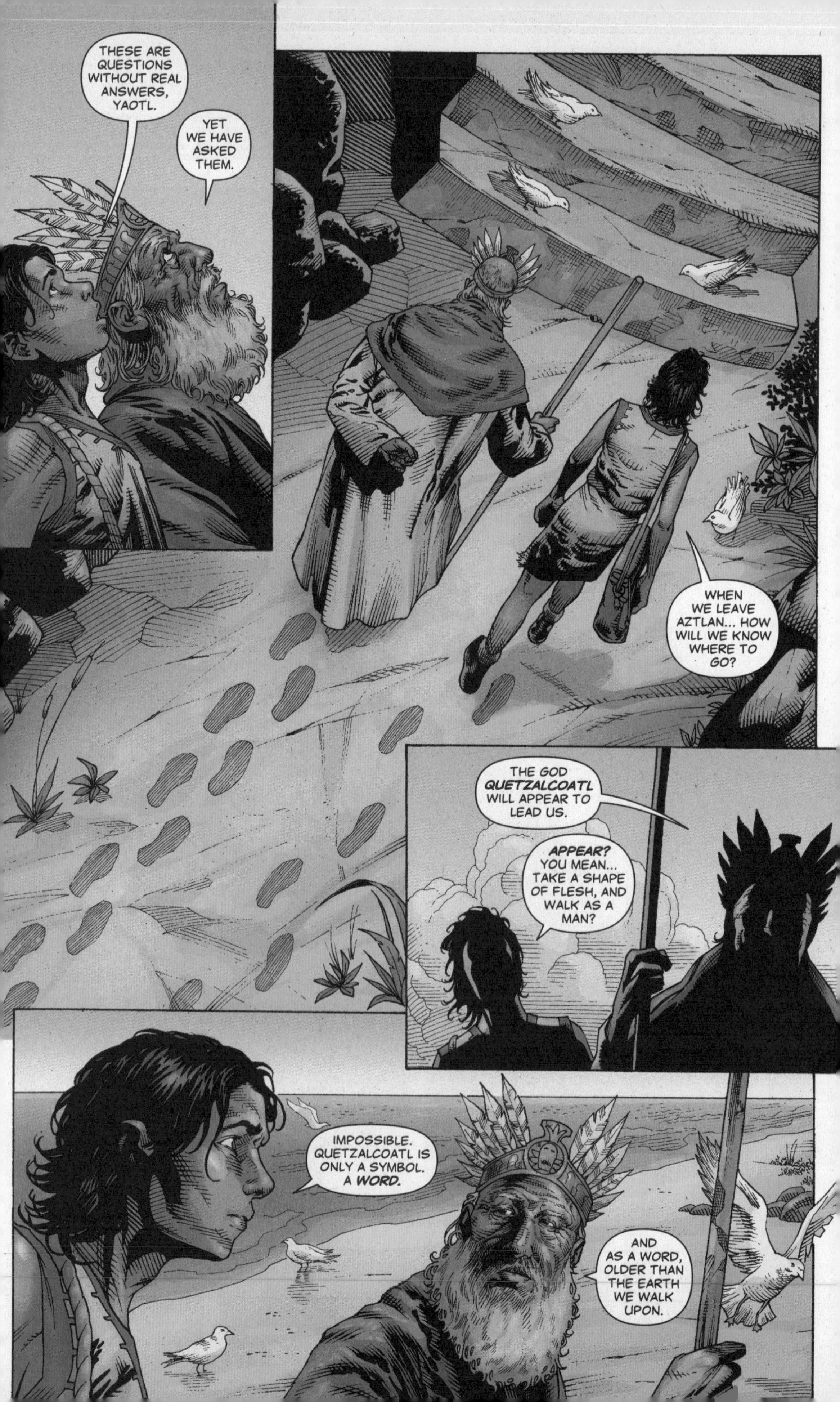

THESE ARE QUESTIONS WITHOUT REAL ANSWERS, YAOTL.
YET WE HAVE ASKED THEM.
WHEN WE LEAVE AZTLAN... HOW WILL WE KNOW WHERE TO GO?
THE GOD QUETZALCOATL WILL APPEAR TO LEAD US.
APPEAR? YOU MEAN... TAKE A SHAPE OF FLESH, AND WALK AS A MAN?
IMPOSSIBLE. QUETZALCOATL IS ONLY A SYMBOL. A WORD.
AND AS A WORD, OLDER THAN THE EARTH WE WALK UPON.

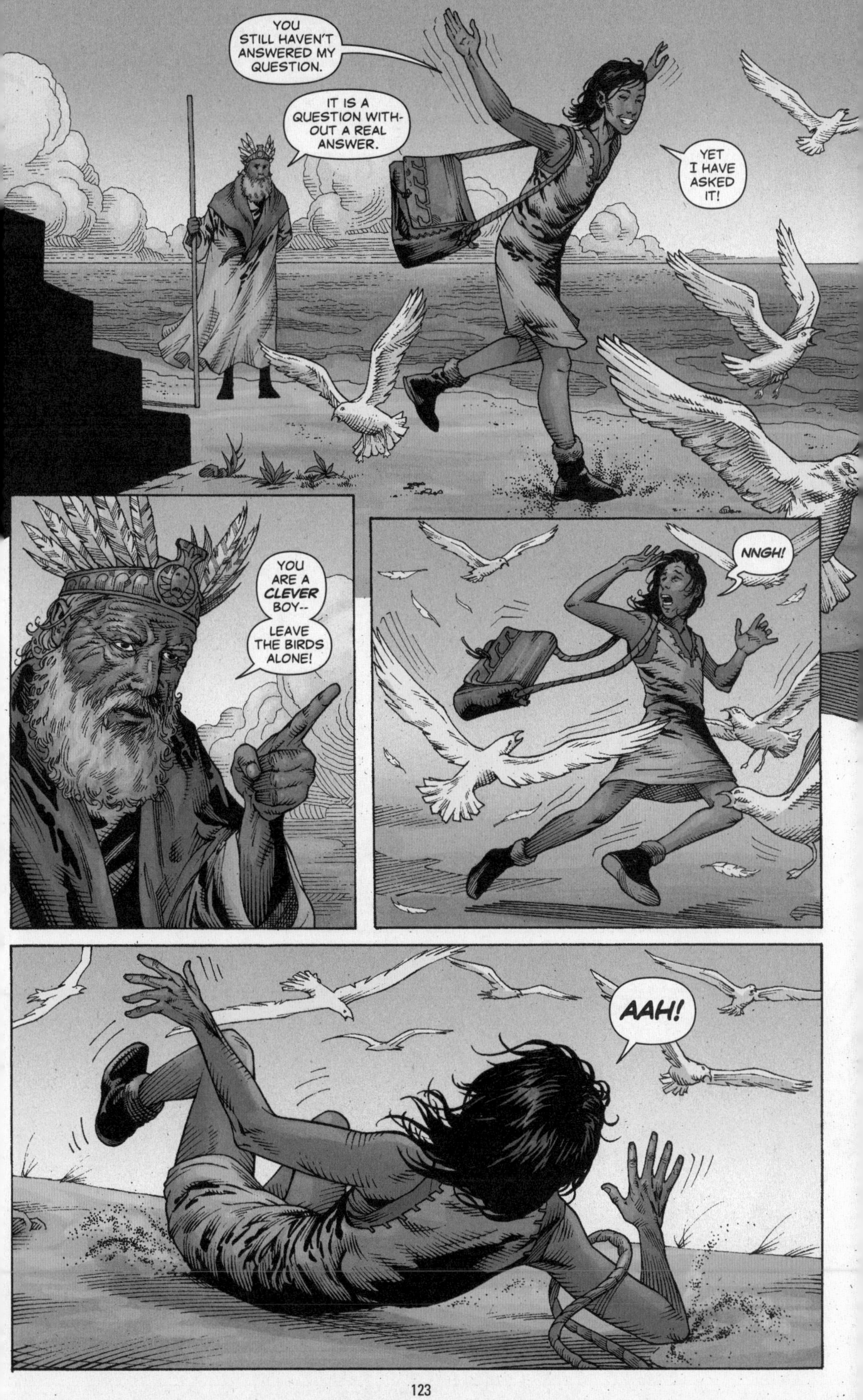
YOU STILL HAVEN'T ANSWERED MY QUESTION.
IT IS A QUESTION WITH-OUT A REAL ANSWER.
YET I HAVE ASKED IT!
YOU ARE A *CLEVER* BOY--
LEAVE THE BIRDS ALONE!
NNGH!
AAH!

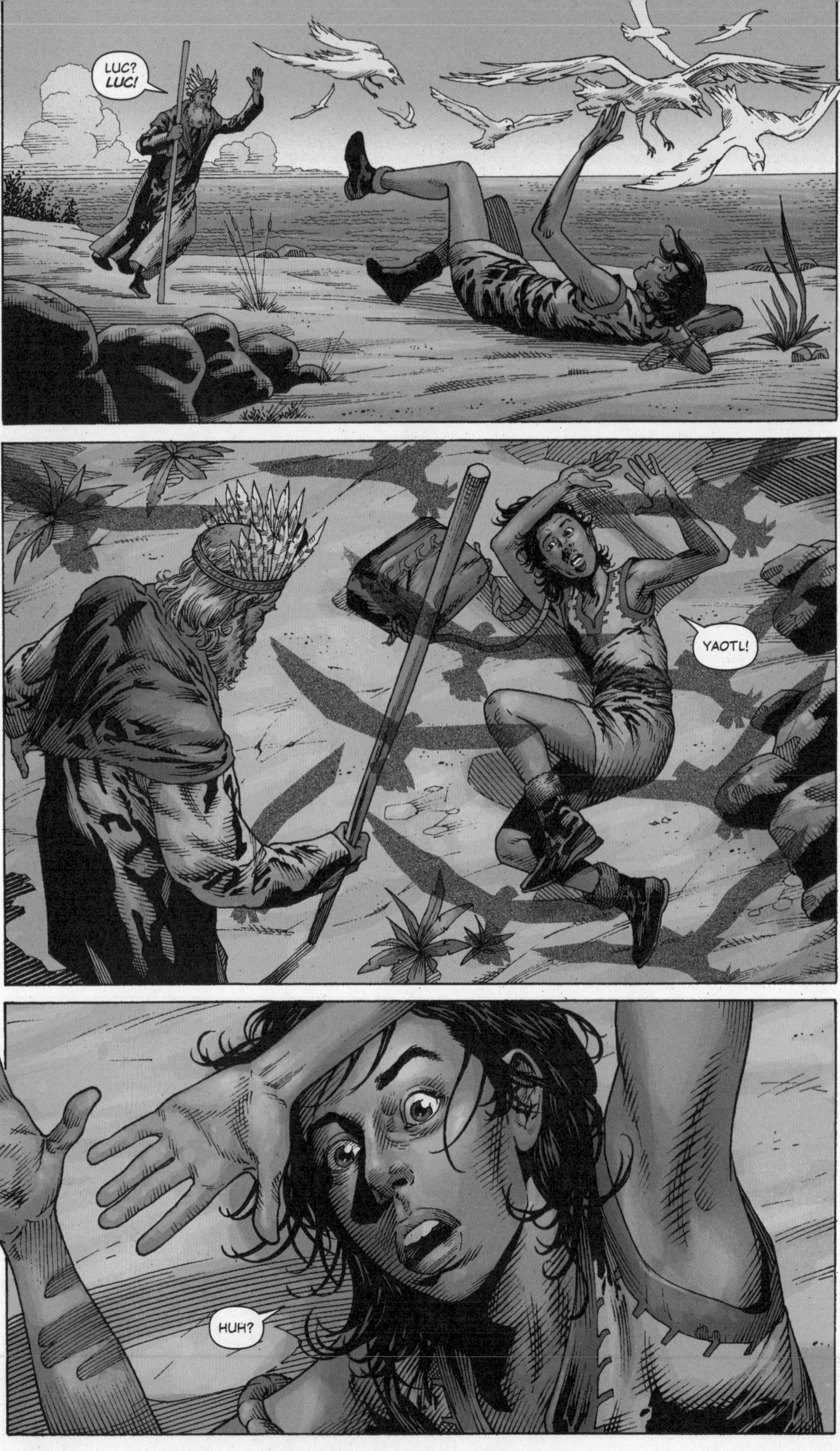
LUC? LUC!
YAOTL!
HUH?

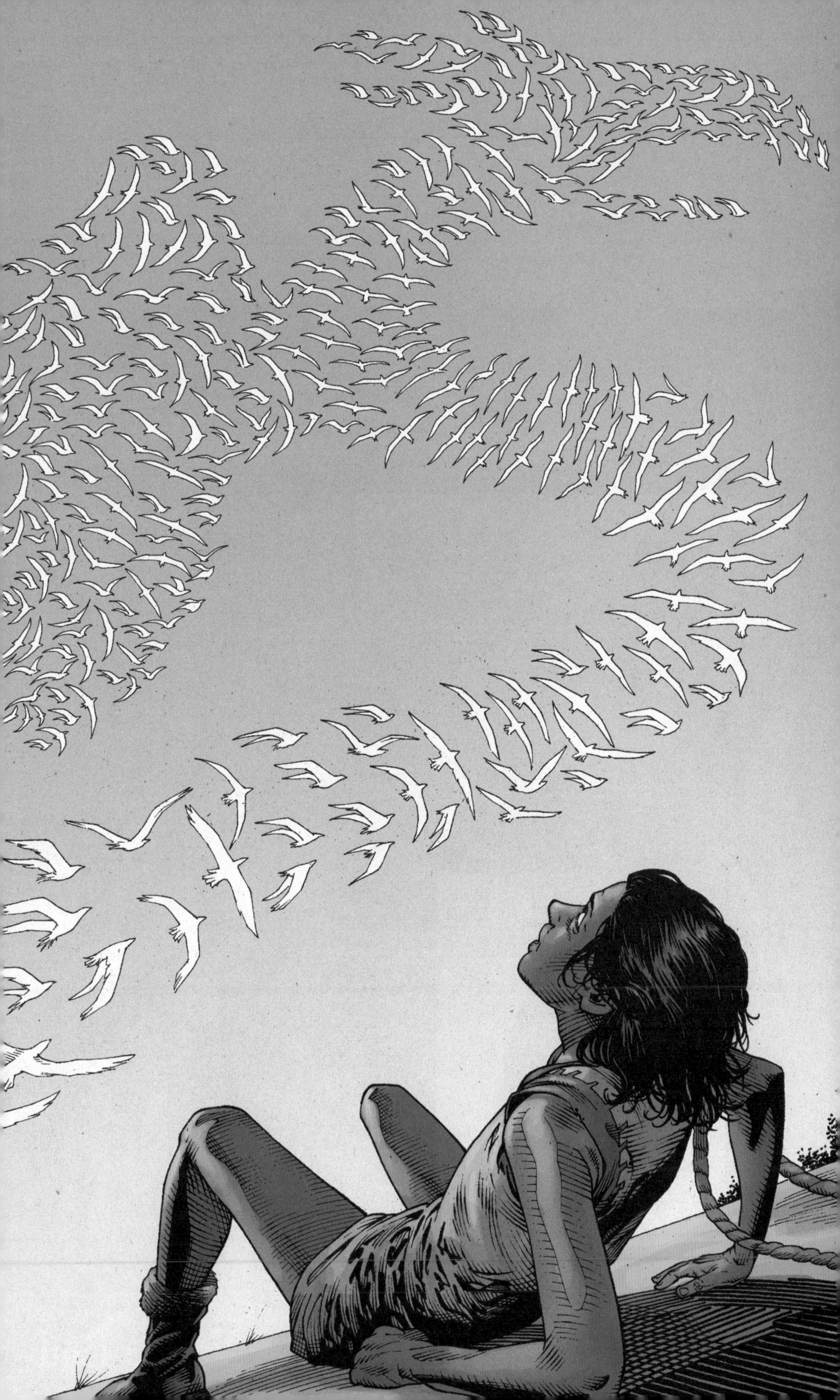

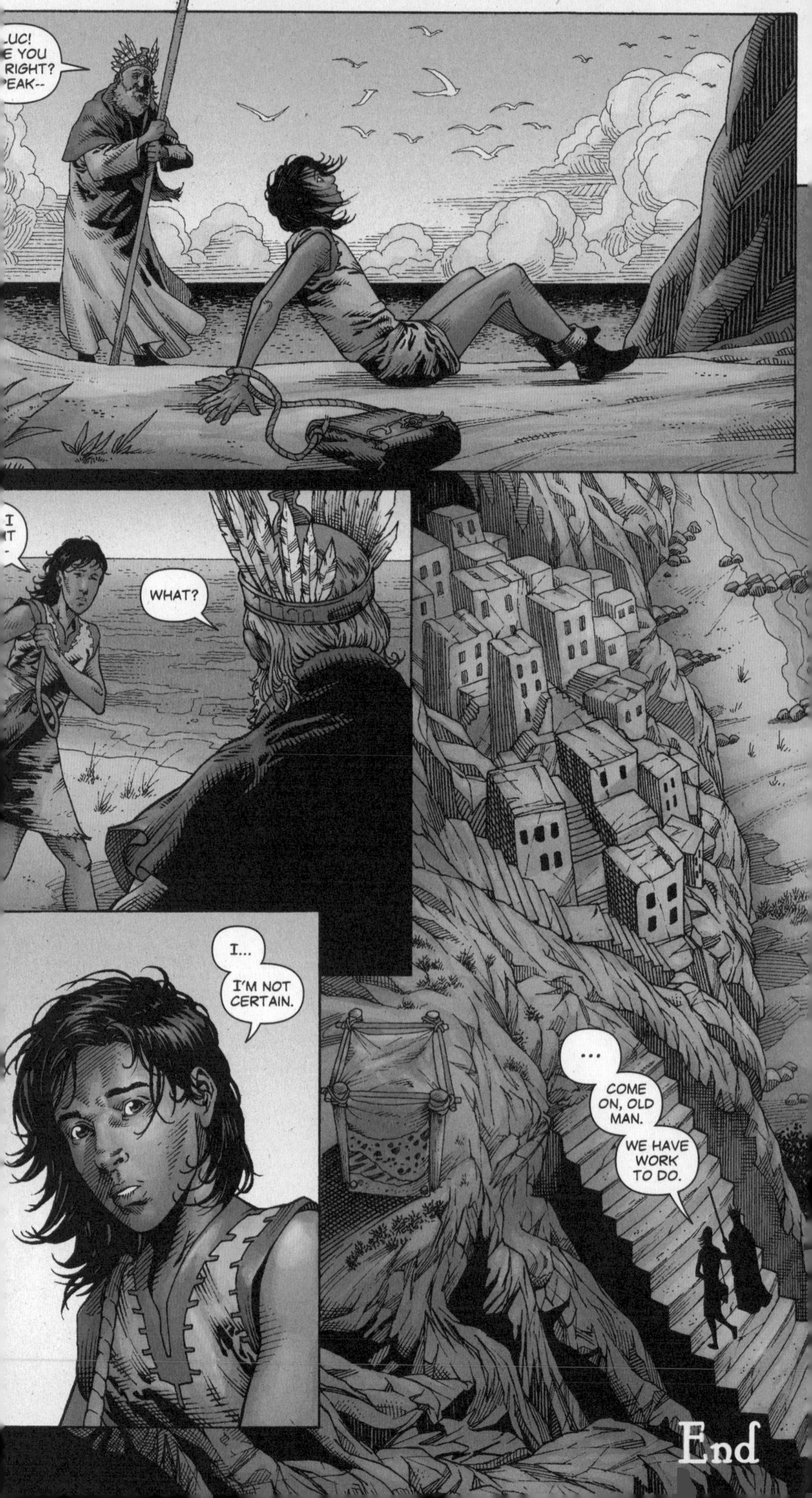
LUC! E YOU RIGHT? PEAK--
WHAT?
I...
I'M NOT CERTAIN.
...
COME ON, OLD MAN.
WE HAVE WORK TO DO.
End

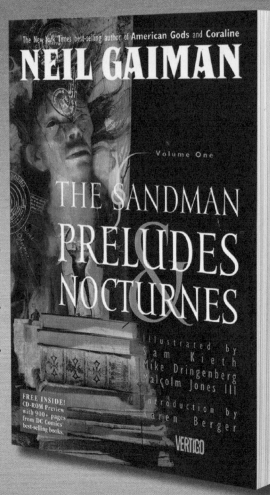
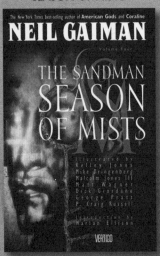
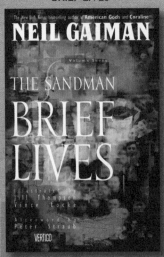
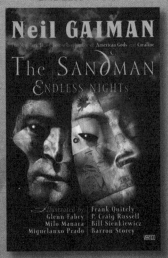

Jossey-Bass Teacher

Jossey-Bass Teacher provides K–12 teachers with essential knowledge and tools to create a positive and lifelong impact on student learning. Trusted and experienced educational mentors offer practical classroom-tested and theory-based teaching resources for improving teaching practice in a broad range of grade levels and subject areas. From one educator to another, we want to be your first source to make every day your best day in teaching. *Jossey-Bass Teacher* resources serve two types of informational needs—essential knowledge and essential tools.

Essential knowledge resources provide the foundation, strategies, and methods from which teachers may design curriculum and instruction to challenge and excite their students. Connecting theory to practice, essential knowledge books rely on a solid research base and time-tested methods, offering the best ideas and guidance from many of the most experienced and well-respected experts in the field.

Essential tools save teachers time and effort by offering proven, ready-to-use materials for in-class use. Our publications include activities, assessments, exercises, instruments, games, ready reference, and more. They enhance an entire course of study, a weekly lesson, or a daily plan. These essential tools provide insightful, practical, and comprehensive materials on topics that matter most to K–12 teachers.

GEOMETRY OUT LOUD

Learning Mathematics Through Reading and Writing Activities

PAT MOWER

JOSSEY-BASS
A Wiley Imprint
www.josseybass.com

Copyright © 2006 by John Wiley & Sons, Inc. All rights reserved.

Published by Jossey-Bass
A Wiley Imprint
989 Market Street, San Francisco, CA 94103-1741   www.josseybass.com

No part of this publication may be reproduced, stored in a retrieval system, or transmitted in any form or by any means, electronic, mechanical, photocopying, recording, scanning, or otherwise, except as permitted under Section 107 or 108 of the 1976 United States Copyright Act, without either the prior written permission of the publisher, or authorization through payment of the appropriate per-copy fee to the Copyright Clearance Center, Inc., 222 Rosewood Drive, Danvers, MA 01923, 978-750-8400, fax 978-646-8600, or on the Web at www.copyright.com. Requests to the publisher for permission should be addressed to the Permissions Department, John Wiley & Sons, Inc., 111 River Street, Hoboken, NJ 07030, 201-748-6011, fax 201-748-6008, or online at http://www.wiley.com/go/permissions.

Limit of Liability/Disclaimer of Warranty: While the publisher and author have used their best efforts in preparing this book, they make no representations or warranties with respect to the accuracy or completeness of the contents of this book and specifically disclaim any implied warranties of merchantability or fitness for a particular purpose. No warranty may be created or extended by sales representatives or written sales materials. The advice and strategies contained herein may not be suitable for your situation. You should consult with a professional where appropriate. Neither the publisher nor author shall be liable for any loss of profit or any other commercial damages, including but not limited to special, incidental, consequential, or other damages.

Permission is given for individual classroom teachers to reproduce the pages and illustrations for classroom use. Reproduction of these materials for an entire school system is strictly forbidden.

Jossey-Bass books and products are available through most bookstores. To contact Jossey-Bass directly call our Customer Care Department within the U.S. at 800-956-7739, outside the U.S. at 317-572-3986, or fax 317-572-4002.

Jossey-Bass also publishes its books in a variety of electronic formats. Some content that appears in print may not be available in electronic books.

ISBN 10: 0-7879-7601-6
ISBN 13: 978-0-7879-7601-9

Printed in the United States of America
FIRST EDITION
PB Printing   10 9 8 7 6 5 4 3 2 1

The Author

Pat Mower is an associate professor in the Department of Mathematics and Statistics, Washburn University, in Topeka, Kansas. She earned a B.S. with a double major in mathematics and English from Dickinson State University in North Dakota, an M.S. in mathematics with a minor in statistics, and a Ph.D. in teacher education with specialization in mathematics education at the University of North Dakota. Currently, she prepares preservice teachers to teach mathematics in elementary, middle, and secondary school. Her interests include reading and writing in mathematics, alternative methods regarding the teaching and learning of mathematics, and basset hounds.

Acknowledgments

This book would not have been written without the love and support of my husband, Derek; my mother; my sons; and my basset hounds. My gratitude goes out to you all. Also, thanks to my illustrator, Toni Mower, and my editors, Steve, Jeff, and Kate, for all their help and for keeping the vision of the book in mind.

Contents

3 Postreading Strategies and Activities

4 Readings in Geometry

PART TWO Writing to Learn Geometry

5 Writing to Understand Geometry

6 Writing to Communicate Geometry

7 Writing as Authentic Assessment

Introduction

Geometry Out Loud follows *Algebra Out Loud* as the second book of the Math Out Loud series. This book introduces reading and writing strategies and activities that are appropriate for geometry courses at the secondary and college levels. It is my contention, and that of many other mathematics instructors, that learning to read and write efficiently regarding mathematics helps students to understand the mathematics at a deeper level. Courses that focus on reading in the content area stress that reading- and writing-to-learn strategies are effective practices for learning any content of any course. Geometry may seem different from many other courses, including other mathematics courses; in fact, the actual learning procedures are very much alike. Reading, listening, writing, communicating, and problem solving are all parts of education.

The uniqueness of geometry lies in the notion that geometry means visual thinking, which is actually part of many other studies. Along with several reading and writing strategies, this book refers to much of the history of geometry. The progression of axiomatic geometry to transformational geometry, which includes many other geometries, shows the differences in visual thinking that have occurred over the years. The variety of reading and writing activities in this book reflect this change in thinking and practice. Some strategies deal with geometric construction and others with geometric vocabulary.

Communication is the major underlying theme of this book. Students who read out loud, write out loud, and think out loud are communicators of mathematics—in this case, geometry. I hope that this book will help you help students become successful learners of geometry.

This book is divided into two parts, "Reading to Learn Geometry" and "Writing to Learn Geometry," each comprising four chapters with strategies and activities for learning geometry, numerous examples, and ready-to-use lessons. Each strategy is broken into three parts. The chapters in Part One address prereading, reading to learn, postreading, and particular readings. The chapters in Part Two address writing to learn, writing to communicate, writing for assessment, and writing for authentic assessment. At the end of the book are tessellations, works of patterned geometric art made by former students. Enjoy!

Geometry Time Line

The time line on the following pages identifies the most important geometers and the concepts they discovered or researched and published on. It is not meant to be exhaustive, and focuses on the geometers and the discoveries that have influenced my geometrical education and interests the most. There is some overlap in the time periods; this was done on purpose so as to place all the geometers with the most appropriate geometric concepts.

Geometry Time Line

Let no man ignorant of geometry enter here.
Plato's inscription over the door to the Academy

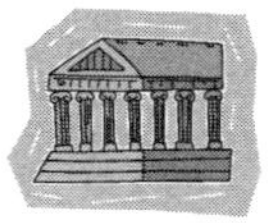
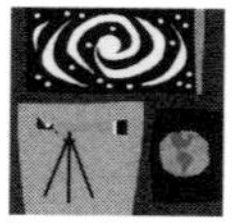
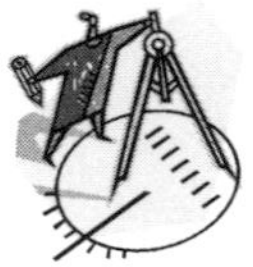

ANCIENTS	GREEKS	ARABS/CHINESE	ASTRONOMERS	ANALYTIC GEOMETRY	NON-EUCLIDEAN GEOMETRY
Babylonians Egyptians 2500–700 B.C.	Pythagoras Euclid Hypatia Archimedes Apollonius Thales 600 B.C.–500 A.D.	Brahmagupta Khayyam 500–1200	Copernicus Galileo Kepler 1400–1600	Descartes Pascal Fermat Newton Leibnitz 1600–1700	Gauss Bolyai Lobachevsky Riemann Saccheri 1775–1870
Hieroglyphics Pyramids Rope stretchers Calendar Pi Volume, area, lines	Pi Elements Geometric proof Axiomatic system Pythagorean theorem Conics Trigonometry Figurative numbers Parallel postulate	Surveying Applications Geometric proofs Symmetry Spherical trigonometry	Heliocentric system Better telescopes Religious persecution Planetary laws Physics	Cartesian coordinate system Calculus Maximum and minimum Celestial mechanics Projective geometry Infinitesimals Fluxions	Attempts to prove PP Hyperbolic geometry Spherical geometry Saccheriś quadrilaterals Differential geometry

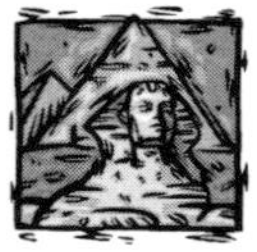
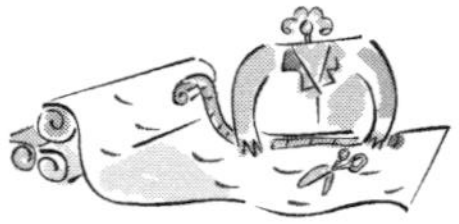
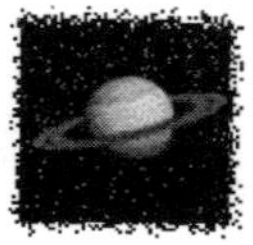
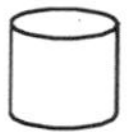

"[Descartes' analytic geometry] is the single greatest step ever made in the progress of the exact sciences."

John Stuart Mills

AXIOMATIC SYSTEMS/RIGOR

Hilbert   Russell   Whitehead

1900–2000

Foundations of geometry
Pi
Philosophy of geometry
Paradoxes
Influence of computers

4-SPACE AND BEYOND

Klein   Mobius   Boole-Stott

1850–1920

Klein bottle
Mobius strip
3D models for 4D figures
Modeling

GRAPH THEORY/PROJECTIVE GEOMETRY

Euler   Hamilton   Desargue

1600–1850

Circuits
Networks
Maps
Pi to 23 digits
Applications
Topology

APPLICATIONS OF CALCULUS

Bernoulli   l'Hospital   LaPlace
Agnesi   Fourier   Cauchy
Legendre
1700–1850

Partial derivatives
Probability
Geometric probability
Antiderivative
Calculus texts
"Witch of Agnesi"

Part One

Reading to Learn Geometry

The No Child Left Behind (NCLB) Act of 2001 calls for changes in mathematics and reading. Although the focus on reading targets early readers and seeks to improve literacy for students by the end of third grade, its call for reformation resonates for readers at all levels. The availability of large monetary grants and program development incentives reinforce the concern of educators, citizens, and politicians regarding the reading skills of our youth. I believe it is never too late to address poor reading and retention skills in any academic field.

In *Principles and Standards for School Mathematics of 2000,* the National Council of Teachers of Mathematics (NCTM) gives four broad goals in the Geometry Standard:

Instructional programs from prekindergarten through grade 12 should enable all students to:

- Analyze characteristics and properties of two- and three-dimensional shapes and develop mathematical arguments about geometric relationships.
- Specify locations and describe spatial relationships using coordinate geometry and other representational systems.

- Apply transformations and use symmetry to analyze mathematical situations.
- Use visualization, spatial reasoning, and geometric modeling to solve problems [p. 308].

There is little doubt that successful geometry students read and retain geometric content well. In the first goal of the Geometry Standard, reading is cited as the first step: "Finding precise descriptions of conditions that characterize a class of objects [two- or three- dimensional] is an important first step" (NCTM, 2000, p. 42).

I have found that I must guide my students to read mathematics and geometry effectively. Thus, the chapters in Part One give a portfolio of strategies and activities that target the integration of reading and geometry at the secondary and early college levels. My colleagues and I have used all of them in our classrooms. They cover prereading, reading to understand, and postreading and are used in many subject areas. They will motivate your students to read and retain geometry content with ease and confidence.

1

Prereading Strategies and Activities

Review/Preview Process
Knowledge Ratings
Anticipation Guides
PreP (Prereading Plan)
Problem-Solving PreP
Wordsmithing

Chapter One begins with the Review/Preview process. Later strategies and activities refer back to this process.

Quick Teaching Tip: Expect resistance.

Students often balk at reading geometric content. I try to focus on the notion that many of my students resist out of fear of the unknown or of failure and I am the motivator and guide who will lead them down the path to success. Therefore, at the start of the school year, I use familiar activities or strategies that have yielded success in the past. When I try a new strategy later in the year, I expect I will need to demonstrate to the class how to do it and I also plan on working with some students individually. Incorporating peer work throughout the lesson plans, even during pre-reading activities, can be a great motivator. But remember that *you* are the guide and must keep your students on track.

The strategies and activities explored in this chapter prepare students to read and learn efficiently from the text. Doing activities before reading the lesson may seem backward or at least time-consuming. Students typically skim through the content, perhaps focusing on some of the worked-out examples, and then go right to the assigned problems. If they instead prepare themselves to learn, they change their thinking from what they were doing last to what they need to do next: read and retain the content.

Every subject in academia is unique in terms of what students learn, why they learn it, and how they learn it. Geometry is the science or study of visual thinking. Thus, the geometry textbook often looks different from an algebra or an English textbook. Certainly there are more diagrams. Many pages contain long processes and proofs spelled out in logical and numbered steps. Other geometry texts contain paragraph-style proofs that students will need much practice both writing and reading to understand and do correctly. If the section in the textbook contains many written constructions, students will find it helpful to have pencil, paper, straightedge, and compass handy. Even if the prereading strategy is merely to scan topics, titles, captions, and diagrams, students who do this preparation will be better able to read and reflect on the content.

As teachers of mathematics, we are often limited by time constraints and the amount of content we are obliged to cover. Some of us may feel that teaching reading is not a priority. In fact, we are actually preparing students to read and learn from reading geometric text. If we choose one or two prereading strategies and assign these often and regularly, students may naturally incorporate this strategy into their personal learning or studying process. A good learning process for a day in geometry class would have students complete the prereading activity, read the lesson, reflect and share with the class what they have learned, and do the assigned homework problems as a class, in small groups, or individually. Moreover, if we address the reading of content early and regularly in the course, we may instill learning habits that successfully carry over to other courses. Our students may become effective readers and successful communicators of geometry and mathematics.

The *Principles and Standards for School Mathematics of 2000* (NCTM, 2000) encourage students to "understand how mathematical ideas interconnect and build on one another to produce a coherent whole" (p. 354). It is essential that the geometry lessons enable students to focus their potential. The lessons should be selected with these criteria in mind:

- Does the lesson promote discussion among the students?
- Does the lesson improve students' comprehension of mathematical concepts?

• Does the lesson lend itself to real-world relevance, thus leading students to make important connections?

These may seem like lofty goals, but I am never disappointed when I guide my students in this direction. I've created the following activities and strategies with these criteria in mind.

Review/Preview Process

WHAT? Description

The review/preview process, which takes place prior to the students' reading of the text, has two parts: (1) teachers present a review of the prerequisite or background material needed to understand the new content and (2) students preview the new content.

To review the background content, teachers should do one or more of the following:

- Summarize background material.
- Pose a problem from the background material.
- Share a historical anecdote regarding the new concepts.
- Present an interesting problem for the students to solve after they have read and learned the new content.
- Sketch an appropriate geometric figure, labeling or pointing out the necessary parts.

To preview the assigned reading, students should complete the following tasks:

- Note the title.
- Note all subheads.
- Note all boxed or highlighted definitions and theorems.
- Note all pictures and graphics.
- Note all other boxed or highlighted special sections, such as biographies of mathematicians or special applications.

WHY? Objectives

Geometry students who learn and use the review/preview process can:

- Recall necessary mathematical concepts and processes.
- Connect previously learned concepts with new concepts.

- Approach new content with curiosity and interest.
- Pose questions regarding new concepts and anticipate the answers to these questions.
- Delineate or categorize different methods or concepts regarding the main topics from the text.

HOW? Example

The lesson that follows gives a review/preview worksheet. Students may use the questions in the worksheet to assist in the review/preview process.

Review/Preview Process

NAME _____   DATE _____

ASSIGNMENT: Briefly answer the following questions as you preview the section on _____ on pages _____.

List all titles and subtitles from the new content.
What background concepts do I need to know?
What new geometric shapes or concepts do I anticipate learning?
What questions do I have regarding the new content?

Knowledge Ratings

WHAT? Description

Charts that ask the student to assess their prior knowledge are called *knowledge ratings* (Blachowicz, 1986). The teacher presents students with a list of geometric concepts or topics and surveys their knowledge on these topics.

WHY? Objectives

The knowledge rating process allows geometry students to:

- Understand their capabilities and review their knowledge base.
- Target problem areas and make study plans.
- Point out to the teacher areas that may present difficulties for them.

HOW? Example

The following lessons show how knowledge ratings can be used for different geometry lesson plans. A template for use in creating lessons is included.

Knowledge Ratings: Triangles

NAME _____ DATE _____

ASSIGNMENT: How much do you know about these terms? Put an X in the spaces that signal your knowledge.

	A Lot!	Some	Not Much
Right triangle			
Isosceles triangle			
Acute triangle			
Obtuse triangle			
Scalene triangle			
Sine			
Cosine			

Knowledge Ratings: Lines and Angles

NAME _____   DATE _____

ASSIGNMENT: How much do you know about the geometric concepts listed in the table? Put an X in the spaces that signal your knowledge.

	Can Define	Can Give an Example	Can Sketch Basic Graph	Am Totally Lost
Parallel				
Perpendicular				
Transversal				
Vertical angles				
Alternating interior angles				
Adjacent angles				
Complementary angles				
Supplementary angles				

Knowledge Ratings: Polygons

NAME _____ DATE _____

ASSIGNMENT: How much do you know about the geometric shapes listed below? Put an X in the spaces that best signal your knowledge.

	Can Define	Can Give Formula or Explain How to Find Area	Can Sketch the Basic Shape	Can Give Sum of All Vertex Angles
Quadrilateral				
Rectangle				
Trapezoid				
Pentagon				
Hexagon				
Octagon				

Knowledge Ratings: Template

NAME _____   DATE _____

ASSIGNMENT: How much do you know about _____? Put an X in the space that best describes your knowledge.

Anticipation Guides

WHAT? Description

Anticipation guides (Herber, 1978) are lists of statements that challenge students to explore their knowledge of concepts prior to reading a text. As they then read the text, they discover explanations of the concepts. A mathematical anticipation guide usually contains four to five statements, each with two parts. In the first part, the student is asked to agree or disagree with each statement. The second part then asks the student to read the text. After reading the text, the student determines whether the text agrees or disagrees with each statement.

WHY? Objectives

Anticipation guides allow and motivate geometry students to:

- Complete anticipation charts.
- Explore their opinions and prior knowledge of geometric concepts.
- Read closely to find evidence to support their claims or discover the text's view.
- Uncover and identify any misconceptions regarding these concepts.

HOW? Examples

The following lessons are just a few ways to approach anticipation guides.

Anticipation Guides: Circles

ASSIGNMENT: In the column labeled **Me**, place a check next to any statement with which you **agree**. After reading the section, consider the column labeled **Text** and place a check next to any statement with which the text agrees.

Me	Text	
_____	_____	1. A circle is the set of points that are all the same distance from a center point.
_____	_____	2. Pi is equal to the circumference of a circle divided by its radius.
_____	_____	3. A tangent line touches the circle at exactly one point.
_____	_____	4. The diameter is the longest chord on a circle.
_____	_____	5. The formula for the area of a circle is $A = 2\pi r$.

Anticipation Guides: Polyhedra

NAME _____ DATE _____

ASSIGNMENT: In the column labeled **Me**, place a check next to any statement with which you **agree**. After reading the section, consider the column labeled **Text** and place a check next to any statement with which the text agrees.

Me   **Text**

_____   _____   1. There are exactly five Platonic solids.

_____   _____   2. A Platonic solid is a regular polyhedron.

_____   _____   3. Polyhedra are three-dimensional solids with polygons for faces.

_____   _____   4. A sphere is a polyhedron.

_____   _____   5. $V + F = E - 2$ (where V = number of vertices, F = number of faces, and E = number of edges) holds for all polyhedra.

Anticipation Guides: Euclidean Geometry

NAME _____ DATE _____

ASSIGNMENT: In the column labeled **Me**, place a check next to any statement with which you **agree**. After reading the section, consider the column labeled **Text** and place a check next to any statement with which the text agrees.

Me	Text	
_____	_____	1. Euclid described a point as "that which takes up no space."
_____	_____	2. Euclidean geometry contains five postulates or assumptions.
_____	_____	3. The undefined terms for this geometry are *point, line,* and *angle.*
_____	_____	4. A theorem is a mathematical statement that is proven from the postulates and other proven theorems.
_____	_____	5. The fifth postulate is called the parallel postulate.

PreP (Prereading Plan)

WHAT? Description

The prereading plan (PreP) (Langer, 1981) is a group brainstorming activity. The teacher guides students in activating, sharing, and fine-tuning prior knowledge. Initially, the teacher chooses one of the key concepts of the reading or lesson and then guides the students in brainstorming of this concept. Langer suggests that the teacher follow a three-step process to guide the students' collective thoughts:

1. *Initial associations.* The teacher asks, "What comes to mind when you hear . . . ?" The teacher writes the student responses on the board.
2. *Secondary reflections.* The teacher asks individual students about their responses: "What made you think of . . . ?" The teacher writes these reflections on the board.
3. *Refining knowledge.* The teacher asks, "Do you have any new ideas or thoughts after hearing your peers' ideas?" The teacher writes new ideas on the board.

WHY? Objectives

Through the group brainstorming process, students will:

- Activate prior knowledge.
- Hear and reflect on peers' ideas.
- Clarify, refine, and enlarge their knowledge.

HOW? Example

Here is how the three-step process works with the concept of triangle:

1. *Initial associations.* Students might identify ideas that come to mind with the word *triangle*—for example, a plane figure, a right triangle, and angles.

2. *Secondary reflections.* When the teacher asks the students how they came up with those ideas, the students respond in this way: for *plane figure,* "three sides that are line segments"; for *right triangle,* "has one 90-degree angle"; and for *angles,* "measures sum up to 180 degrees."

3. *Refining knowledge.* The discussion yielded these new ideas from the students: "There are obtuse triangles, containing one angle greater than 90 degrees, and acute triangles, containing one angle less than 90 degrees," and "Trigonometry is used to find measures in right triangles."

Problem-Solving PreP

The National Council of Supervisors of Mathematics (1988) states that the principal reason for studying mathematics is to learn to solve problems.

WHAT? Description

Problem solving is the process of resolving the confusion or mystery of an unfamiliar situation. The twentieth-century mathematician George Polya devoted his life to helping students become good problem solvers. In his famous book *How to Solve It* (Polya, 1973), he outlines a four-step process for solving problems:

1. *Understand the problem.* Read, reread, make a guess, restate the problem, and/or rewrite the question.
2. *Devise a plan.* Draw a picture, construct a table or graph, use a model, find a pattern, work backward, and/or use a formula or equation appropriate to solving the problem.
3. *Carry out the plan.* Write out work, solve an equation, and/or recheck work.
4. *Look back.* Verify or check the solution referring to the initial problem, reread the problem, generalize to a larger problem, pose questions for further exploration, and/or compose related problems.

During the problem-solving prereading (PreP) process, students follow a guided reading format to help hone their problem-solving skills. They can use this process prior to or during a section covering geometric applications.

WHY? Objectives

The problem-solving PreP process asks geometry students to:

• Spend time reading problems for understanding.
• Find personal meaning by rewriting problems in their own words.

- Practice using different strategies to solve problems.
- Focus on the understanding phase of problem solving.
- Build confidence in their ability to solve problems.

HOW? Examples

The lessons that follow provide good examples.

Problem-Solving PreP

NAME _____   DATE _____

ASSIGNMENT: Read the word problem. Then use the instructions in the box to solve it. Refer to the list of problem-solving strategies to complete the "Devise a Plan" section in the box.

Problem: A right triangle with sides that measure 6 inches, 8 inches, and 10 inches has a square constructed off each of the three sides (for example, the 6-inch side has a square with each side length of 6 inches). Which is greater: The sum of the areas of the two squares of the two shorter sides or the square of the longer side?

Problem-Solving Strategies

- Draw a picture.
- Guess and check.
- Sketch a table or graph.
- Find a pattern.
- Work backward.
- Use a formula or equation.
- Use a model.

UNDERSTAND: Rewrite the problem in your own words.
UNDERSTAND: Make a guess, and explain your reasoning.
DEVISE A PLAN: Choose one of the problem-solving strategies listed above.
CARRY OUT THE PLAN: Use the strategy to solve the problem.
LOOK BACK: Create a similar problem.

Problem-Solving PreP

NAME _____ DATE _____

ASSIGNMENT: Read the word problem. Then use the instructions in the box to solve it. Refer to the list of problem-solving strategies to complete the "Devise a Plan" section in the box.

Problem: Imagine that the earth is a perfect sphere and its circumference is exactly 25,000 miles at the equator. Now imagine that a band is placed around the earth directly above the equator. The circumference of the band is 10 feet longer than the circumference of the earth. Is it possible to place a 12-inch ruler between the earth and the band?

Problem-Solving Strategies

- Draw a picture.
- Guess and check.
- Sketch a table or graph.
- Find a pattern.
- Work backward.
- Use a formula or equation.
- Use a model.

UNDERSTAND: Rewrite the problem in your own words.
UNDERSTAND: Make a guess, and explain your reasoning.
DEVISE A PLAN: Choose one of the problem-solving strategies listed above.
CARRY OUT THE PLAN: Use the strategy to solve the problem.
LOOK BACK: Create a similar problem.

Copyright © 2006 by John Wiley & Sons, Inc.

Problem-Solving PreP

NAME _____   DATE _____

ASSIGNMENT: Read the word problem. Then use the instructions in the box to solve it. Refer to the list of problem-solving strategies to complete the "Devise a Plan" section in the box.

Problem: The Hobbits Bilbo, Frodo, and Samwise each live along a circle with a market as the center of the circle. The circumference of the circle is 2 miles. If each of their houses is an equal distance from the center of the circle, what is that distance?

Problem-Solving Strategies

- Draw a picture.
- Guess and check.
- Sketch a table or graph.
- Find a pattern.
- Work backward.
- Use a formula or equation.
- Use a model.

UNDERSTAND: Rewrite the problem in your own words.
UNDERSTAND: Make a guess, and explain your reasoning.
DEVISE A PLAN: Choose one of the problem-solving strategies listed above.
CARRY OUT THE PLAN: Use the strategy to solve the problem.
LOOK BACK: Create a similar problem.

Problem-Solving PreP: Template

NAME _____ DATE _____

ASSIGNMENT: Read the word problem. Then use the instructions in the box to solve it. Refer to the list of problem-solving strategies to complete the "Devise a Plan" section in the box.

Problem:

Problem-Solving Strategies

- Draw a picture.
- Guess and check.
- Sketch a table or graph.
- Find a pattern.
- Work backward.
- Use a formula or equation.
- Use a model.

UNDERSTAND: Rewrite the problem in your own words.
UNDERSTAND: Make a guess, and explain your reasoning.
DEVISE A PLAN: Choose one of the problem-solving strategies listed above.
CARRY OUT THE PLAN: Use the strategy to solve the problem.
LOOK BACK: Create a similar problem.

Wordsmithing

WHAT? Description

A *smith* is someone who makes or works at something specified. A *word-smith* is a person who makes and experiments with new words. Often these words are new terms to the reader, or they might be a corruption or an unusual restating of the original term. For example, a wordsmith might refer to a graphing calculator as a *graphulator*. A geometric wordsmith must have a good grasp on the definition and features of the related geometric term in order to change the term in an appropriate or revealing manner.

In the following wordsmithing activity, students use a three-column matrix and search the text for new geometric terms, which they write in the first column of the matrix. Then they guess what each term means and write this guess in the second column. Next, they look in the text for the definition of the term and write it in the last column. Finally, they choose at least one of the new terms and rewrite it in an interesting or unusual fashion, using words or parts of words that uncover or reveal the often unspoken meaning of the term.

WHY? Objectives

Wordsmithing asks geometry students to:

- Learn the definition of new geometric concepts or terms.
- Self-assess their ability to define new geometric terms.
- Gain confidence in learning new geometric terms.
- Think of themselves as geometric wordsmiths.

HOW? Examples

See the lessons for wordsmithing matrices.

Wordsmithing: Matrix

NAME _____   DATE _____

ASSIGNMENT: Guess what each term means, and write your guess in column 2. Then use the text to find the correct definition, and write it in column 3.

New Term	Your Definition (a good guess)	The Text's Definition
rectangle		
parallelogram		
trapezoid		
rhombus		
kite		
quadrilateral		

Now try your hand at wordsmithing. Two examples are given.

rectangle = _____
parallelogram = ___pairs-o'-parallel_____
trapezoid = _____
rhombus = _____
kite = _____
quadrilateral = ___four-of-sides_____

Wordsmithing: Matrix

ASSIGNMENT: Guess what each term means, and write your guess in column 2. Then use the text to find the correct definition, and write it in column 3.

New Term	Your Definition (a good guess)	The Text's Definition
sphere		
the shell of a ball		
all points in 3-space equidistant from a center point		
prism		
pyramid		
cylinder		
cone		

Now try your hand at wordsmithing. Two examples are given.

sphere = ball-points or ball-shell _____

prism = _____

pyramid = _____

cylinder = rectangle round _____

cone = _____

Wordsmithing: Matrix Template

NAME _____   DATE _____

ASSIGNMENT: Guess what each term means, and write your guess in column 2. Then use the text to find the correct definition, and write it in column 3.

New Term	Your Definition (a good guess)	The Text's Definition

Now try your hand at wordsmithing.

_____ = _____

_____ = _____

_____ = _____

_____ = _____

_____ = _____

_____ = _____

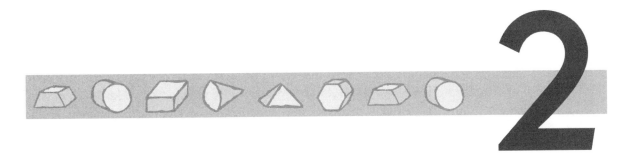

Reading and Vocabulary-Building Strategies and Activities

Quick Teaching Tip: Do not take on too much.

Incorporating a few good reading activities in all mathematics classes or choosing one course with the intent of using several of the strategies and activities is better than trying to do too many reading activities in all of your classes. In that way, the time spent focusing and assessing student success in reading to learn geometry is manageable and well spent.

Prelude

The strategies and activities in this chapter will help students learn to read geometric text effectively and efficiently. The text of geometry is unique in that the readings implicitly or explicitly conjure up images of shapes and parts of shapes. Thus, the reading of geometric content is an active learning experience.

In active learning, students visualize concepts (that is, they sketch shapes and figures literally or in their mind), organize information, pose questions, predict solutions or new knowledge, and make connections with prior and new knowledge. During this process, they make personal meaning of the content through identification with various geometric shapes and figures they are familiar with, like jewelry or cars.

The interactive learning component of reading geometry text consists of the students' reflecting, writing, and talking about geometry. Reflecting on content during and after the reading is part of the reading process. Students often use this time to consider how they will interpret the content in class or on assessments. Some students need help in the reflection process; many of the activities in Chapters One and Two address just this need.

The process of writing, another important component when teaching for deeper understanding, is discussed in Part Two of *Geometry Out Loud*. Writing about geometric concepts helps readers set goals, consider the audience, organize and refine thinking, and summarize and share new knowledge. As they talk about geometry, students compare thinking, obtain and share new ideas, guide and are guided in the reflection and study processes, and see the concepts in a new light. Thus, reading strategies and activities in geometry ultimately push student readers to become student communicators of geometry.

The Communication Standard for Grades 9–12 in the NCTM's *Principles and Standards for School Mathematics of 2000* (2000, p. 348) speaks to the importance of good communication in elementary, middle school, and secondary geometry:

> Instructional programs from prekindergarten through grade 12 should enable all students to:
>
> - Organize and consolidate their mathematical thinking through communication.
> - Communicate their mathematical thinking coherently and clearly to peers, teachers, and others.
> - Analyze and evaluate the mathematical thinking and strategies of others.
> - Use the language of mathematics to express mathematical ideas precisely.

This seems like a large goal, primarily to us as the teachers of these students. It helps me to think of it as a journey, not a destination. Learning is a lifetime process; the importance lies in developing strategies that allow us to be lifelong learners: problem solvers, readers, writers, and communicators. This is accomplished one step at a time. The fallacy lies in thinking we must teach mathematics first and then worry about teaching communication in mathematics. In this book, the strategies and activities are created and presented in such a way that students learn geometry as they learn to communicate geometry.

The strategies and activities contained in this chapter focus on the reading process and on vocabulary building while reading the text. The goals for these activities are to help students:

- Connect prior and new knowledge.
- Reinforce and enlarge their geometric vocabulary.
- Sketch or visualize geometric shapes and figures.
- Break up information into smaller, more manageable pieces.
- Categorize and organize information.
- Select key concepts.
- Interpret definitions, theorems, and processes.
- Follow and generalize from examples.
- Construct study guides.
- Understand directions or what type of answer the problem is asking for.

Magic Square Activity

WHAT? Description

The magic square activity combines a matching activity with the intrigue and mathematics of a magic square (Vacca and Vacca, 1999). The write-up of the matching activity consists of two columns: one lists concepts and one lists definitions, facts, examples, or descriptions. As the student solves the matching activity, he or she places the numbers in the proper square inside the magic square:

A	B	C
D	E	F
G	H	I

To see if the answers are correct, the student adds the numbers in each row, each column, and each diagonal. These sums should be equal. This sum is referred to as the square's *magic number.*

WHY? Objectives

Completing the magic square activity will reinforce students' understanding of the concepts or word meaning:

- As they work on this activity, students will feel intrigued by what might otherwise be considered a mundane activity.
- When they complete the magic square activity, students will have a stronger grasp of concept or word meaning. They will understand the concept and properties of magic squares.

The magic squares that follow use the magic number of 15.

7	3	5
2	4	9
6	8	1

8	1	6
3	5	7
4	9	2

6	1	8
7	5	3
2	9	4

The magic square that follows has the magic number of 39. Note that the diagonal sums do not yield the same sum as rows and columns; this is true of some magic squares.

2	7	18	12
8	5	11	15
13	17	6	3
16	10	4	9

Magic Square Activity

NAME _____   DATE _____

ASSIGNMENT: Select the best answer for each of the terms in the Concepts column from the lettered items in the Defining Feature column. Put the number in the corresponding square in the magic square. Add each row, and add each column. If these sums are the same number, then you have found the magic number and matched the correct terms with their rules.

Concepts	Defining Feature
_____ 1. hexagon	A. polygon with all congruent sides
_____ 2. polygon	B. sum of length of two sides greater than the length of the other side
_____ 3. square	C. set of all points that are equidistant from a center point
_____ 4. trapezoid	D. any *n*-gon
_____ 5. rhombus	E. a regular rhombus
_____ 6. circle	F. may have three sets of parallel sides
_____ 7. pentagon	G. maximum of two pairs of parallel sides
_____ 8. regular 6-gon	H. exactly one pair of parallel sides
_____ 9. triangle	I. a square is one

A	B	C
D	E	F
G	H	I

Magic number = _____

Magic Square Activity

ASSIGNMENT: Select the best answer for each of the terms in the Concepts column from the lettered items in the Defining Features column. Put the number in the corresponding square in the magic square. Add each row and add each column. If these sums are the same number, then you have found the magic number and matched the correct terms with their rules.

Concepts

_____ 1. straight angle

_____ 2. acute angle

_____ 3. supplementary angles

_____ 4. obtuse angle

_____ 5. scalene triangle

_____ 6. equilateral triangle

_____ 7. isosceles triangle

_____ 8. right triangle

_____ 9. complimentary angles

Defining Feature

A. measure of angle less than 90 degrees

B. triangle with exactly two congruent sides

C. triangle with all sides congruent

D. sum of measures of angles = 90 degrees

E. triangle with no sides congruent

F. 180-degree angle

G. angle whose measure is more than 90 degrees

H. sum of measures of angles = 180 degrees

I. triangle with 90-degree angle

A	B	C
D	E	F
G	H	I

Magic number = _____

Copyright © 2006 by John Wiley & Sons, Inc.

Magic Square Activity

NAME _____   DATE _____

ASSIGNMENT: Read each statement below and decide which of the following geometries the statement refers to. Then write the correct letter on the line provided:

> Euclidean: E
>
> Non-Euclidean, Hyperbolic: H
>
> Non-Euclidean, Spherical: S

Each statement refers to only one type of geometry. However, more than one statement refers to each type of geometry. Use the letters in the magic square below to figure out the correct numbers from 1 to 9 that make it a magic square.

Example: The upper-left corner square contains an E. If statements 1 and 6 refer to E (Euclidean geometry), then you can place a *1* or *6* in that top square. Recall the rules for magic squares (each row and each column must sum up to the same number).

_____ 1. Through a point not on a given line, there exist at least two lines that are parallel to the given line.

_____ 2. Lines in this geometry are portions of great circles.

_____ 3. Triangles in this geometry have angles whose sum is less than 180 degrees.

_____ 4. Line segments in this geometry are portions of orthogonal circles.

_____ 5. A right triangle may contain three right angles.

_____ 6. The sum of the angles of a triangle is 180 degrees.

_____ 7. A great circle is an equator or circle whose center is the center of a sphere.

_____ 8. Through a point not on a given line, there exists exactly one line parallel to the given line.

_____ 9. A 30–60–90 triangle exists in this geometry.

E	H	E
H	S	S
H	E	S

Magic number = _____

Vocabulary Scramble

WHAT? Description

In this activity, students unscramble geometry terms from a particular unit in the course. Using the numbers placed below the correctly unscrambled word and their related letters, students discover a problem they are to solve. This activity reinforces the understanding and spelling of the most significant topics or words from that section.

WHY? Objectives

The vocabulary scramble activities ask the geometry students to:

- Identify and define the major geometric terms from a unit or chapter in the text.
- Use the new terms to discover and solve the hidden problem.
- Consider and identify the correct spelling of the new terms.

HOW? Example

This example of scrambled terms comes from a unit on symmetry or transformational geometry:

> ttoare =
>
> clefret =
>
> evrovel =
>
> leatstran =
>
> mystermy =

The correct terms are, in the order above, *rotate, reflect, revolve, translate,* and *symmetry.*

Vocabulary Scramble

NAME _____   DATE _____

ASSIGNMENT: Unscramble the following twelve words from the unit on right triangles. Then use the numbers under each letter to decode the problem statement below. Use the terms and what you've learned about right triangles to answer the problem.

e x v e r t   _____   o l e s s i c e s   _____
5–24–22–5–18–20   15–12–5–19–19–9–3–5–19

a n d i m e   _____   g r e e d e s   _____
1–14–4–9–13–5   7–18–5–5–4–5–18

t r o d e c n i   _____   h y p o t e e n s u e_____
20–18–15–4–5–3–14–9   8–25–16–15–20–5–5–14–19–21–5

c l e e n a s   _____   t h i r g   _____
3–12–5–5–14–1–19   20–8–9–18–7

i n f l e c t o r e _____   t e r r i o x e   _____
9–14–6–12–5–3–20–15–18–5   20–5–18–18–9–15- 24- 5

m i s l a i r   _____   r e q u i t a l l e   _____
13–9–19–12–1–9–18   18–5–17–21–9–20–1–12–12–5

___ ___   ___ ___ ___ ___ ___ ___ ___ ___ ___
1 – 14   9 – 19 – 15 – 19 – 3 – 5 – 12 – 5 – 19

___ ___ ___ ___ ___ ___ ___ ___   ___ ___ ___   ___ ___ ___ ___
15 – 7 – 9 – 1 – 14 – 7 – 12 – 5   8 – 1 – 19   20 – 8 – 9 – 19

___ ___ ___ ___   ___ ___ ___ ___ ___ ___ ___ ___ ___
13 – 1 – 14 – 25   3 – 15 – 14 – 7 – 18 –21 – 5 – 14 – 20

___ ___ ___ ___ ___ ___.
1 – 14 – 7 – 12 – 5 – 19

Concept Circles

WHAT? Description

Concept circles are a versatile reading and postreading activity (Vacca and Vacca, 1999). A concept circle usually focuses on one concept and its important features. The circle is generally divided into quarters, though more than four sectors may be used, and features or descriptors of the concept are placed in each sector of the circle.

Concept circles may be teacher-created and used to quiz students—for example:

- Given the descriptors contained in the sections of the circle, students identify the concept.
- Given the concept and descriptors, students select which of the descriptors is incorrect.
- Given the concept and a few descriptors, students fill in the rest of the circle.

Concept circles may also be student-created—for example:

- The teacher provides the concept, and students fill in the sections of the circle.
- Students select a concept from their reading and fill in the sections of the circle.
- The teacher gives one or more features written in the sections of the circle, and students write in the correct concept and other features of the concept.

Note there may be several correct answers or features for the appropriate concept.

WHY? Objectives

The use of concept circles allows the geometry students to:

- Categorize information from the reading.
- Review features and descriptors of a geometric concept.
- Self-assess their reading comprehension.
- Create study guides for upcoming assessments.

HOW? Example

This example uses a geometric concept circle:

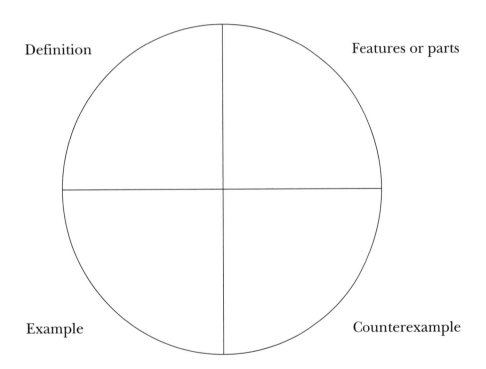

Definition   Features or parts

Example   Counterexample

The concept is _____.

K-W-L

WHAT? Description

K-W-L (Ogle, 1986) is a reading strategy involving note taking prior to, during, and after reading:

K stands for "What I *Know*"

W stands for "What I *Want* to Know"

L stands for "What I *Learned*"

Students write notes in a three-column grid, using the following format:

K **What I *Know***	W **What I *Want* to Know**	L **What I *Learned***
During prereading, write notes about what you already know about the concepts presented.	During prereading, write questions about what you want to know about the concepts presented.	As you read or after reading, write answers to questions posed in column 2 or notes regarding what you have learned.

WHY? Objectives

The use of K-W-L guides geometry students by asking them to:

• Reflect on prior and new knowledge.

• Merge prior knowledge with new knowledge.

• Summarize prior and new knowledge.

• Authentically assess (that is, self-assess) their learning process.

HOW? An Example and a Lesson

Following is an example of a completed K-W-L chart that students might complete if they were reading a text on the Golden Ratio. If the students' questions are not answered in the text, encourage them to consult other sources to find the answers.

Fibonacci, the Greeks, and a Divine Ratio

Leonardo de Pisa, nicknamed Fibonacci, was an Italian mathematician who lived during the Middle Ages. While contemplating the mating habits of a pair of rabbits and their descendants, Fibonacci created the following sequence:

$$1, 1, 2, 3, 5, 8, 13, 21, 34, 55, 89, 144, \ldots$$

The Fibonacci sequence is a recursive sequence. Starting with the third term, each term is the sum of the two terms preceding it:

$$1 + 1 = 2, \quad 1 + 2 = 3, \quad 2 + 3 = 5, \quad 3 + 5 = 8, \quad 5 + 8 = 13, \quad 8 + 13 = 21, \ldots$$

This sequence has many extraordinary properties. One such property pertains to the ratios of consecutive pairs. Note the following ratios:

$$1/1 = 1$$
$$\frac{1}{2} = .5$$
$$2/3 = .666\ldots$$
$$3/5 = .6$$
$$5/8 = .625$$
$$13/8 = .6153846154$$
$$21/13 \approx .619047619$$
$$34/21 \approx .6176470588$$

If we were to continue in this pattern, we would see that the ratios would tend toward (get closer and closer to) the irrational number $\frac{\sqrt{5}-1}{2} \approx .6180339887$. Note that the consecutive ratios vacillate between being either smaller than or larger than .6180339887.

Fibonacci was delighted to discover that his sequence contained this special property. He knew that the Greeks had long thought of this ratio as a divine number and had aptly titled it the Golden Ratio. As early as 350 B.C., Greek artists and architects believed that figures and structures displaying proportions that approximated this ratio were pleasing to the eye. The Parthenon in Athens, Greece, was built with many features using dimensions whose ratios tend toward the Golden Ratio. For example, the height compared to the width of the front of the Parthenon approximates .618. Also, many sculptures of Greek gods and goddesses display proportions close to this divine ratio.

To see if you have goddess- or god-like proportions, use the formula:

$$r = \frac{navel\ height}{height}$$

(Your navel height is the distance from the floor to your belly button.) If your ratio is close to the Golden Ratio of .618, then you are proportionally divine, at least by the standards of Fibonacci and the ancient Greeks.

The following table shows how the K-W-L strategy can be applied to the reading. The K and W columns are completed prior to reading, and the L column is completed during and after reading the piece.

K **What I *Know***	W **What I *Want* to Know**	L **What I *Learned***
A ratio is a fraction.	Why is the Golden Ratio considered divine?	The Greeks used this ratio in their famous sculptures and buildings.
Fibonacci invented a sequence.	How is the Fibonacci sequence related to the Golden Ratio?	Consecutive pairs form ratios that tend to the Golden Ratio.

K-W-L

NAME _____ DATE _____

The K-W-L reading strategy follows this format:

K What I Know	W What I Want to Know	L What I Learned
During prereading, write notes about what you already know about the concepts presented.	During prereading, write questions about what you want to know about the concepts presented.	As you read or after reading, write answers to questions posed in column 2 or notes regarding what you have learned.

ASSIGNMENT: Use the reading titled _____
on page _____ to complete the table.

K What I Know	W What I Want to Know	L What I Learned

Semantic Feature Analysis

WHAT? Description

Semantic feature analysis (Baldwin, Ford, and Readance, 1981) is a reading strategy that has students complete a matrix showing how various terms and concepts are alike or different. The terms or concepts are related or fall under a particular category. The matrix itself consists of several columns. The first column contains the terms. The other columns contain headings spelling out features that the terms or concepts might have in common.

WHY? Objectives

Using the semantic feature activity, students will:

- Fill out semantic feature charts to demonstrate their knowledge of the lesson's topics.
- Compare and contrast features of related mathematical concepts.
- Refer back to the completed matrix when reviewing for exams.

HOW? Example

An X placed in a particular space indicates that the feature applies to the given quadrilateral. If the best response is "not necessarily," the space is left blank—for example:

Quadrilateral	Four-Sided Polygon	Opposite Sides Are Congruent	Opposite Sides Are Parallel	Exactly One Pair of Parallel Sides	Vertex Angles Are Congruent
Square	X	X	X		X
Rectangle	X	X	X		X
Parallelogram	X	X	X		
Rhombus	X	X	X		
Trapezoid	X			X	

Another version of semantic feature analysis has the student fill in answers to questions regarding various features of related concepts: for example, how many sides a square has.

Regular Polygons	Number of Sides	Number of Vertex Angles	Degree Measure of Each Vertex Angle	Number of Reflection Symmetries
Equilateral triangle	3	3	60	3
Square	4	4	90	4
Regular pentagon	5	5	108	5
Regular hexagon	6	6	120	6
Regular n-gon	N	N	$(180n - 360)/n$	N

Semantic Feature Analysis

NAME _____ DATE _____

ASSIGNMENT: Place an X in the space provided if the indicated feature applies to the given concept.

Regular Polygons (*n*-gons)	Diagonals Exist	Diagonals Meet at Right Angle	Diagonals Are Congruent Angles	Vertex Angles Are Congruent	Sides Are Congruent
Equilateral triangle (3-gon)					
Square (4-gon)					
Regular Pentagon (5-gon)					
Regular Hexagon (6-gon)					

Semantic Feature Analysis

NAME _____   DATE _____

ASSIGNMENT: Fill in the matrix.

Regular Polygons	Number of Sides	Number of Vertex Angles	Sum of All Degree Measures of All Vertex Angles	Degree Measure of Vertex Angle
Equilateral triangle				
Square				
Regular pentagon				
Regular hexagon				
Regular *n*-gon	N			

Semantic Feature Analysis

NAME _____   DATE _____

ASSIGNMENT: Place an X in the space provided if the indicated feature applies to the given concept. If the best response is "not necessarily," leave the space blank.

Quadrilateral	Four-Sided Polygon	Opposite Sides Are Congruent	Opposite Sides Are Parallel	Exactly One Pair of Parallel Sides	Vertex Angles Are Congruent
Square					
Rectangle					
Parallelogram					
Rhombus					
Trapezoid					

Semantic Feature Analysis

NAME _____   DATE _____

ASSIGNMENT: Write *yes* or *no* in the space provided in response to whether the indicated feature applies to the given geometric concept. If the best response is "not necessarily," write NN. Note that *no* and *NN* do not have the same meaning. *No* means the feature is never true for that shape or solid.

Shape or Solid	Two-Dimensional?	Three-Dimensional?	Platonic Solid?	Regular?
Cube				
Tetrahedron				
Quadrilateral				
Square				
Equilateral triangle				
Sphere				
Equilateral triangular pyramid				

Semantic Feature Analysis

ASSIGNMENT: Place an X in the space provided if the indicated feature applies to the given concept. If the best response is "not necessarily," leave the space blank.

	Number of Sides	Number of Vertex Angles	Sketch of Polygon	Measure of Vertex Angle
Equilateral triangle				
Square				
Regular pentagon				
Regular hexagon				
Regular octagon				

The instructions below demonstrate how to find the measure of the vertex angle for the table:

1. Sketch a figure (a triangle or square, for example).
2. Draw as many triangles inside the figure as there are sides.
3. Multiply the number of triangles by 180.
4. Subtract 360 from this number.
5. Divide the result by the number of sides.

For example:

1.
2. [This square has four triangles.]
3. $4 \times 180 = 720$
4. $720 - 360 = 360$
5. $360/4 = 90$

Each vertex angle of a square has a measure of 90 degrees.

Graphic Organizers

WHAT? Description

Graphic organizers (Barron, 1969) are schematics created to show connections between key concepts, much as semantic word maps do. Mathematical graphic organizers often are constructed using a mathematical figure or graphic.

Graphic organizers may be created by teacher or student, and they may be used during prereading, reading, or postreading. Teachers might present a graphic organizer to the class as a prereading demonstration to elicit students' prior knowledge of the concepts to be studied. Working in groups, students might brainstorm terms related to some larger concept and create their own graphic organizers. A graphic organizer may be a circle, square, hexagon, or any other plane figure.

WHY? Objectives

Learning about graphic organizers will help mathematics students to:

- Create graphic organizers.
- Activate prior knowledge of concepts.
- Make effective connections between key concepts.
- Summarize or organize main ideas from the reading for reviewing purposes.

HOW? Examples

The lessons that follow show how to use graphic organizers. Here is a template for the circle graphic organizer.

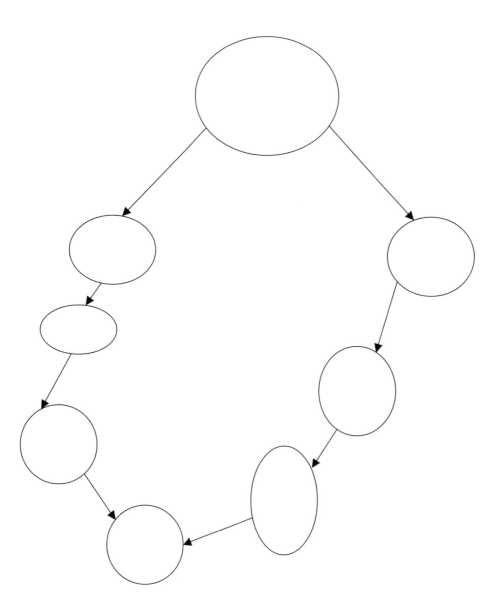

Graphic Organizers

NAME _____ DATE _____

ASSIGNMENT

1. Scan the list of terms below.

2. Write each term on a 3- by 5-inch index card.

3. Select the term(s) that all of the other terms might fall under.

4. Sort the cards with the terms, and place the cards showing any connections you see between the terms.

5. Choose an appropriate mathematical figure and sketch the organizer, writing the terms in the proper sites. Or use the circle graphic organizer to help place the terms in the appropriate circles.

There is not just one way to complete this assignment. Be creative!

Terms

circumference

circle

diameter

secant line

radius

diameter

area

tangent line

chord

sector

arc

Graphic Organizers

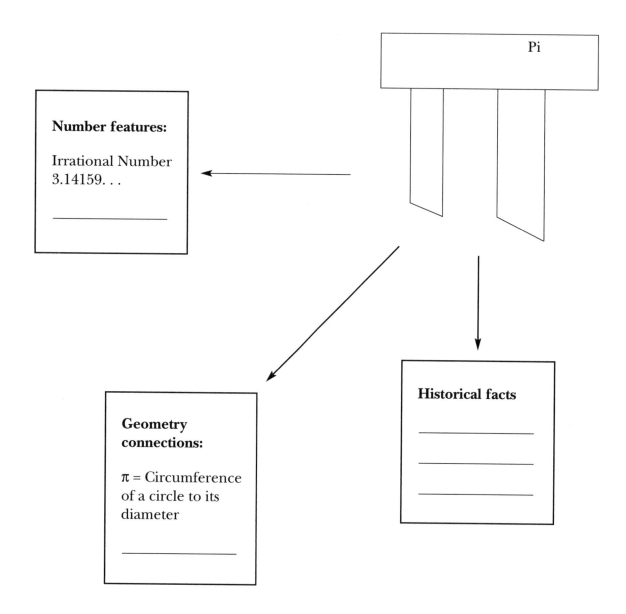

ASSIGNMENT: Fill in the blanks with features and/or descriptors of pi.

Pi

Number features:

Irrational Number
3.14159...

_____

Geometry connections:

π = Circumference of a circle to its diameter

_____

Historical facts

_____

_____

_____

Reading Math Symbols

WHAT? Description

Creating a witty short story using math symbols is one way of reinforcing student recognition of these symbols. For example, consider these symbols:

∞	infinity		∃	there exists
≈	approximately equal to		±	plus or minus
⇒	implies		∀	for all
⇔	if and only if		∴	therefore; since
∈	is an element of		. . .	goes on forever
≠	is not equal to		∅	empty set
>	greater than		Σ	summation
≥	greater than or equal to			

WHY? Objectives

Requiring students to use math symbols to create a story involving geometry will:

• Reinforce the meaning of symbols and geometric concepts.

• Help students reflect on and retain math symbols.

HOW? Example

Here is an example of a story created using symbols:

On a scalene-triangular island ∃ a city called ∅. This is a misnomer, since the population, which consists of persons with perfectly spherical-shaped heads, of the city of ∅ was always to be ≥ Σ of the number of short and cylindrical-shaped dogs alive in ∅. Should it ≠ the number of these strangely symmetrically shaped dogs, the appropriate creature(s), human or canine, would be massacred, deleted, erased, rubbed out, squelched, or killed, which made for paranoia and fear on the day of the yearly census. ∴ the number of dogs was great, so many of the geo-cylindrical dogs would die! This caused great sadness, ∀ of the members ∈ of the set of dog lovers and perhaps not as loving toward their peers, who all shared the perfectly rounded head feature with its ∞ number of lines of symmetry. How might the citizens of ∅ arrive at the perfect number of citizens: the equally ideal number of dogs > 0?

Reading Proofs

WHAT? Description

Reading proofs is a reading activity designed for introducing students to mathematical proof. Without proof, we are destined to arrive at incorrect conclusions. In 1989, the NCTM suggested that teachers move away from two-column proofs to short sequences of theorems written in paragraph or sentence form. Eventually students need to know how to read and compose this type of proof. To succeed, they must understand definitions and logic and have the insight and ability to make connections between theorems and concepts. This activity is a good starting point for developing the skills needed for writing geometric proofs.

The activity encourages students to look at mathematical statements in various forms. Ideally, students refashion these statements in four formats: verbal, numerical, visual, and geometric. It should be pointed out to the students that the numerical form gives only particular cases, while the visual and geometric forms give the general cases that constitute proofs. Of course, the visual type of proof is the preferred type for geometric proof.

For example, let ☺ = unknown number and ● = a constant:

Verbal form	Add 3 to a number.	
Visual form	☺ ● ● ●	
Numerical form	[if the number = 4]	$4 + 3 = 7$
Algebraic form	$x + 3$	

WHY? Objectives

The activity of reading proof will:

- Teach students the rudiments of proof.
- Give students practice with basic proof writing and reading.
- Allow mathematics students to see what forms constitute proof.
- Encourage students to consider various approaches to proof writing.
- Teach students how to make connections between mathematical statements.

HOW? Examples

The examples show proofs in the various formats: numerical, visual, and geometric.

Example 1

Consider the mathematical "trick" spelled out in the Verbal column of the table below.

Verbal	Numerical (one case)	Visual (geometric proof)	Algebraic (algebraic proof)
Pick a number.	2	–	x
Add 3 to the number.	$2 + 3 = 5$	____	$x + 3$
Multiply by 2.	$2 \times 5 = 10$	_____	$2(x + 3) = 2x + 6$
Subtract 6.	$10 - 6 = 4$	–	$2x + 6 - 6 = 2x$
Take $\frac{1}{2}$ of the result.	$\frac{1}{2}$ of $4 = 2$	–	$\frac{1}{2}(2x) = x$

The answer will be the original number. After students complete a few tables similar to this one, they should be able to create their own math trick.

Example 2

Prove: $(a + b)^2 = a^2 + 2ab + b^2$.

Numerical: Let $a = 2$ and $b = 3$ (this gives only one case):

$$(2 + 3)^2 = 5^2 = 25$$
$$2^2 + 2(2)(3) + 3^2 = 4 + 12 + 9 = 25$$

Visual: This is a geometric proof, originating with the ancient Greeks.

Note that the sides are of length $A + B$. So the area of the square is:

$$(A + B)(A + B)$$
$$= A^2 + (A \times B) + (A \times B) + B^2$$
$$= A^2 + 2(A \times B) + B^2$$

Example 3

Consider the mathematical trick given in the "Verbal" column of the table below. Then fill in the last three columns.

Verbal	Numerical	Visual or Geometric	Algebraic
Pick a number.			
Add 3.			
Multiply by 2.			
Take $\frac{1}{2}$ of result.			
Subtract your original number.			

The result will always be _____.

Semantic Word Maps

WHAT? Description

Semantic word maps (Johnson and Pearson, 1984) are graphics used to depict and display relationships between key concepts and terms. The semantic word map often resembles a flowchart or a web connecting mathematical terms. Arrows connect related concepts and often display a hierarchy of the terms.

WHY? Objectives

Constructing semantic word maps allows mathematics students to:

- Construct semantic word maps to explore relationships between mathematical concepts and terms.
- Consider the hierarchy of key concepts.
- Create study guides displaying key concepts.

HOW? Example

Consider the following related geometric concepts:

polyhedra	octahedron
tetrahedron	cube
platonic solids	prism
pyramid	sphere
duodecahedron	cylinder
icosohedron	nonregular polyhedron
regular polyhedron	
cone	
conic solids	

First, we note that the two main concepts seem to be "regular polyhedron," which are the same as platonic solids, and "nonregular polyhedron." The remaining terms appear to be conic solids. The first step in creating an appropriate semantic word map is to list the terms in a usable format, showing the hierarchy of the terms. From this listing, a word map is constructed. The following semantic word map clearly shows the relationship between and the hierarchy of the terms:

3D Objects

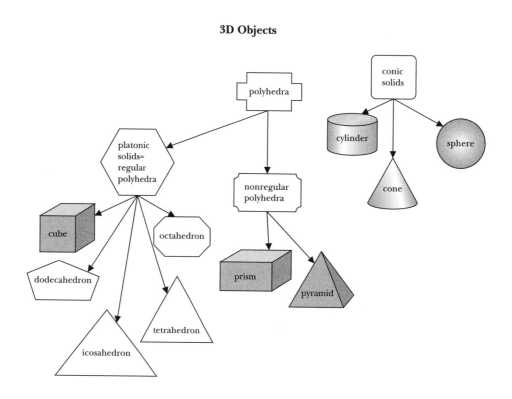

Semantic Word Maps

ASSIGNMENT: Sketch a semantic word map showing the relationship of these terms:

polygon	plane figure	rhombus
pentagon	hexagon	parallelogram
square	rhombus	rectangle
quadrilateral	trapezoid	
circle	triangle	

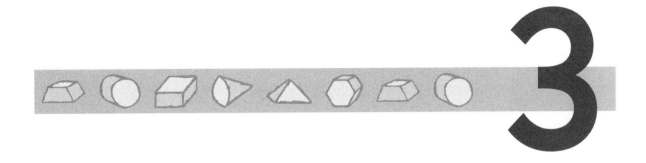

Postreading Strategies and Activities

Fill in the Picture
Concept Cards
Frayer Model
Question-Answer Relationship (QAR)
Comparison and Contrast Matrix

Quick Teaching Tip: Use a successful activity many times over the course.

When you find postreading strategies that are particularly successful, use them several times during the course. Students get better at communication when they are on familiar ground.

Prelude

Chapter Three contains strategies and activities that ask students to revisit the content an hour or even days after they have read it thoroughly. The purpose of these postreading activities, which are easily adapted to reflect the content the students are learning, is to help students retain the lessons learned, as well as to remind them of important concepts. Reflection, retention, and communication are the goals of postreading activities. Ultimately you will ask your students to demonstrate or describe the geometric content (see Chapters Five to Eight for activities). Most geometry teachers will agree that practicing geometric problem solving or doing many different constructions reinforces the students' retention of that content. This practice, combined with a postreading activity, works as an effective and powerful learning strategy.

Some students easily visualize geometric figures and others do better with verbal descriptions. What is vital is that each learner spends some time reflecting on the reading.

Fill in the Picture

WHAT? Description

This postreading strategy works best at the end of a chapter in a geometry text that deals with figures—for example, circles, triangles, polygons, and prisms. The figures allow the student to easily visualize the important geometric features. The activity can be done with small groups working at the board or on transparencies to be shown on an overhead.

The activity begins with a student sketching the main figure on the board. Then another student draws a related figure in or on the original figure and labels it; for example, if the first student sketches a right triangle, the second student may add the right angle and label it 90 degrees. Encouraging students to come up with as many related parts or facts about the figure is a superb motivator. Consider the right triangle again. Another student may label the hypotenuse and the legs. Still another may write the Pythagorean theorem on the board, and another a set of Pythagorean triples, which leads into trying to find as many triples as possible.

The directions this activity may take seem endless. Students may compare their group's work with other groups' work. Even if this activity is done individually, it's a great way for students to study for a test.

WHY? Objectives

This postreading strategy allows geometry students to:

- Visualize and sketch key geometric concepts.
- Work together to study and learn concepts.
- Challenge themselves and work competitively.
- Discover how geometric concepts and parts fit into the whole.

HOW? Example

For an example from a unit on circles, students would be asked to label each of the lines and parts of the circle shown here. (There are at least seven.) To get started in this activity, it is best to choose a plane (two-dimensional) figure that students will easily recognize. For example, in a beginning geometry course, a square or parallelogram would be an appropriate shape to use first because students would know some facts about the measure of the angles or congruency of the sides.

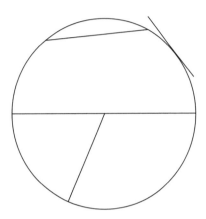

Fill in the Picture

ASSIGNMENT: Label all lines (L_1, L_2, L_3, L_4) and angles (A, B, C, D, E, F, . . .) on the figure below. Then give all congruent angles and parallel lines.

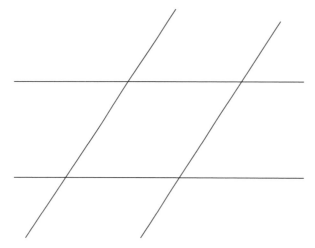

Fill in the Picture

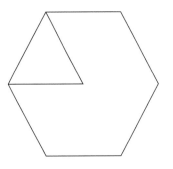

ASSIGNMENT: Consider each of the shapes shown here regular (all sides are congruent and all angles are congruent). Give all angle measures, and show all sides that are congruent.

The lines on the sides of the regular triangle indicate the sides are all congruent. Mark the other polygons in the same manner, showing which sides are congruent to each other.

Note that on three of the polygons, a wedge is shown in the interior of the polygon; it is not part of the polygon. When giving angle measures, you will have to consider the interior angles, that is, the angles from all possible wedges in the interiors. However, give only the vertex angles' measures.

vertex angle measure = _____

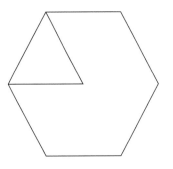

vertex angle measure = _____

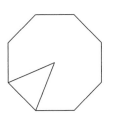

vertex angle measure = _____

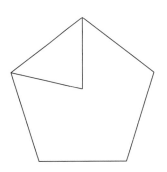

vertex angle measure = _____

Concept Cards

WHAT? Description

The construction of concept cards is an excellent way for students to make study aids for exams or other assessments. Index cards (3 by 5 or 5 by 7 inches) work well for this activity. After reading the text and doing any assigned problems, students go back over the content looking for key concepts. They then write each concept on one side of an index card and the definition, features, facts, or theorems regarding the concept on the other side.

Then they sort the concepts or cards into piles of related concepts. These concepts may be used to construct a geometry glossary for the entire course. The most common use of the concepts is as a study guide before a chapter or unit exam. Moreover, the cards can become part of a game where each student reads the back of a card and another student guesses which concept the verbal information is about.

WHY? Objectives

Concept cards are a postreading strategy that allows the geometry students to:

- Identify the key concepts and terms from the text and use these terms to create concept cards.
- Define the concepts in their own words, promoting ownership of the knowledge.
- Create a useful study guide for upcoming assessments.
- Complete a glossary for future use on final assessments or new courses.

HOW? Examples

The examples are contained in two lessons.

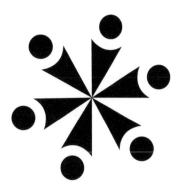

ASSIGNMENT: Consider the following two readings looking for the key concepts. When you are finished, construct at least six concept cards. See the next page for one set of concepts. Remember to write out the definition and important facts or features about the concept on the back of each card.

Reading 1: Euclidean Geometry: The First Geometry

In 350 B.C. Euclid, a famous Greek mathematician, wrote a text, *The Elements,* on all that was known about mathematics at the time. *The Elements* is divided into thirteen books. Books 1 to 6 deal with plane geometry, books 7 to 9 deal with number theory, book 10 deals with irrational numbers, and books 11 to 13 deal with three-dimensional geometry. Euclid's text is the second most reproduced, read, and studied book in history, second only to the Bible.

Euclidean geometry begins with definitions and five postulates (assumptions, or axioms) and also includes over 240 theorems (facts that are proven from the postulates and already proven theorems). The beauty of Euclid's geometry is that it does not make use of numbers to measure lengths or angles or areas or volumes. Instead, it deals with points, lines, triangles, circles, and the relationships among these. The undefined terms are points, lines, and planes. Euclid made some effort to describe these terms. He refers to a point as that which takes up no space and a line as that which has no breadth. Euclid also defines many terms in the treatise— for example:

> *Line segment:* any section of a line with two end points
>
> *Circle:* sets of all points in a plane in 2-space equidistant from a center point
>
> *Polygon:* a closed figure in the plane with line segments as sides
>
> *Sphere:* sets of all points in 3-space that are equidistant from a center point

Euclid's invention of an axiomatic geometry has been used and taught in schools for over two thousand years. Euclidean geometry presents over two hundred theorems, and their proofs, which are based on a finite number of postulates (axioms). Postulates are general assumptions, or as Euclid referred to them, "common notions"—for example, *things which are equal to the same thing are equal to each other.*

The foundation of Euclidean geometry is based on Euclid's five axioms (or postulates):

1. To draw a straight line from any point to any point.
2. To produce a finite straight line continuously in a straight line.
3. To describe a circle with any center and radius.
4. That all right angles are equal to one another.
5. That if a straight line falling on two straight lines makes the interior angles on the same side less than two right angles, the two straight lines, if produced indefinitely, meet on that side on which are the angles less than the two right angles (Burton, 2005).

John Playfair, a nineteenth-century mathematician, rewrote the five postulates in a form that is easy to understand and has been used in high school geometry texts ever since:

1. A line may be drawn between any two points.
2. A segment of any length may be constructed in any line.
3. A circle with any radius and center may be drawn.
4. All right angles are equal.
5. Through a point not on a given line, exactly one line may be drawn parallel to the given point.

Euclid's fifth postulate was considered wordy and not easily understood. For this reason, mathematicians have challenged this postulate ever since *The Elements* was published. Many mathematicians believed that the fifth postulate was actually a theorem and thus could be proved. Hours, days, years, and even lifetimes were spent on this endeavor. However, all efforts failed. In 1767, d'Alembert, a famous mathematician, called this controversy "the scandal of elementary geometry."

One thing did become clear: Euclidean geometry was not the only consistent geometry. Axiomatic geometries must be consistent (meaning no axiom or theorem conflicts with any others), and each axiom must be independent of the others. It was not until the early 1800s that it became clear that another axiom about parallelism could be substituted for the original fifth postulate and a new consistent geometry could be formed.

Reading 2: Non–Euclidean Geometries

There are many different types of geometry, and some are referred to as non-Euclidean. Many mathematicians, however, believe there are only two true non–Euclidean geometries: the hyperbolic and spherical. (There are several variations of these two geometries, but the basic ideas are given below.)

Non–Euclidean geometry, as in other fields or concepts of mathematics, was simultaneously discovered by mathematicians who had no contact with each other. Carl Friedrich Gauss in Germany, John Bolyai in Hungary, and Nicolai Lobachevsky in Russia all simultaneously (around 1830) uncovered a new fifth postulate. Bolyai's father was also a renowned mathematician. So, when the younger Bolyai made his discovery, he went to his father and excitedly told him the news. The senior Bolyai told his good friend Gauss, who claimed he had realized this fact some time ago and just did not publish it. After John's father told him that Gauss had already discovered this postulate, John got angry, thinking that Gauss was belittling or upstaging him. For this reason, Bolyai never did anything about his discovery. Therefore, when Lobachevsky did publish his findings, he immediately received credit for discovering the first non–Euclidean geometry. Time has been nicer to the younger Bolyai, and he is now considered one of the three persons credited with discovering what is now called *hyperbolic geometry*.

Hyperbolic geometry has many of the same features as Euclidean geometry: points, many theorems, and the first four postulates. However, the fifth postulate for this new geometry is called the Lobachevskian Parallel Postulate and reads, "There exist two lines parallel to a given line through a given point not on the line." Perhaps the other major change between the two geometries is the fact that the concepts of a plane and a line are different. The Euclidean plane is a slice of 3-space, or flat surface, and goes on indefinitely in all directions. The hyperbolic plane is the interior of a piece of the Euclidean plane. Let us consider it circular. There are no bounds to the hyperbolic plane. However, a larger circle could be drawn around our hyperbolic plane. Lines are also different in this geometry.

To think of this new geometry in its simplest version, consider the sketch below. Note that line 1 (L_1) goes through the center of the plane. Above L_1, there exist two lines, L_2 and L_3, that intersect each other but do not intersect L_1. Thus, L_1 has two lines passing through a common point, labeled P, that are nonintersecting and parallel to L_1.

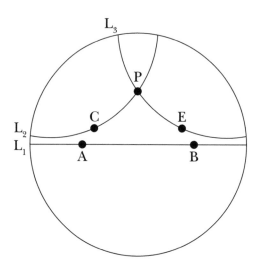

In the mid-1800s, Bernhard Riemann discovered what is now known as spherical geometry. Again, Riemann came up with a third fifth postulate: "There exist no lines parallel to a given line through a given point not on the line." The major differences are the plane and lines. Riemann's plane is the surface of a sphere, and his lines are great circles, circles on the surface of the spherical plane with the center of the sphere being the center of the great circle. Notice in the sketch below how all great circles intersect each other in two points:

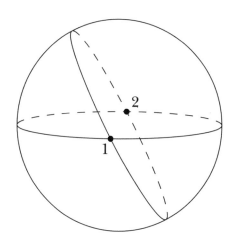

SOLUTION: Here is one set of key concepts covered in the reading (there are, of course, many others):

Euclidean geometry

hyperbolic geometry

spherical geometry

postulates

undefined terms

defined terms

planes

lines

Write each concept on one side of a card and the definitions and facts on the other side.

Frayer Model

WHAT? Description

The Frayer model (Frayer, Frederick, and Klausmeier, 1969) is a writing strategy that uses word categorization. The student defines a concept and considers its attributes, nonattributes, examples, nonexamples, and other important features of it. This is an excellent postreading strategy that requires students to review, reflect on, and study the key concepts of a unit. The Frayer model is an activity whose strategy is to have students define, describe, and sketch various geometric objects on a matrix and in their own words. It is an excellent tool for teaching new terms and assists students in building a strong foundation for geometric concepts. As the students use and reuse the terms when problem solving, they display a greater sophistication when using geometric terms.

WHY? Objectives

Using the Frayer model, students will:

- Read to search for the facts or features of the concept.
- Analyze and write out the attributes and nonattributes of the concept.
- Complete a graphic that may be used as a study aid.

HOW? Example

The example here is for the concept of a regular polygon.

Your Definition	Important Features
Many-sided two-dimensional closed and convex shape with line segments as sides. Regular means that all sides and all angles are congruent, making the polygon convex.	Vertex angles are all congruent and can be found using this formula where n = number of sides. $n = 180n - 360n$ Triangles = 3-gons Quadrilaterals = 4-gons Pentagons = 5-gons Hexagons = 6-gons
Examples	**Nonexamples**
Equilateral triangle Square Regular octagon	Isosceles triangle Scalene triangle Trapezoid

Frayer Model

ASSIGNMENT: The concept is reflection symmetry. Use your text and other resources to help you fill in the matrix below. First, give a definition for reflection symmetry in your own words. Then list at least three important features regarding this concept; think about rules and facts. In the lower two boxes, give an example (it might be a picture) and a nonexample of reflection symmetry.

Your Definition	**Important Features**
Example	**Nonexample**

Frayer Model: Template

NAME _____   DATE _____

ASSIGNMENT: Concept = _____.
Use your text and other resources to help you fill in the matrix below. First, give a definition for the concept in your own words. Then list at least three important features regarding this concept; think about rules and facts. In the lower two boxes, give an example (it might be a picture) and a nonexample of this concept.

Your Definition	**Important Features**
Example	**Nonexample**

Question-Answer Relationship (QAR)

WHAT? Description

Question-answer relationship (QAR; Raphael, 1986) is a postreading or reflection strategy. Raphael came up with four types of questions: two are text based and two are knowledge based. The question types are labeled as follows: *right there, think and search, author and you,* and *on your own.* (See the student handout that follows for descriptions of the types of questions.)

To use this strategy, students are introduced to the types of questions and asked to identify particular questions by these labels. By giving the students a handout like the one in the upcoming lesson, they will have a reference sheet for question types. By being able to identify the types, they become more skilled at finding the information or knowing when to reflect on the question and answer.

WHY? Objectives

By using the QAR strategy, students will:

- Become aware of and identify different types of questions.
- Hone their question-answering skills.
- Explore their prior knowledge or opinions on the content.
- Become more efficient and effective at studying content.
- Become better at understanding and responding to questions.

HOW? Examples

The questions that follow refer to Readings 1 and 2 in this chapter.

Right there	What are three types of geometry?
Think and search	Why did Bolyai not receive credit for the discovery of hyperbolic geometry?
Author and you	Would this scandal be considered a scandal in today's world?
On your own	How do you feel about inventions, inventors, and publications about inventions? Negative or positive, and why?

Question-Answer Relationship (QAR)

Where are the answers to questions found?

In the text:

Right there: The answer is found in the text. The wording of the question parallels the wording of the answer in the text.

Think and search: The answer is also in the text. However, the question and the answer in the text may be in different words. You will need to think about the ideas in the text and put the answer in your own words.

In your head:

Author and you: The answer is not in the text. You need to put together what the author says with what you think to answer the question.

On your own: The answer is not in the text. The text should have prompted you to think about the content. Use your background knowledge and insight to answer the question.

Question-Answer Relationship (QAR): Cartesian Coordinate System

NAME _____ DATE _____

ASSIGNMENT: Read each paragraph below. State what type of question each one is. Then answer the question.

René Descartes (pronounced *day cart'*) was a seventeenth-century mathematician and philosopher. It was not unusual for mathematicians in those days to be philosophers, for the invention or discovery of mathematics involved deep thought and intuition. Descartes was believed to have coined the phrase "I think; therefore I am."

Question: How does mathematical invention influence the field of philosophy?

QAR = _____

Answer = _____

Descartes is credited with developing the rectangular coordinate system that we call the Cartesian coordinate system. This system consists of a grid of squares sketched on a plane. The Cartesian coordinate system, also called the rectangular coordinate system or the xy plane, contains two perpendicular axes: a vertical line called the y-axis and a horizontal line called the x-axis.

Question: What are the two axes called in the Cartesian coordinate system?

QAR = _____

Answer = _____

The *origin* is the point at which the two axes meet. Points are plotted in the xy plane by locating the point of intersection for the line containing the x value and the line containing the y value. Ordered pair notation (x,y) is used to denote each point. For example, the origin is denoted $(0,0)$.

Question: How would you denote the point that sits at the number 2 on the x-axis?

QAR = _____

Answer = _____

Question: Why is the Cartesian coordinate system called the xy plane?

QAR = _____

Answer = _____

Question-Answer Relationship (QAR): Points of Concurrency in Triangles

NAME _____   DATE _____

ASSIGNMENT: Read each of the following paragraphs. State what type of question each one is. Then answer the question.

Each triangle has three angles and three vertices. If you bisect each angle and sketch the bisector, it will be a line segment that meets the other side of the triangle. Each of these three lines meets at a point of concurrency called the incenter.

   Question: What is a point of concurrency?

QAR = _____

Answer = _____

_____

_____

A perpendicular bisector is the midpoint of a line segment or side of a triangle that is perpendicular to the line segment. The three perpendicular bisectors of a triangle will always meet, and the point they meet at is called a circumcenter.

   Question: What is the point of concurrency for the three perpendicular bisectors of a
            triangle called?

QAR = _____

Answer = _____

_____

_____

Question-Answer Relationship (QAR): Points of Concurrency in Triangles (continued)

Each side of a triangle has an altitude. Take one of the sides, and consider it the base of the triangle. Find the altitude or height of the triangle from that base by finding a perpendicular from the base or extension of the base to the opposite point. The point of concurrency for all three altitudes is called the orthocenter.

Question: Will the orthocenter always be in the interior of the triangle?

QAR = _____

Answer = _____

_____

_____

Many regular polygons have points of concurrency. Consider a square. All four angle bisectors meet at the same interior point.

Question: What point(s) of concurrency does a regular hexagon have?

QAR = _____

Answer = _____

_____

_____

Comparison and Contrast Matrix

WHAT? Description

The comparison and contrast matrix (Vacca and Vacca, 1999) is a matrix for students to compare and contrast related features of related geometric concepts—for example, for a polygon, features might be the number of sides, angles, or diagonals. Usually the teacher chooses the concept and the features, and the student fills in the blank squares in the matrix. The completed matrix may then be used as a study guide or turned in as an assignment. The answers may be objective or subjective depending on the concepts or features to be compared.

WHY? Objectives

Completing the comparison and contrast matrix will allow mathematics students to:

- Research and reflect on the similarities and differences of geometric concepts.
- Complete a comparison and contrast matrix and use the matrix as a study guide.
- Receive feedback from the teacher about the validity of the facts in their matrices.

HOW? Examples

The next two pages have reproducible comparison and contrast lessons for students to complete. Note the differences and similarities in the features from both matrices.

Geometry Out Loud

Comparison and Contrast Matrix: Analytical Geometry—Triangles

NAME _____ DATE _____

ASSIGNMENT: The matrix below gives directions on the left and concepts across the top. Some directions ask for a sketch, and others ask for an amount. Read the directions carefully, and do only what is asked.

	Equilateral Triangle	Isosceles Triangle	Scalene Triangle
Sketch in quadrant I where all points are positive. Use the origin (0,0) as one of the vertices.			
Find the length of the base.			
Find the length of the height. Sketch the height in the graph above in row 1.			
Find the area of the triangle.			

Comparison and Contrast Matrix: Conics—Volume and Surface Area

NAME _____   DATE _____

ASSIGNMENT: The matrix below has directions across the top and geometric objects along the left side. Follow the directions as completely as possible. Show all work.

	Sketch	Find volume when height = 2 in. and base radius = 2 in.	Find surface area when height = 2 in. and base radius = 2 in.
Cylinder			
Cone			
$\frac{1}{2}$ sphere			
$\frac{1}{2}$ sphere seated atop a cylinder			

Geometry Out Loud

4

Readings in Geometry

Quick Teaching Tip: Assign only readings or reading activities that refer to and enhance the learning of the content.

A reading that would work well after a lesson on tessellations might be a piece on Arabian designs in rugs and architecture. The Arabs used only geometric patterns, not animals or people, in their art. Some of the most beautiful symmetrical drawings or designs are Arabic. (See the student examples at the end of Chapter Eight.)

Prelude

Chapter Four consists of four readings: two short essays, a listing and brief description of most of the geometries, and a prose poem. Each reading may be used as part of an assignment where students are assigned to read the piece and use one or more of the reading or writing strategy exercises from other chapters in this book. Also, the first reading contains questions to consider during or after the reading of each piece.

Three of the readings focus on the history and development of geometry. The term *geometry* comes from "geo" meaning earth and "metric" meaning measure. A textbook definition for the word *geometry* is visual thinking. The recorded beginnings of the study of geometry date back to Egypt and Babylon (4000–5000 B.C.) with some records from India and China (1000 B.C.). Understanding how a field of study such as geometry came into being is an effective way to learn about the field itself.

Writings about geometry often focus at least in part on the aesthetics of geometry or the topics that refer to the artistic flair of geometry, such as the Golden Ratio or tessellations. In *Principles and Standards for School Mathematics of 2000* (NCTM, 2000), the NCTM states, "Geometry offers a means of describing, analyzing, and understanding the world and seeing beauty in its structures" (p. 309). These readings may also describe geometric patterns, architecture, or geometric connections. They may be used as motivators to encourage students to search for a topic that tweaks their interest. We can set up the classroom in such a way that there are materials, space, and time allotted for the student to begin the creative process. The third piece in this chapter is a listing of geometries and their important facts or features. This list gives topics for students to explore and perhaps write about.

Reading 1: Early Geometry

Embedded in this reading are three numbered questions in bold type. Address each question as it arises.

The earliest recorded human history dates back to 4241 B.C. in the form of an Egyptian calendar. The calendar contained eighteen months of twenty days each plus five feast days. The Babylonian civilization also was quite prosperous at this time, with its own written language and mathematical system.

Historians offer two reasons they believe are the rationale for both peoples' creation of a written language and invention of a number system:

- There was more time for leisure, so people had time to invent.
- There were great needs for systems that enabled individuals and governments to compute taxes, survey lands, count materials, keep records, and engage in other business.

Most mathematics historians agree that the main reason was practical needs of the people.

The earliest mathematics known to humans was geometry, discovered by the Babylonians and Egyptians. They used two types of geometry: subconscious (intuitive figures and their shapes and size) and scientific (empirical, based on observations and experiments). There were also two strands of geometry developing during these ancient times: more and more content of geometry and the changing nature of the existing geometry.

Today pieces of two papyri scrolls, referred to as the Rhind Papyrus and Golenischev Papyrus, remain and are studied in an effort to understand the mathematics and geometry that the Egyptians used. One famous formula given is that for finding the area of a quadrilateral: $A = \frac{1}{4}(a + c)(b + d)$, where a and c, and b and d are the lengths of opposite sides, and the area is the product of the averages of two sets of opposite sides' lengths.

1. **Try some different four-sided figures such as squares or trapezoids, and their modern formulas to see if this original formula always works.**

Reading 1 (continued)

Perhaps the best achievement given on the Rhind Papyrus was the use of a formula for finding the area of a circle: $A = (8d/9)^2$.

2. Compare this formula with the actual formula to see how close the Egyptians came in their approximation for π. Note that the actual formula is $A = \pi r^2$, where r = radius.

One of the many uses of geometry was for surveying, called rope stretching. Rope stretchers used ropes with knots tied in them to measure land area. These men were considered specialists and geometers.

The first large-scale geometric project in Egypt was the planning and construction of the pyramids. The building of the pyramids began around 2900 B.C. Along the fertile valley of the Nile River, the Egyptians built huge tombs of stone (pyramids mostly) as resting places for their rulers. For thirty-five hundred years, these pyramids have stood majestically as if they ruled the desert just as the Egyptian pharaohs ruled their people. In fact, the Great Sphinx, a statue of a king with the body of a lion, was considered the guard of the pyramids of Giza. In its prime, it stood 66 feet tall and 240 feet long.

About 2600 B.C., the Great Pyramid, a monumental creation of geometric art, engineering, and long-term workmanship, was constructed at Giza. The ancient historian Herodotus wrote that 400,000 workmen labored for 30 years on the pyramid. They carried 2.3 million blocks that weighed 2.5 tons each to the work site, where each block fit so tightly together that a knife blade could not fit into any joint. The Great Pyramid is known for its size, not its beauty. In its early days, the pyramid rose 481.2 feet, and its base area covered 13 acres. Many mysterious qualities surround the mystique of the Great Pyramid. A few are given below:

- Egyptian priests contend that the area of each face is equal to the area of a square with sides equal to the pyramid's height. This notion implies that the pyramid's engineers planned to use the golden ratio in the pyramid's construction. To see this, consider the right triangle with the pyramid's height as one leg and the other leg as $b = \frac{1}{2}$ the length of the pyramid's base and a = hypotenuse which is the length of one triangular side of the pyramid and $a \approx 915.3$ feet. Thus, b/a approximates 1.618, an approximation of the golden ratio (considered the most pleasing proportion).

Reading 1 (continued)

3. Coincidence or by plan: What do you think? Finish the algebra to find the ratio $b/a \approx 1.618$.

• Some people maintained the pyramids were erected as dikes to keep the sands from moving and covering the cultivated parts of the Nile Valley. Others believed that captive Hebrews built the pyramids to serve as granaries for storing corn for years of need.

• Charles Piazzi Smyth (1819–1900), a Scottish royal astronomer, spent a great deal of time studying the pyramids and discovered a unit of measurement he called the pyramid inch, which is approximately 1.001 inch. Using this pyramid inch to measure the bumps and cracks amid the hieroglyphics on the interior walls, Smyth concluded that the Great Pyramid was designed by God to document prophecy or as a "Bible in Stone" (Burton, 1999, p. 56).

Possible Reading and Writing Assignments

Choose one of the following strategies and use it on this reading:

> semantic feature analysis
>
> concept cards
>
> graphic organizer
>
> Frayer model
>
> comparison and contrast matrix
>
> semantic word maps

Copyright © 2006 by John Wiley & Sons, Inc.

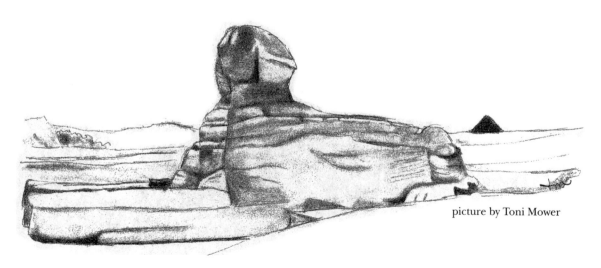

picture by Toni Mower

Geometry Out Loud

Reading 2: Types of Geometries

There are a number of different geometries, some of which share common concepts, terminology, and theorems, but mathematicians do not agree on how many there are. This difference of opinion may stem from the ambiguity of the term *geometry*.

The word *geometry* taken literally means earth measure. However, the concept of geometry could be generally defined as visual thinking. Geometry is derived from inductive reasoning. The first recordings of geometry came from the Egyptians and Babylonians over three thousand years ago. The geometry of these ancient peoples was a collection of measurements and processes used to solve practical problems. After observing and collecting geometric data, they formed conjectures, which led to generalizations. The next geometry came from the early Greeks and included proof. As more and more geometric discoveries were made, different geometries were formed and titled.

The lists that follow give many of these geometries. For each there is a brief definition or description, some vital features, or an application of the given geometry.

Euclidean Geometry

Description: Axiomatic system discovered by Euclid in about 300 B.C. Euclidean geometry is based on undefined and defined terms, 5 axioms (assumptions), and more than 240 theorems (propositions proven based on terms, axioms, and any previously proven theorems). This is the geometry taught in high school. Euclidean geometry has evolved over the centuries. It is often referred to as plane (two-dimensional) and solid (three-dimensional) geometry.

Application: Parallel lines have the same slope. This simple Euclidean geometric theorem is vital to the construction of buildings and highways and has been used for thousands of years.

Projective or Perspective Geometry

Description: Projective geometry is used to obtain the correct perspective of what we see. Artists use this geometry, which was discovered in the sixteenth century, to represent three-dimensional objects on a two-dimensional surface. A vanishing point is often used in scenic artwork where objects seem to converge to a fixed (vanishing) point.

Reading 2 (continued)

Application: This geometry is the basis for architectural and mechanical drawing and might be considered an aesthetic geometry.

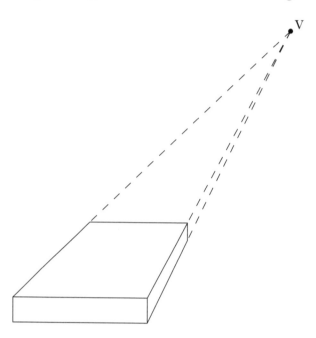

Transformational Geometry

Description: This geometry is based on transformations called rigid symmetries. Four of these symmetries are translations (slides, like a trail of bread crumbs might look), rotations (turns, a figure that looks the same when rotated), reflection (mirror images or flips), and glide reflections (combinations of a translation and then a reflection, like a set of footprints in the snow).

Application: Tessellations or tilings are repetitive patterns based on symmetries. Wallpaper, borders, rugs, floor tiles, and carpet designs are just a few examples of this aesthetic geometry. See the examples of tessellations at the end of Chapter Eight.

Reading 2 (continued)

Non–Euclidean Geometry

Description: Hyperbolic and spherical geometry. These two non–Euclidean geometries were discovered as a result of challenges to Euclid's fifth postulate (the parallel postulate). Mathematicians had long challenged Euclid's contention that the fifth postulate was an independent assumption. They believed it was a theorem and could be proven based on the other four postulates. When several of them realized they could not do so, they looked for other approaches to this challenge. A few of them realized that by changing the wording of the fifth postulate, they had discovered a consistent and viable geometry.

Application: Euclid's geometry said that the shortest distance between two points is a straight line (as the crow flies). However, the shortest flying distance from Los Angeles to New York would be an arc or curved "line" and not a straight line. This is an example of spherical geometry, where the lines are called *great circles;* they have their center at the center of the sphere (in our example, the earth). AB and CD are great circles in the sketch below.

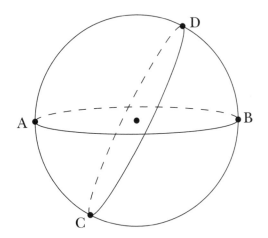

Synthetic Geometry

Description: Euclidean geometry where shapes or solids are not on any grid. For example, triangles can be drawn on any plane. However, a solid, like a cylinder, is a three-dimensional and tangible object.

Application: The ancient Greeks believed in using only a straight-edge and compass to construct a synthetic figure like a line

segment, perpendicular bisector, or right triangle. Today, many artists use many shapes as part of a painting without considering a grid or coordinate plane. Of course, some artists do use a grid for their beginning sketch.

Analytic Geometry

Description: In the seventeenth century, the French mathematician René Descartes discovered the two-dimensional coordinate system with two number lines (axes) perpendicular to each other and meeting at the point (0,0). This grid is called the *Cartesian coordinate system* or the *rectangular coordinate* system or simply the *xy plane*. Each point on the grid is an ordered pair (x,y), and all valid algebraic equations in two variables can be graphed on the grid.

Application: The discovery of the Cartesian coordinate system was necessary to the discovery or invention of calculus. Moreover, calculus is used to find rates of speed and the area under a curve that may represent a particular probability distribution.

Topology

Description: Analysis of position. Topology is the study of the abstract concepts of continuity and nearness. A popular term for topology is *rubber sheet geometry*—the study of properties that do not change the sheet (surface) when it is distorted.

Application: Graph theory and map coloring problems were at first interesting yet isolated problems. In the eighteenth century, a few mathematicians noted that these problems were based on position alone and not magnitude. It was not until the late nineteenth and early twentieth centuries that these subjects became part of a larger field of geometry called topology.

Taxicab Geometry

Description: A geometry whose model is a map of perpendicular and parallel "streets" as lines that run as a taxicab would take you over the streets to your destination. The shortest distance between two sites may include many turns, as the taxi cannot drive through a building or city lot. Taxicab circles look similar to the sketch here. Note the rotated square. There may be more than one route that gives the shortest distance between two sites (points.)

Reading 2 (continued)

Application: Taxicab geometry can be used to determine the school boundaries based on the number of students living on the streets by the school or where the most effective site is to place a restaurant.

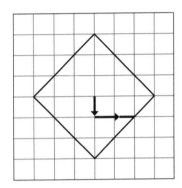

Differential Geometry

Description: The study of relations between the local and global properties of surfaces. Geodesics are curves used in differential geometry that are analogous to Euclidean lines.

Application: Given any two points (A and B) on a sphere, there exist special arcs called geodesics that are arcs of shortest distance joining A and B.

Finite Geometries

Description: An axiomatic geometry has a finite number of assumptions, lines, and points. The undefined terms include points, lines, and words like *on* or *adjacent to.*

Application: By understanding and being able to sketch a finite geometry correctly, students often can understand the properties necessary for valid geometry: consistency (no theorems or rules contradict each other in the geometry), completeness (all definitions, facts, and theorems are included in the geometry), and independence (each axiom must be independent from each other axiom).

Reading 3: Important Women Geometers

This reading introduces four brilliant female mathematicians and geometers. We start with **Hypatia**, the first female author in advanced mathematics, who was born in Alexandria in about 355 A.D. Her father, Theon, was a prominent mathematician, commentator, and astronomer. He was Hypatia's main teacher, and in later years she evolved into one of his major collaborators. One of her own major writings was a commendation of Apollonius's *Conics*, dating from the second century B.C. Hypatia was a popular teacher and helped invent and construct a hydrometer and astrolabe. For these reasons, she could be considered the first female geometer we know about. Since she lived during the decline of the Greek Empire and studied and taught in the Greek manner, she was considered a pagan by the Romans (Christians), although there is no proof of her religious or paganistic leanings at all.

One day, she was teaching in the park to a small group of mathematics students when a group of Roman citizens came upon her. They suddenly began stoning Hypatia as she ran through the park to a common temple, where she became trapped and was stoned to death. These misguided Christians believed this was what God would expect good Romans to do to any pagans and especially pagan women who were flouting tradition regarding women's roles in life.

Maria Agnesi (1718–1799) is considered the first great female mathematician in the modern Western world. She was born in Italy and was considered a gifted child. When her father realized her gifts in mathematics and in mastering new languages, he hired distinguished professors as her tutors. Under their tutelage, she mastered seven languages and became famous for writing what is considered one of the best and clearest calculus with analytic geometry texts. Agnesi is said to have unified calculus by connecting the inventions of calculus with the original problems of geometry and physics. One of her passions was to investigate analytic geometric curves. She is best known for a complex curve she explored that, because of a mistake in translation, is known as "The Witch of Agnesi."

After her father's death in 1752, Agnesi retired from the academic world and turned to religious studies and charitable work. She spent the last forty years of her life and all of her money helping those in need. During her years as a geometer and author, she also used those skills to help others. There was a need for a calculus text that students could understand. At this same time many other mathematical writers were

Reading 3 (continued)

attempting to write this text. Agnesi's *Instituzioni Analitiche* (1748) turned out to be the best.

Sofya Kovalevskaya was born in Moscow, Russia, in 1850. Her father had a love for mathematics and hired a tutor to teach this subject to Sofya beginning at a young age. Her bedroom walls were said to have been papered with her tutor's math notes. Since Russian schools did not allow female students and her parents did not want her to go off alone to study in another country, she married a friend, Vladimir Kovalevskaya. This marriage of convenience allowed her to go abroad, first to Berlin to study with Karl Weierstrass, one of the leading mathematicians of the 1800s. In 1874 Sofya received her doctorate from the University of Göttingen; she was the first woman to earn a Ph.D. in mathematics since the Renaissance.

Sofya was interested in applied mathematics as well as analytic geometry. In 1888 she won the Prix Bordin of the French Academy of Sciences for her work on the revolution of a solid body around a fixed point.

In 1858 **Charlotte Angas Scott** was born in Lincoln, England. Her father was the minister of the Congregational church and a principal of Lancashire Independent College. Non-Anglicans and women had little education available to them, so essentially she learned from her father, although her family did play mathematical games for entertainment. At age eighteen, Charlotte won a scholarship to Girton College, England's first women's college, which had opened in 1869. By 1885 she had earned her doctorate while studying under the famous algebraist Arthur Cayley.

Byrn Mawr College opened its doors to students in Philadelphia in 1885, and Scott was hired to run the mathematics department. Actually, she *was* the mathematics department. She published several articles on plane geometry and two texts on geometry. To her peers, mostly men, since there were not very many women at this time who were her peers, she was considered an excellent geometer. Over her adult life, Charlotte fought for greater opportunities for women in education and the workplace.

These geometers were brilliant women who had opportunities to learn only through family members and their willingness to teach. The schools and colleges around them were for males only, and even if they were allowed to sit in on classes, they were not allowed to earn a degree. All were highly motivated, and once they found what they considered their life's work, they taught themselves or sought out experts. Each woman faced some form of discrimination. All in all, these four women shared many of the same opportunities, challenges, and characteristics. However, their personalities were their own.

Reading 4: A Geometric Awakening

Standing at the window, peering through a visual tunnel of geometry.
A myriad of rhombi and prisms implodes
As a pattern of polygonal jewels suddenly splays across the screen,
Circles inside circles of light explode into gems of turquoise and jade.
Twisting the cylinder with childlike expectation and delight
A transformation of colors and shapes tessellate.
Orange, rust embedded with black and gold stripes,
Arced sides from hyperbolic triangles within hyperbolic triangles.
Moving with the sunset, pointing the tool toward the red-orange hues
Rainbows of royal blue and bright
    pink reproduce.
Stars turn to flowers to pentagons
    to links of glowing chains
A theater of symmetry: reflections,
    rotations, translations.
Reminiscent of earlier times and
    toys, childhood joys
A motif of stained glass designs
    duplicates.
The changing of rainbowed colors
    caused by shaken chips of glass
A tessellating experience, coloring
    the patterns in my mind with glee.

Pat Mower

picture by Toni Mower

Part Two

Writing to Learn Geometry

Writing across the curriculum is a movement that has been around since the 1970s; more than two thousand colleges and secondary and middle schools are involved at some level. The movement was a push for the use of writing as a teaching strategy in disciplines where writing creatively was considered time wasted. The federal No Child Left Behind Act (2001) with its call for literacy reform and greater professional standards has inspired school boards, administrators, and college professors to create and teach courses that use reading and writing, along with other innovative teaching and learning strategies, to help bring up student scores on state and other assessments.

Part Two of this book presents a portfolio of writing to understand, communicate, and assess geometry. We begin with strategies and activities that allow students to learn geometry and build geometric vocabulary. Once they have explored the geometry—its shapes, features, and definitions—and added new geometric knowledge and its connections to their repertoire, they are ready to practice communicating this knowledge to others. The communication process may then become an opportunity for students to open a dialogue with the instructor regarding content, grades, or personal issues. Not least of all, the writing can and will be used on assessment problems.

The National Council of Teachers of Mathematics (NCTM), in its *Principles and Standards for School Mathematics of 2000,* gives four broad strands in the Communications Standard:

Instructional programs from prekindergarten through grade 12 should enable all students to:

- Organize and consolidate their mathematical thinking and communication.
- Communicate their mathematical thinking coherently and clearly to peers, teachers, others.
- Analyze and evaluate the mathematical thinking and strategies of others.
- Use the language of mathematics to express mathematical ideas precisely.

Some of the larger obstacles I have had to face teaching lower-level college mathematics classes deal with getting students to write or explain their work and then write or explain why the process that they have used works. Often the problem lies in the fact that the student does not know how to work the problem or has memorized or guessed what to do. These facts have led me to believe that good communication is based on a good understanding of and confidence in that understanding of the mathematics (geometry) studies.

The strategies and activities in Part Two follow the standards set by the *Principles and Standards for School Mathematics of 2000.* I have enjoyed experimenting with these activities for writing to learn mathematics over more than fifteen years of teaching. More important, I believe that many of the activities have helped motivate my students to have fun while learning mathematics.

5

Writing to Understand Geometry

Many of the activities in Chapter Eight could also be used for writing to understand geometry.

Quick Teaching Tip: Display an example of what you consider to be a very good paper.

I usually do not show examples of bad papers, but I may list guidelines:

- Do not use a pen!
- Follow directions, especially since this is a new assignment.
- It is okay to start over, but watch the time.
- This paper is due on _____.
- Use the dictionary or spellcheck often.
- Do not judge anyone else's work negatively.
- Use any of the resource books at the math center in the corner of the classroom.
- Return all materials and books and clean up your workspace when you are finished.

Prelude

The strategies and activities in this chapter assist students in understanding geometry and writing about that knowledge, categorizing and creating graphic organizers to display that categorization, problem solving and communicating the problem-solving process used on paper, and creating amusing writings about a geometric concept to entertain as well as learn, among many other related activities.

Much of geometry is visual. In fact, one definition for geometry used in this book is visual thinking. It seems natural that once students have mastered reading about and understanding geometry, along with visualizing and interpreting the geometric contents, they would move on to writing about the content. This chapter offers opportunities to students to learn more about geometry through writing and using the vocabulary that we explored in Chapter Two.

Over the past twenty years, writing to learn has become a well-established pedagogy for many disciplines. Writing to learn as a pedagogical tool arose out of the writing across the curriculum (WAC) movement. Since the early 1980s, WAC advocates have been active in promoting instructional techniques that include writing, and writing to learn mathematics is part of this movement. Many mathematics instructors are committed to the use of writing for the enhancement of students' comprehension of mathematical concepts and processes. In 1990, I attended a two-week seminar put on by WAC and became committed to the idea that writing to learn mathematics is a powerful form of instruction that students for the most part relate well to. This pedagogy carries over nicely into the teaching and learning of geometry.

The first chapter of the NCTM's *Principles and Standards for School Mathematics of 2000* contains this eloquent opener: "Imagine a classroom, a school or school district where . . . orally and in writings, students communicate their ideas and results effectively" (NCTM, 2000, p. 3).

The writing process encompasses research, reflection, analysis, synthesis, rewriting, and communicating—skills that are equally valuable for learning geometry. The cognitive processes required in the writing process cause students to think before they proceed to use geometric algorithms or solve geometric problems. Often problem solving in mathematics can become a mechanical process in which the student may learn how to do it but not why it (the process) works. Memorizing a finite number of problem-solving processes and when to use them does not work for every student or for every problem. If the student comes across a problem with an unanticipated twist, being able to think logically and beyond the memorized processes and algorithms might prove a better route to take. The activities in this chapter encourage students to do so.

The writing-to-learn strategies and activities that follow speak to why algorithms work, encourage student reflection, demand analysis of geometric processes, and require that students explore and discover the fine points of and logic behind the mathematics. These activities are usually read and assessed by the teacher. Kiniry and Rose (1990) suggest the following writing-to-learn strategies: defining, serializing, classifying, summarizing, comparing, and analyzing. Other important writing-to-learn strategies are narrating, paraphrasing, detailing, recounting, illustrating, depicting, and characterizing. This chapter contains activities that address many of these strategies.

In Your Own Words: A Paraphrasing Activity

WHAT? Description

One of the most common excuses that students give for not reading the text is that they do not understand the language of the text. The paraphrasing activity helps students to target and interpret the key concepts. By rewriting portions of the text, they demystify and make personal meaning of mathematical content.

Students are assigned small portions of the text to read and translate into their own words. This activity works equally well with concept definitions, theorems, and examples. Having students read their translations to each other allows student writers to consider different interpretations and pinpoint misconceptions. If the translations are handed in, the teacher-reader can correct faulty thinking.

WHY? Objectives

The paraphrasing activity encourages students to:

- Read the text.
- Examine content closely and ask questions when necessary.
- Gain ownership of geometry by translating it into their own language.
- Consider peers' interpretations of the content.
- Identify and correct misconceptions.

HOW? Examples

See the examples in the lessons that follow.

In Your Own Words: A Paraphrasing Activity

NAME _____   DATE _____

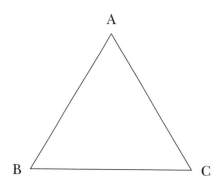

ASSIGNMENT: Read the passage that follows. Then write your definition of an equilateral triangle. Be clear, and use at least two complete sentences. Be prepared to share your definition with your peers. You may use other sources to help develop your definition.

Equilateral triangle: An equilateral triangle is a triangle with three sides of equal length or three congruent (same size and same shape) sides. By using the following theorem, we can show that all equilateral triangles are equiangular.

Theorem: The two base angles of an isosceles triangle with the congruent sides meeting at the apex (top vertex) of the triangle are congruent.

You can show that all equilateral triangles are equiangular by using the theorem above for each pair of sides of an equilateral triangle.

Your definition of an equilateral triangle:

_____

_____

_____

_____

For _____ bonus points, write out the point of the theorem above, using A, B, and C for the angles and AB, AC, and BC for the sides:

_____

_____

_____

_____

In Your Own Words: A Paraphrasing Activity on Transformational Geometry

NAME _____ DATE _____

ASSIGNMENT: Read the section in the text on transformational geometry on pages _____. Then paraphrase the section by answering the following questions. Be clear and address the items below in your description. Write as if you were writing or talking to a classmate who was absent the day we covered this section.

What is a transformation?

_____

_____

_____

Give the four basic transformations:

1. _____

2. _____

3. _____

4. _____

Only one of the transformations changes the orientation of the figure in one step. Name it.

_____

Chicken tracks in the dirt are an example of which transformation? (Note that this transformation has two steps.)

_____

_____

In Your Own Words: A Paraphrasing Activity on Transformational Geometry (continued)

NAME _____ DATE _____

In middle school geometry, three of the transformations are called slide, turn, and flip. Which transformation does each stand for?

slide = _____

turn = _____

flip = _____

Definition in your own words: Transformational geometry is

_____

_____

_____

Method of Operation

WHAT? Description

Much of geometric and mathematical content consists of processes. Students need to know the methods for simplifying or arriving at solutions. Having students write out processes (methods of operation) reinforces their understanding of how to solve problems and helps them to consider the fine points of or exceptions to the rule. If we consider the text or the classroom to be the scene of the crime and the problems to be the criminals, then the problem-solving processes are the modus operandi, or the MO, for problem solving.

Students might be asked to write out the MO for finding the midpoint of a line segment using only a straightedge and a compass. They also should be encouraged to write out the MO as if they were talking to a student who is just learning this process. This motivates the writer to be clear and complete, and consider the geometric vocabulary the student-reader should know.

WHY? Objectives

The method of operation activity will teach students to:

- Use a completed MO to conduct a geometric process.
- Share their MOs with their peers.

HOW? Examples

Here are some examples for student assignments:

- Write out the MO for finding the area of any triangle.
- Write out the MO for finding all lines of reflection symmetry of a regular octagon.

- Research and find the method President Garfield invented in 1876 for proving the Pythagorean theorem: $a^2 + b^2 = c^2$, where a, b, and c, respectively, are the two legs and hypotenuse of a right triangle. Then write out the MO for this proof in your own words.

A student who was asked to provide a method of operation for finding the circumference of a circle with radius of 4 inches came up with these steps:

1. The formula for the circumference is $C = 2\pi r$.
2. Decide on the accuracy you require for π, such as: let $\pi = 3.14$.
3. Apply the formula, that is, multiply: $2 \times (3.14) \times 4 = 50.24$.
4. Consider the correct label or unit of measurement: in^2.
5. Then give the solution: $C = 50.24 \text{ in}^2$.

Method of Operation: A Dissection Proof of the Pythagorean Formula

NAME _____   DATE _____

ASSIGNMENT: Follow the directions (the MO for the proof of the Pythagorean formula) to show a unique proof:

1. Sketch a right triangle, labeling a and b as the length of the legs and c as the length of the hypotenuse.

2. Sketch a square off the triangle's hypotenuse where one side of the square is the hypotenuse of your triangle. Label all lengths of all sides.

3. Sketch three more right triangles congruent to the original triangle, placing each with c as a side of the square. Again, label all sides. You should end up with a square with sides of length $a + b$. You may have to rearrange the four triangles to get them in the correct places. Remember that you need to end up with a large square with each side of square having a length of $a + b$.

4. Set up an algebraic equation with the left side being $(a + b)^2 = $ _____. You will need to fill in the blank. (*Hint:* You will need to use the formula for area of a triangle for part of this equation.) Solve and see if you end up with $a^2 + b^2 = c^2$. If you do, you have successfully proven the Pythagorean theorem. Congratulations!!

5. Find another geometric proof for the Pythagorean theorem. Write out the proof in your own words, using sketches when you need to. Recall there are at least 370 of these proofs!

Method of Operation: Constructions

ASSIGNMENT: Consider a line segment, AB:

A————————————B

Write out the steps for finding the perpendicular bisector of AB using a compass and a straightedge. Use sketches in the space below to support your steps. Explain each step as you would to another student who missed this lesson. Step 1 is given to get you started.

1. Place the point of the compass on the left end point of the line segment AB and open the compass to the length of AB. Draw an arc.

2. _____

   _____

3. _____

   _____

4. _____

   _____

5. _____

   _____

Method of Operation: Constructions (continued)

NAME _____   DATE _____

Write out the steps for constructing an equilateral triangle. Use sketches in the space below to support your steps.

1. _____

   _____

2. _____

   _____

3. _____

   _____

4. _____

   _____

5. _____

   _____

Method of Operation: Finding the Sum of Degrees of a Triangle

NAME _____ DATE _____

ASSIGNMENT: You will need a sheet of paper, scissors, and a ruler for this activity.

In elementary school we learned that the sum of the measure of all three angles in any triangle is 180 degrees. Think of other geometric concepts that have that same measure—for example, a straight angle, one-half the measure of the sum of all central angles of a circle, or the measure of the central angles off the diameter of a circle. Consider how to use sketches to show the congruence of these examples and the three angles of a triangle. For example, place the three angles next to each other to see if they form a straight angle.

Sketch several different-sized triangles with different angle measures, such as 30–60–90 degrees or 45–45–90 degrees. Then cut each corner of the triangle, with each cutout showing the angle and its measure. Place each of the cutout angles next to each other. Do they form a straight angle of 180 degrees?

1. Will this activity work for all triangles? In other words, if you cut around each of the three angles and lay them next to each other, will they form a straight line? Write this conjecture below.

    _____

    _____

2. Explain your reasoning for your answer to question 1.

    _____

    _____

3. Have you proven this conjecture above? Why or why not?

    _____

    _____

4. What is the sum of all four angles of any quadrilaterals? Why do you believe this conjecture?

    _____

Copyright © 2006 by John Wiley & Sons, Inc.

Geometric Figure Description Activity

WHAT? Description

This activity encourages students to reflect on and choose appropriate terms to describe the specific features of a geometric figure. First, the teacher sketches two different geometric figures and makes copies for each student. The students are divided into two groups of equal size. Each student in each group is given a copy of one of the figures to observe and write a description of on a separate sheet of paper. The descriptions are then traded with the members of the opposite group. Each student attempts to sketch the figure based on the written description he or she receives. The original version of the geometric figure is then viewed and students are encouraged to discuss their descriptions and sketches in pairs. This activity helps students enlarge their geometric vocabulary.

WHY? Objectives

The geometric description activity will guide the students to:

- Describe given geometric figures using vocabulary their peers will understand.
- Sketch a geometric figure given only its written description.

HOW? Examples

Students are given the following instructions: "Write out a description of the given figure in at least two complete sentences. Use language that your peers will understand and from which they will be able to sketch the figure." Possible descriptions follow.

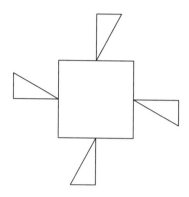

"This is a two-dimensional figure. It has a square in the middle of the figure and four triangles of equal size and shape coming out of each side. Each triangle meets the side of the square at one vertex."

"There is a large square in the center of the drawing. Around the square are right triangles that are about one-half of the size of the center square. The triangles are attached to the middle of the sides of the square, and each seems to be rotated about 90 degrees compared to the prior one."

"This is a picture of a propeller with four blades around a square. Each blade meets each side of the square at a corner. The blades are smaller than the square."

Geometric Figure Description Activity

NAME _____   DATE _____

ASSIGNMENT: Consider the three-dimensional figure below. On a separate sheet of paper, write out a description of the figure. Choose your vocabulary carefully so that another student can use your description to sketch the figure.

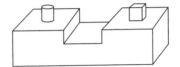

Geometric Figure Description Activity

ASSIGNMENT: Consider the three-dimensional figure below. On a separate sheet of paper, write out a description of the figure. Choose your vocabulary carefully so that another student can use your written description to sketch the figure.

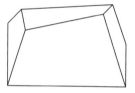

Crib Sheets

WHAT? Description

The creation of a crib sheet is an excellent study strategy for students preparing for an exam. The crib sheet is a one-page document containing the important information from a particular chapter, a section of the mathematics text, or related class discussions and lectures. Each student must select and summarize the key concepts, along with definitions, theorems, features, and examples. Each student's crib sheet will be unique, containing content and examples that make sense to that particular student. Teachers decide whether students will be permitted to use crib sheets during quizzes or exams. Students often say that creating a crib sheet is one of the best study methods they have used.

The crib sheet format may be predetermined or left up to the student. Consider the two different formats below and on the next two pages.

WHY? Objectives

The crib sheet activity allows the students to:

- Choose the key concepts from the unit's content.
- Complete a detailed summarization of a chapter or unit's geometric content
- Use the crib sheet as a study guide for upcoming assessments.

HOW? Example

Here is the partially completed example of a crib sheet from a chapter on triangles.

Concept	Description or Definition	Sketch
Incenter	Point of concurrency of angle bisectors	
Orthocenter	Point of concurrency of altitudes	
Centroid	Balancing point or point of concurrency of medians	
Circumcenter	Point of concurrency of perpendicular bisectors	
Median	Midpoint of the side of a triangle	

Crib Sheet

NAME _____ DATE _____

ASSIGNMENT: Fill in the following table with content that will help you prepare for the upcoming exam. Use language that makes sense to you.

Section	Concept	Description	Example	Notes/Facts

Crib Sheet

NAME _____   DATE _____

Review Chapter _____ and your class notes to find all key concepts and processes. Then fill this side of the paper with all vital content (content you anticipate will be on the exam). List all definitions, methods of operation, and examples in a manner that makes sense to you and will help you prepare for this exam.

Math Story Activity

WHAT? Description

Students are given a list of geometry terms or concepts and asked to use all of the terms correctly to create a short story. This activity may be used during or after the lesson containing the specified terms. Asking students to use geometry terms or concepts to create stories requires that they learn the meaning of these terms.

Student writers are encouraged to be creative but also to pay close attention to the meanings of the geometrical terms. The stories may be fiction or nonfiction. They may be witty, silly, sad, or dramatic.

WHY? Objectives

The math story activity will require the students to:

- Create a short story using geometric terms.
- Follow all directions, and use a dictionary or text to find correct definitions for terms.

HOW? Assignment Criteria

Students should be given some guidelines to follow when writing. Being explicit about what constitutes a paper that deserves an A is equally important to the student writer and the teacher reader-grader. Here is one example of teacher guidelines for this activity:

1. Use all of the listed terms.
2. Use each term correctly. Consult the text or a dictionary to check on definitions and correct use of terms. You may be creative with each term, but in at least one place use the term correctly or in a manner that clearly demonstrates what the term means.

3. Your story may be fiction or nonfiction.

4. Your story should contain an introduction and conclusion, and follow a logical story line.

5. Your story should be at least one page but no more than two pages.

6. Be creative, and choose a theme that has relevance for you.

Math Story Activity

ASSIGNMENT: Use the following terms to create a short story:

circle
radius
pi
diameter
chord
tangent
secant
circumference
area
central angle
inscribed angle

Follow these directions to earn full credit:

1. Use at least nine of the eleven listed terms.

2. Use each term correctly. Consult the text or a dictionary to check on definitions and correct word use. You may be creative with each term, but in at least one place use the term correctly or in a manner that clearly demonstrates what the term means.

3. Your story may be fiction or non-fiction.

4. Your story should contain an introduction and a conclusion, and follow a logical story line.

5. Your story should be at least one page but no more than two pages.

6. Be creative, and choose a theme that has relevance to you.

My lifelines are circles!

Writing to Understand Geometry   133

Math Story Activity

ASSIGNMENT: Use the following terms to create a short story:

line
point
angle
plane
parallel
perpendicular
bisect
midpoint
median
line segment
right angle
straight angle

Follow these directions to earn full credit:

1. Use at least ten of the twelve listed terms.
2. Use each term correctly. Consult the text or a dictionary to check on definitions and correct use of terms. You may be creative with each term, but in at least one place use the term correctly or in a manner that clearly demonstrates what the term means.
3. Your story may be fiction or nonfiction.
4. Your story should contain an introduction and a conclusion, and follow a logical story line.
5. Your story should be at least one page but no more than two pages.
6. Be creative, and choose a theme that has relevance to you.

Math Story Activity

ASSIGNMENT: Use the following terms to create a short story.

Platonic solid
cube
sphere
cylinder
prism
pyramid
polyhedron
cone
octahedron
rectangular prism
rectangular pyramid

Follow these directions to earn full credit:

1. Use at least nine of the eleven listed terms.
2. Use each term correctly. Consult the text or a dictionary to check on definitions and correct use of terms. You may be creative with each term, but in at least one place use the term correctly or in a manner that clearly demonstrates what the term means.
3. Your story may be fiction or nonfiction.
4. Your story should contain an introduction and a conclusion, and follow a logical story line.
5. Your story should be at least one page but no more than two pages.
6. Be creative, and choose a theme that has relevance to you.

Math Advertisements

WHAT? Description

Having students write advertisements for geometric concepts is an excellent way to encourage them to research these topics. Students become salespersons or promoters for the concept they choose to promote. To be effective salespersons, they must become experts on their products. They must sell the audience on the usefulness, uniqueness, and beauty of their geometric concept.

During this activity, students should have access to several different resources containing the appropriate content, such as several geometry texts and a mathematics dictionary. They will learn to research geometric topics as they are introduced to different interpretations of these topics. Students then collect and adapt this information into a format fitting for advertisement.

Tips

• Present students with multiple resources.

• Show students an example of what you consider to be a good ad, and explain why you think the ad is successful.

• Encourage students to be creative.

WHY? Objectives

The math ad activity will allow the students to:

• Research a geometric concept of their choosing.
• Create an advertisement using the geometric concept in creative ways.

Several examples of good ads for geometry concepts follow.

Math Advertisement

Centroid: $25

The balancing point of any triangle!
Now on Sale
The point of concurrency of all three medians!
Face it! We all need more balance
in our lives!

Use it for balance

- In all your affairs!
- For all your triangular relationships!
- To keep your work and love lives perfectly balanced!
- To help rid your life of those unnecessary moments!

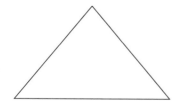

You will wonder how you ever
survived life without it!
So, get your centroids
while they last.
Hint: Centroids are great
stocking stuffers for your
stressed-out friends!

Math Advertisement

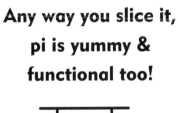

**Any way you slice it,
pi is yummy &
functional too!**

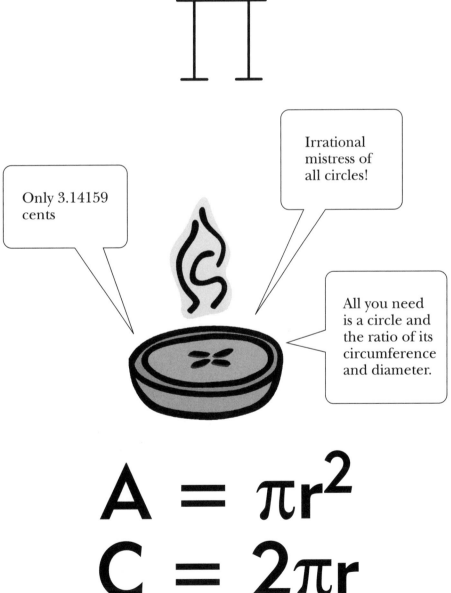

Only 3.14159 cents

Irrational mistress of all circles!

All you need is a circle and the ratio of its circumference and diameter.

$$A = \pi r^2$$
$$C = 2\pi r$$

The Writing Is on the Wall

WHAT? Description

Elementary teachers often post new words on a word wall or bulletin board to help students learn them. A more sophisticated version of the word wall is the posting of the Top Ten, Fabulous Five, or Foremost Four geometric concepts from each lesson or chapter on a bulletin board or poster board. As the word wall is being constructed, students are asked to give the key concepts and discuss the definition and hierarchy of the terms they identify.

In this way, students collect significant geometric concepts and terms that they can use to construct their own glossaries and thus become word-smiths. Students might be allowed to use their glossaries during special quizzes or exams or for studying for exams.

WHY? Objectives

This activity allows the students to:

- Choose key concepts from a section in the text or that day's lesson.
- Construct a geometry glossary over the entire course.
- Choose related terms and place them under witty titles (for example, Top Ten, Fab Five).

HOW? Examples

Here are two examples of word walls.

Fabulous Five Terms from a Lesson on Quadrilaterals

square

rectangle

parallelogram

rhombus

trapezoid

Top Ten Concepts from a Lesson on Circles

circumference

area

pi

radius

diameter

sector

central angle

inscribed angle

semicircle

chord

Creating a Math Mnemonic

WHAT? Description

Mnemonics are devices such as rhymes used as memory aids. One example of a mnemonic is an acronym, or a word formed from the first letters or parts of words. A popular mnemonic is the phrase "Please Excuse My Dear Aunt Sally," an aid for memorizing the order of operations: P stands for parentheses, E for exponents, M for multiplication, D for division, A for addition, and S for subtraction. Although memorizing is only one of the many strategies for learning mathematics, it is nonetheless vital to the learning of certain problem-solving processes.

This activity works well when the lesson involves a sequential process, such as the construction of a perpendicular bisector of a line segment. First, the process is demonstrated. Then the students work together or separately to create mnemonics that will help them memorize the steps of the process. The mnemonic might be an acronym, a rhyme, a rap song, or any other catchy wording that is easily remembered.

WHY? Objectives

This activity allows the students to:

- Choose a geometric process, and write it out in as few words as possible.
- Create a mnemonic using leading letters from each step of the process.

HOW? Examples

The lessons that follow are examples of assignments.

Creating a Math Mnemonic

NAME_____   DATE_____

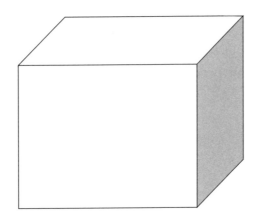

ASSIGNMENT: Create a mnemonic to help you remember how to find the surface area for a rectangular box without using the formula.

Consider the rectangular prism below.

The base of the prism is a rectangle with side lengths of 10 inches and 6 inches The sides of the rectangular prism are also rectangles. The height of the prism is 8 inches.

Rule	Mnemonic
Find the area of the base. A = 10 × 6 = 60	Base area B A
Double it. 60 × 2 = 120	Double D
Find the area of the front and back lateral sides. A = 10 × 8 = 80	Lateral area L A

Creating a Math Mnemonic (continued)

NAME _____   DATE _____

Rule	Mnemonic
Double it. $80 \times 2 = 160$	Double D
Find the area of the other two lateral sides. $A = 6 \times 8 = 48$	Lateral area L A
Double it. $48 \times 2 = 96$	Double D
Add all doubles. $120 + 160 + 48 = 328$	Add doubles A D
Give the final solution with a label. $328 \ in^2$	BAD double LAD AD

Creating a Math Mnemonic

NAME _____   DATE _____

ASSIGNMENT: Create a mnemonic to assist in finding the orthocenter of a circle. Recall that the orthocenter is the point where the altitude from each of the three sides meets.

1. Find the altitude of the triangle using one side as the base. Construct a perpendicular line segment (using a compass to establish the right angle) from this side to the opposite vertex (using a straightedge).

2. Repeat step 1 using a second side as a base, connecting a perpendicular on this base to its opposite vertex.

3. Repeat step 1 using the third side as a base.

Note that these three lines have one point in common, generally called a point of concurrency and specifically called an orthocenter.

Steps	Mnemonic
Find the altitude for side 1.	Alt, side 1
Find the altitude for side 2.	Alt, side 2
Find the altitude for side 3.	Alt, side 3
Find the point of concurrency = orthocenter.	Point of concurrency of alt = orthocenter
(Point of concurrency = point of intersection)	

Your mnemonic:

_____

_____

Creating a Math Mnemonic

NAME _____   DATE _____

ASSIGNMENT: Create a mnemonic to help you remember how to find the area of a circle.

Steps	Mnemonics
Sketch and cut out a circle with a 6-inch radius, using cardstock or construction paper.	
Divide the circle into 12 congruent sectors, cutting each one out.	
Place each of the wedges next to each other with the vertex of one next to the arc of the next one. Repeat.	
You will end up with a rectangle of sorts. Note that the short side = radius of the circle (r), and the long side will be $\frac{1}{2}$ of the circumference, (C), of the circle.	
Note that $C = 2\pi r$ and the area of the sector-rectangle is $A = \left(\frac{1}{2}\right)2\pi r \times r = \pi r^2$, which is the formula for the area of the circle.	

Use this space to sketch the work for each step of the process.

Your mnemonic:

_____

_____

Creation of Written Problems

WHAT? Description

Often geometry students say that they find word problems difficult and confusing. This activity asks students to create their own applications, which allows them to look at solving written problems from a different angle. Students do best with this activity when the geometric content is specific, such as solving problems that use right triangles.

Students work in pairs or small groups of three or four to create the problem. Groups then exchange problems and work solutions out on the board.

WHY? Objectives

This activity allows the students to:

- Work together and research applications of geometry.
- Create a written problem that is of interest to them.
- Share their creations with each other.

HOW? Examples

An example of a student-generated problem follows:

A swimming pool in the shape of a rectangle is 35 feet by 15 feet. There is a walkway around the pool that has the same width all around. The swimming pool and the walkway form a large rectangle with an area of 800 square feet. Find the width of the walkway.

After I guided a group of students through this process, we came to the following realizations:

- You must work backward to get the numbers to work out nicely.
- You must choose the words you use carefully so students will understand the question posed.
- You must understand why, and not just how, the problem works (Mower, 1995).

Geometric Concept Paragraphs

WHAT? Description

A concept paragraph is a paragraph written by the student describing a geometric concept or a feature of the concept using as many mathematical or geometric terms as possible. Prior to the assignment of the concept paragraph, the teacher and students review the rudiments of the concept paragraph:

- A thesis statement that introduces the concept
- One to three sentences about the thesis sentence that describe the features or characteristics of the concept

The teacher might encourage students to use as many mathematical terms as possible by awarding them points for each term used. This assignment may be enhanced by asking the student to include an example of the concept alluded to in the paragraph—for example, a two-dimensional or three-dimensional figure, a geometric proof or process, or a particular feature from a geometric sketch.

WHY? Objectives

This activity allows students to:

- Review the rudiments of constructing a good paragraph.
- Create paragraphs using as many geometric terms as possible.

HOW? Examples

The following geometric concepts could be used for concept paragraphs:

    reflection symmetry

    rotation symmetry

    circumcircle

    incircle

    inscribed angle

    scalene triangle

    regular rhombus

    tessellation

This example of a good concept paragraph is on the topic of reflection symmetry:

Many geometric figures have reflection symmetry, meaning that if the figure is folded over a line of symmetry, the sides will match. Another way to think about reflection symmetry is to place a mirror on the line of symmetry and note that the rest of the figure will reflect in the mirror. Consider a square. One of its lines of symmetry is a vertical line in the center of the square, running from top to bottom. The square also contains three more lines of symmetry: a horizontal line and two diagonal lines. If the square is folded over each of these lines, the sides will align exactly. An equilateral triangle has three reflection symmetries, a regular pentagon has five reflection symmetries, and a regular hexagon has six reflection symmetries. In fact, all regular polygons (n-gons) have n reflection symmetries.

Geometric Concept Paragraphs

NAME _____   DATE _____

ASSIGNMENT: Write a concept paragraph about one of the key concepts from Chapter _____.

Guidelines

Each concept paragraph must contain the following:

- A thesis statement that introduces the concept
- Two to three sentences that describe features or characteristics of the concept
- At least ten mathematical terms
- Complete, clear sentences

Grading

Each paragraph is worth 25 points, according to the following criteria:

Thesis statement is clear and accurate, and introduces the theme of the paragraph.	5 points
At least 10 math terms are used correctly.	10 points
Paragraph contains 2 to 3 clear and accurate sentences describing features.	5 points
Mechanics, grammar, and spelling are correct.	5 points

Biographies of Geometers

WHAT? Description

One way to understand geometry is to explore the history of the field of geometry. Several ancient men contributed to the development of the field of mathematics called geometry. Geometry may be generally defined as the systematic study of the physical world. *Merriam-Webster's Collegiate Dictionary* defines geometry as the mathematics of the properties, measurement, and relationships of points, lines, angles, surfaces, and solids. In 350 B.C. Euclid wrote *The Elements,* which details his axiomatic geometry based on these undefined terms: points, lines, and planes, five postulates (assumptions), and more than two hundred theorems. Each of the theorems is based on the undefined terms, postulates, and the theorems that came before the theorem in question.

Researching a geometer's life and geometric contributions helps us to understand the background and the step-by-step development of the various geometries and geometric processes. Several of the geometers and their contributions to the field of geometry are listed below. Students may be assigned a particular geometer or choose one of their liking. Also, having students peer-teach about their geometer is an excellent way to teach the class this knowledge.

Geometer	Contribution
Pythagoras	Geometric proofs
Euclid	Euclidean geometry
Erastosthenes	Good approximation of the circumference of the earth at the equator
Archimedes	Considered the greatest mathematical genius of antiquity; volume of the sphere, physics
Nicolai Lobachevsky	Non–Euclidean geometry (hyperbolic geometry)

Geometer	Contribution
Carl Friedrich Gauss	Hyperbolic geometry
John Bolyai	Hyperbolic geometry
Bernhard Riemann	Non–Euclidean geometry (spherical or elliptical geometry)
Jacob Steiner	Projective geometry
Hermann Minkowski	Taxicab metric

A biography is the write-up of a person's life story. The research, writing, and sharing of a biography of a mathematician who contributed to the development of geometry helps students to consider how and why the field of geometry arose. The development of geometry, like any other field of mathematics, is a step-by-step process of discovery or invention.

The assignment of a biography of a mathematician should include the format for the write-up. For example, each biography might consist of the following parts:

- Early life
- Education and career
- Family or social life
- Geometric contributions
- Later life

WHY? Objectives

This activity will require the students to:

- Research, take notes on, and learn about a mathematician of his or her own choosing.
- Write a mathematician's life story.

HOW? Example

The following lesson provides an example.

Biographies of Geometers

NAME _____   DATE _____

ASSIGNMENT: Write a four- to six-page biography of one of the following mathematicians:

Geometer	Contribution
Pythagoras	Geometric proofs
Euclid	Euclidean geometry
Erastosthenes	Good approximation of the circumference of the earth at the equator
Archimedes	Considered greatest mathematical genius of antiquity; volume of the sphere, physics

Guidelines

1. Each biography must contain the following parts of your geometer's life:

   Early life

   Education and career

   Family or social life

   Geometric contributions

   Later life

   Resource list

2. Conclude with your geometer's influence on the field of geometry.

3. Use at least three different sources with one source from the school's library.

4. Prepare a bibliography of the sources you consulted at the library.

5. Prepare the biography using a computer.

6. The report should be a minimum of four pages and a maximum of six pages in length.

Biographies of Geometers (continued)

NAME _____   DATE _____

Grading

Content score = _____
  Contains all required parts?
  Contains accurate information?

Mechanics score = _____
  Grammar, spelling, clarity, transitions, introduction, conclusion?
  Follows guidelines?

Resources score = _____
  Format? Number of sources, library source?

Final grade = _____

Experimenting-to-Learn-Geometry Reports

WHAT? Description

The National Council of Teachers of Mathematics (NCTM) has a Geometry Standard for Pre-K through grade 12 students in its *Principles and Standards for School Mathematics of 2000:*

> Instructional programs from prekindergarten through grade 12 should enable all students to:
>
> - Analyze characteristics and properties of two- and three-dimensional geometric shapes and develop mathematical arguments about geometric relationships.
> - Specify locations and describe spatial relationships using coordinate geometry and other representational systems.
> - Apply transformations and use symmetry to analyze mathematical situations.
> - Use visualization, spatial reasoning, and geometric modeling to solve problems [p. 308].

The study of geometry lends itself well to experimentation and discovery learning experiences. Students might be asked to sketch all of the different types of quadrilaterals and the diagonals inside each one. During this process, students will come to several conclusions and make several conjectures. In the write-up of this experiment, students should show all work and list all conclusions and conjectures. In this experiment and in all other types, the format of the write-up should be well laid out for the student. A fill-in-the-blanks form is the one way to encourage consistency and completeness.

WHY? Objectives

This activity assists students to:

- Complete geometric experiments.
- Fill out technical reports on the process and outcome of their experiments.

HOW? Examples

The lessons that follow provide examples.

Experimenting-to-Learn-Geometry Reports: Constructing Angles

NAME _____   DATE _____

Materials

One sheet of typing paper
Pencil and paper for sketch and recording
Straightedge and compass
Graphing calculator

Experiment

1. Trace a line segment using a straightedge. _____

2. Use a compass to sketch an arc above the line segment, starting with the end point of the left side of the line segment.

3. Use a compass (at the same setting as above) to sketch an arc, starting with the end point of the right side of the line segment.

4. Repeat this process to find a point of intersection below the line segment.

5. Join the two points of intersection on top and on bottom using a straightedge.

What angle have you constructed? _____

6. Use the compass to choose a certain distance from the origin to a point on the vertical axis, and sketch the arc.

7. Repeat this step using the same compass setting to sketch an arc from the origin to a point on the horizontal axis.

8. Join this upper point of intersection to the origin.

What size angle(s) have you constructed now? _____

9. Repeat this process and fill in the following table with the size of each new angle.

Experimenting-to-Learn-Geometry Reports: Constructing Angles (continued)

NAME _____   DATE _____

Number of Step in Process	Size of Angles in Degrees
1	90
2	45
3	
4	

Give any conclusions or realizations you came to during this experiment.

_____

_____

_____

Consider the process above, and write out the process for trisecting an angle.

_____

_____

_____

Give any conjectures or realizations you came to during this experiment.

_____

_____

_____

Experimenting-to-Learn-Geometry Reports: Building the Perfect Candy Box

NAME _____   DATE _____

ASSIGNMENT: Your boss has asked you to construct an open box that will hold a maximum amount of candy. You have decided to use analytic geometry (geometry on a grid) to solve this problem.

Requirements

1. Find the dimensions for an open box that will maximize volume.

2. Each box is to be made from precut squares that are 2 feet by 2 feet of predecorated cardboard.

3. The box will be made by cutting out a square of side length x in each of the four corners and folding up the edges.

Sketch

Draw a sketch of the problem.

Equation

Find a function for the volume of the box. Call the function $h(x)$, with x the length and width of the corner square.

$h(x) =$ _____

Explanation of Process

Give all steps for maximizing the volume. Explain each step clearly so your boss will understand the process. You may use your graphing calculator or calculus if you wish.

Final Report

On another sheet of paper, summarize your findings in a clear report using two or three paragraphs.

Experimenting-to-Learn-Geometry Reports: Networks

NAME _____ DATE _____

The Swiss mathematician Euler invented what is now known as graph theory in the 1700s while considering the answer to a problem involving seven bridges. The problem at hand was whether a person could cross all seven bridges while going over every bridge just once. Euler sketched a simple model, making the problem less complex and allowing generalization. Consider the problem below and its corresponding model. Note that the landmasses become the points, and the bridges become the paths.

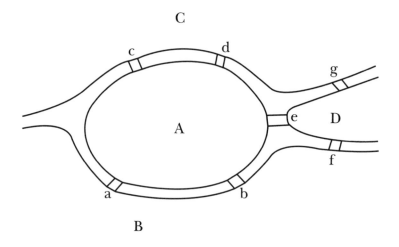

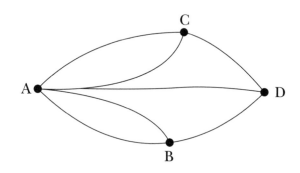

Experimenting-to-Learn-Geometry Reports: Networks (continued)

NAME _____   DATE _____

Now consider this problem:

The drawing below gives the "blueprint" for a house. Each room is labeled from A to E, and the doors are the paths. Is it possible to enter one door from the outside, go through every door exactly one time, and leave the house through an outside door?

Sketch a model here, and answer the question. Then write out any conclusions or realizations that you came to while attempting to solve this problem.

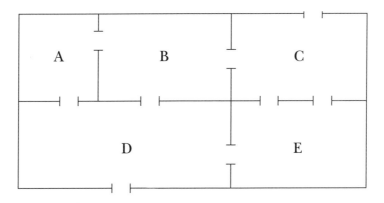

Concept Math

WHAT? Description

Concept math is an activity that invites the student to choose a concept, and then research and write about the mathematics related to this concept. This activity encompasses several steps: choosing the concept, researching the concept and the mathematics, freewriting or brainstorming the writing, writing a rough draft, polishing the paper, and sharing the report with peers and teacher. If the teacher chooses to be a part of each step, the final writing becomes much better. In this case, the concept math paper could be considered a mini research paper.

After students finish writing the paper, they should be encouraged to read the paper out loud to themselves or to a peer. Then after the papers are graded, students might read their papers out loud to the class and demonstrate any mathematics they wrote about in the paper.

WHY? Objectives

This activity requires students to:

- Choose and research a geometric concept.
- Complete a rough and a final draft of the paper.
- Share their work with peers and teacher.

HOW? Examples of Topics

The topics listed below are ideas of how a student might choose a topic of interest and write a paper exploring the geometry related to that topic. For example, a student might write a paper on softball and present the geometric features related to the ball, ball field, and ball game.

The Geometry of Dogs	The Geometry of Quilts
The Geometry of Basset Hounds	Kaleidoscope Math
Baseball Geometry	Building the Perfect Kite
Islamic Art	Pyramids

Concept Math: Basset Math

NAME _____   DATE _____

ASSIGNMENT: Read this passage, and answer the questions that follow.

Basset hounds are short-legged, long-bodied canines of the utmost character. The breed was developed by the French several centuries ago to hunt game in fields or woods with heavy ground cover. Their long ears (five to twelve inches in length) aid in the hunting of small game as the ears scoop up and big snouts take in the scent of their prey. Their short barrel-shaped bodies have huge breasts that often rub up against the ground, especially when climbing stairs. Even the basset puppy has huge feet for his or her body. These huge feet are attached to short, crooked legs, giving the dog a comical yet adorable appearance.

Female bassets are shorter, weigh less, and tend to have prettier faces than their male counterparts. Only rarely do you see symmetry in the bicolored or tricolored basset. An adult basset hound weighs between 40 and 100 pounds generally. Bassets tend to live to the ages of twelve to fourteen years.

These dogs are people dogs, very social and loyal. However, the basset can be stubborn and responds best when offered treats. They see themselves as lap dogs, no matter their size. Their bark turns swiftly into a deep howl when anticipating their master's arrival home or hearing bad guys, such as mail carriers or the garbage guys. Many bassets' masters register their pure-breed basset hound with the American Kennel Club and name their pets with such titles as King Ralph or Frederick the Great.

Two female bassets named Samantha and Sadie Sue live together. Sam is 14 years old, 57 pounds, and short and chubby, and loves to ride in the back of trucks, sleep, and eat treats. Sadie Sue is 3 years old, weighs 45 pounds, is taller than Sam and quite lean, and loves to play and terrorize Sam. At least once a day, Sam and Sadie play together, with Sadie doing most of the running and Sam most of the barking. The rest of the time Sadie tries to get Sam's attention and Sam just tolerates Sadie.

Concept Math: Basset Math (continued)

1. Given the information in the passage, can you describe the symmetry of a basset hound's body?

_____

_____

2. Describe the geometric qualities of basset hounds in general.

_____

_____

3. Sam and Sadie Sue are tricolored bassets, with white, brown, and black as their configuration. This means they each have mostly white fur and more brown than black fur. Is it possible to sketch a basset face that has reflection symmetry? Try it!

4. What geometric features or attributes do basset hounds have that make them good rabbit hunters?

_____

_____

Concept Math

NAME _____   DATE _____

ASSIGNMENT: Choose a concept from the list given below or another of your own liking. Research your concept, focusing on the geometric attributes, the shape and size, the symmetry or lack of, or any other geometry related to your concept. Take notes on index cards, labeling the back of the card with a category title, such as shape and size, or symmetry. Sort your cards by category, and use this information to write a rough draft of your concept paper.

Your paper must be between 100 and 250 words and contain at least three paragraphs. Begin with an introduction and summary of the topics you address in each of the paragraphs. End with a summary and a conclusion that ties back to your introduction.

Your paper must (1) address at least three different areas of mathematics or geometry and (2) contain at least ten mathematical or geometric terms or words.

Examples of Topics

Poolroom Math
Tessellations
The Symmetry of Flowers
Your Face's Symmetry

Crystal Prisms
Shadows and Right Triangles
Mirrors and Miras
Pizza Math

Grading

Each paper is worth 100 points, with the following breakdown:

Mechanics, grammar, transitions, spelling	25 points
Use of math and geometry terms: number accuracy	25 points
Creativity in topic or in writing	25 points
Accuracy of concept, effort, and effectiveness	25 points

Learning Logs

WHAT? Description

The creation of a learning log is a writing-to-learn activity that promotes student reflection and analysis of content. A learning log is similar to a journal; however, the emphasis is on content as opposed to students' feelings and opinions of content. Technically, a log is a record of progress or occurrences. In a mathematical or geometric learning log, students take notes in writing and sketches and answer teacher-generated questions daily, weekly, or periodically. The log is turned in periodically and assigned a grade based mainly on completion rather than accuracy of content.

The learning log may take several different forms: a spiral notebook, a binder of paper, or a file of note cards.

WHY? Objectives

This activity requires the students to:

- Complete a learning log by recording notes, sketches, and progress in the course.
- Share their learning log with the teacher periodically.

Here is a partial example of a double-entry learning log:

DATE: *Sept. 14, 2006*

Questions	*Answers*
Give your definition of parallel lines.	Two lines are parallel, if when cut by a transversal, opposite interior angles are congruent.
	Two parallel lines are lines that never meet.
	Two parallel lines are equidistant from each other when transversals meet the lines are right angles.
Name features of parallel lines.	Parallel lines have equal slopes.
	Horizontal lines have slope = 0.
	Vertical lines have undefined slopes.

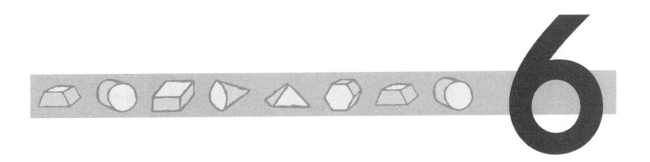

Writing to Communicate Geometry

Quick Teaching Tip: Give students several options for the types of writing explored in this chapter.

Students usually have few forums or opportunities in which they may write creatively. Remember that our goal as teachers is to get them to think of geometry in another light, and we have a better chance of doing that if the student writers enjoy the assignment.

Prelude

The strategies and activities in this chapter allow students to think out loud regarding their understanding of geometric content. By writing to communicate geometry activities, students share moments of mathematical clarity, entertainment, or even genius with their peers or instructor. Describing and communicating these thoughts on paper helps them organize their thoughts and use mathematical vocabulary to enhance and enlarge their geometric world. Communicating through writing in mathematics is intertwined through all chapters of this book. This chapter focuses on the more aesthetic part of communication through writing.

The first chapter of the NCTM's *Principles and Standards for School Mathematics of 2000* contains an eloquent opener: "Imagine a classroom, a school or school district where . . . orally and in writings, students communicate their ideas and results effectively" (2000, p. 3). The Standards go on to explain that teachers can create an environment where students feel safe enough to share "comments, conclusions, and explanations" (p. 351). We are their guides and must teach them first to appreciate the aesthetics of mathematics and then to communicate mathematically through choosing their forum, refining their language, considering the audience, and setting and reaching appropriate goals.

One way we think of communicating mathematically is participating in the aesthetic endeavors of geometry. Artwork, poems, short stories, letters, and advertisements are activities that allow the writer to be creative and consider the artistic qualities of geometry. See the tessellations created by future elementary educators at the end of Chapter Eight.

Writing to communicate geometry is a writing-in-mathematics strategy itself. Student writers must consider the audience and make appropriate choices in mathematical and geometric vocabulary and content. When composing a letter to his parents, a student must use more general mathematical terms unless one of his parents has a good understanding of the geometry alluded to. Moreover, if a student is composing a poem on the concavity of a polygon to be read at a campuswide poetry reading, she might begin by explaining the basic idea of concavity.

Writing Across Campus

WHAT? Description

Writing Across Campus Coffeehouse Readings is an activity that might take place on the campus of a high school or college. Professors and instructors from all disciplines assign a writing piece about some concept explored in one of their classes. The piece should demonstrate the student's understanding of the chosen concept and may be any writing that can be read in two to three minutes: a poem, rap song, letter, or short story, for example. Once a year, students from across the disciplines come together for coffee, pastries, and poetry and prose readings. The writings are selected by teachers who are committed to the writing-to-learn philosophy.

This is only one model used for this activity. Instructors should feel free to create their own coffeehouse readings activity or interdisciplinary writing program.

The readings can be funny, sad, enlightening, or even creepy. One year on the Washburn University campus in Topeka, Kansas, the majority of the readers came from a course called "Bugs and Society." That night, the air was full of the imagery of arachnids and creepy crawling things, and everyone left feeling just a little itchy.

WHY? Objectives

The writing across campus activity asks students to:

- Create a writing piece about a concept explored in one of their courses.

- Read their piece, and listen to other students share their work at a reading.

HOW? Examples

The poems that follow were composed by two freshmen enrolled in a geometry course. They read their work at a college Writing Across the Campus Coffeehouse Reading.

Geometry Out Loud

The Empty Set

Oh, empty set, how lonely you must be,
With nothing between your parenthesy.
Barren and abandoned, dreary and dull,
To bear such a name as null.

When not a number solves the case,
When all other answers are erased,
Without a seven, eight, or nine,
Then it is your time to shine.

You are the answer when there is no solution,
And so I draw the following conclusion:
That you must be important, though you stand alone,
You are well respected and known.

When finding the slope of a vertical line,
No other answer will be mine.
Never to be confused with zero,
Oh, empty set, you are my hero.

Untitled:

Triangles tangle,
Squares box,
Circles surround,
Rectangles reckon, and
Trapezoids trap in
Euclid's Geometry

Group Exposition

WHAT? Description

A typical geometry course covers from six to twelve chapters in a textbook and at least fifty different geometric concepts. Often there is little time to include historical anecdotes or real-world applications of the concepts presented. One solution to this dilemma is to require small groups of students to research and write up this material and then present it to their peers.

The group exposition activity works best with groups of two or three students with clearly defined roles—for example, researcher, writer, and editor-reporter. The assigned roles ensure that everyone in the group contributes to the exposition. Small amounts of class time should be allocated for groups to choose roles, brainstorm, assign tasks, and share work that has been completed outside class. Students may choose the format for the presentation: essay or speech, poster presentation, and skit or play are a few ideas. Students can build on the talents of the group members and choose a format that is compatible with those talents.

For example, the exposition topic might be the history of the number pi. The researcher gathers, reads, and takes notes from resources related to this history. The writer uses this material to compose the essay, poster presentation, or play. Finally, the editor-reporter edits the writer's work and presents the finished exposition to the class.

In a class of twenty-four students, eight expositions could be assigned over the semester. Approximately every other week, a different group could present an exposition on a concept being taught during that period. Students could use allocated class time or time when other students are doing seat work to prepare. Multiple resources should be made available to students for this preparation.

WHY? Objectives

The group exposition activity has students:

- Work together in groups of two to three, each with an assigned role to create an exposition.
- Research the history or an application of a geometric concept.
- Present their expositions to the class.

HOW? Examples of Geometric Exposition Topics

History of Pi

History of Non–Euclidean Geometry

Historical Applications of Geometry

History of Greek Geometric Proofs

Applications of the Transformational Geometry in Today's World

History of the Pythagorean Theorem

Group Exposition

NAME _____   DATE _____

ASSIGNMENT: Each group will be given one chapter to choose a topic from for a presentation to the class. The topic might be the history of one of the geometric concepts or an application that uses the geometry introduced in the chapter.

Your group must choose the format for the presentation: you could write an essay, deliver a speech, present a poster, or perform a skit or play, for example. Your presentation will take place during the time that we cover that particular chapter. When you have selected a topic and format, come visit with me.

Assign the following roles in your group: researcher, writer, and editor/reporter. Some class time will be allocated for work on this project; see the class calendar for these dates.

Listed below are the chapters to be covered in the text and some suggested topics.

Chapter	Chapter Title	Suggested Topics
1		History of ancient geometers History of Euclid's geometry Application of Euclid's geometry
2		Babylonians and geometry History of Platonic solids Early applications of Platonic solids
3		History of tessellations The geometry of Arabic art History of symmetry Application of symmetry
4		History of non–Euclidean geometry Today's applications of non–Euclidean geometry
5		History of finite geometries Euclidean geometry versus finite geometry

Geometry Out Loud

Group Exposition (continued)

NAME _____ DATE _____

Chapter	Chapter Title	Suggested Topics
6		History of projective geometry Applications of projective geometry
7		Geometric probability and Dr. Cardan History of geometric probability Application of geometric probability
8		History of trigonometry History of radian measure Application of right triangle trigonometry

Chapters from the following sources: Thomas (2002), Henderson & Taimina (2005), and Seydel (1980).

Guided Math Poetry

WHAT? Description

The creation and sharing of mathematical poetry can be an extraordinary learning experience for both teacher and students. This writing activity has the teacher guide student writers through the process of creating their own mathematical poems. Writing math poems can provide students with a forum for expressing themselves, as well as considering the vocabulary related to a geometric concept. It can prove to be a pleasant respite from the daily routine. By reading or listening to students' poems, teachers are able to pinpoint student misconceptions about the chosen concepts and experience the mathematics through the words of the student poets.

Two guided poem formats are explained here: the cinquain (MacBeth and others, 1997) and wordplay (Fleury, 2000).

WHY? Objectives

The guided math poetry activity asks the students to:

- Create poetry about geometry during a guided poetry experience.
- Research and experiment with geometry vocabulary and concepts.
- Share their poems in class.

HOW? Examples

The two lessons give the prompts used to guide students through the creation of poems about geometry.

Guided Math Poetry: Creating Geometric Cinquains

A cinquain is a five-line stanza or portion of a poem. The teacher guides the students with these directions:

"Think of a noun from geometry. Recall that a noun is the name of a person, place, or thing. Write it down."
Example: lines

"Now write out two words that describe your noun."
Example: parallel, perpendicular

"Okay, now write three verbs that go with your noun. Recall that verbs are action words."
Example: ascend, descend, extend

"Now write a phrase that says something about your original noun."
Example: dashing, slashing, and underscoring our lives

"Finally, rewrite your noun or a synonym of your noun."
Example: streaks

"Now, put it all together and you have created a poem!"

> Lines
> Parallel, perpendicular
> Ascend, descend, extend
> Dashing, slashing, and underscoring our lives
> Streaks

Here are some other examples of geometric cinquains:

Geometry
Euclidean, non-Euclidean
Shape, draft, construct
The mathematics of figures, proof, and symmetry
Earth study

Graph
Linear, parabolic
Planed, coordinated, plotted
A model of life as points on a plane
Graph

Triangle
Scalene, isosceles, equilateral
Angled, sided
A polygon whose angles measure up to 180 degrees
3-gon

Transformation
Rigid, tessellated, tiled
Reflect, rotate
A kaleidoscopic view of the images of life
Symmetry

Empty set
Vacuous, illusive
Hides, plunders, assassinates
A black hole of confusion and mind pirates
No solution

Guided Math Poetry: Wordplay

Wordplay is a form of poetry or writing where words are made up or used in unusual ways. The teacher guides the students with these directions:

"Write down three nouns from geometry. Recall that nouns are people, places, or things."
Example: polygon, sphere, point

"Change each noun to a verb by adding a suffix. Made-up words are allowed."
Example: polygoned, sphering, pointer

"Now, use at least two of your words in phrases."
Example: The women polygoned the floor.
     All young men must attend the sphering ceremony.

"Write down three geometric verbs. Recall that verbs are action words."
Example: reflect, rotate, glide

"Change each verb to a noun by adding prefixes or suffixes."
Example: reflecting, rotation, glideness

"Now, use two of these nouns in phrases that might fit with your last phrases."
Example: It was a night of reflecting and rotation.
     The boys marched with a proud glideness to their steps.

"Write down three geometric adjectives. Recall that adjectives are words that describe."
Example: concave, convex, congruent

"Change each adjective to either a noun or a verb."
Example: concavity, convexation, congruentness

"Now, use two of these in phrases."
Example: This rite of passage caused a congruentness among the young men,
     causing a certain convexation to the night's ambience.

"Finally, use some or all of your phrases to put together a prose poem."

The women polygoned the floor, preparing for the night's events
For all the young men were to attend the sphering ceremony.
It would be a night of reflecting and rotation.
As the boys dance with a proud glideness to their steps
As this rite of passage causes them to experience a congruentness with each other
Giving a sense of convexation to the night's affair.

Math Letters

WHAT? Description

One of the more obvious vehicles for communication is the written letter. Asking students to write letters about particular topics in geometry is asking them to communicate what they have learned. Student letter writers must research and reflect on content, summarize their understanding of the topics, and compose a writing that is readable and understandable to the reader.

Math letters may be composed for real or imaginary recipients. When students compose and send their letters to friends or family, they take great care in choosing the words to clearly explain their topic. They then must consider their audience's knowledge or lack of knowledge of geometry. Often high school and college geometry students know more mathematics than their parents ever will.

The assignment should be explicit in terms of audience, theme, and format (length, typed or long hand, formal or informal, and so forth). After giving the assignment, share with students an example of a letter that received a grade of A.

WHY? Objectives

The math letter activity necessitates that the students:

- Write a real or fictitious letter describing geometric content.
- Use language that is appropriate for their audience.

HOW? Examples

Here are some examples of assignments to various audiences:

- Write a letter to an absent student explaining the process of constructing a perpendicular bisector of a line segment.
- Write a letter to a prospective boss detailing your knowledge of geometric software and how that knowledge will help her company.
- Write a letter to your parents to convince them to buy you a graphing calculator; explain how it will help you learn geometry.
- Write a letter to your teacher comparing and contrasting concave and convex polygons.
- Write a letter to the president explaining how geometry could help him or her win the next election.
- Write a letter to your last high school geometry teacher detailing what you have learned about proof in your college geometry course.

Directions to students should cover the length of the letter, how it should be prepared (for example, typed and single-spaced with an extra space between paragraphs), and advice about choosing vocabulary based on the knowledge of the audience for the letter.

Math Letters: Memo to Your Boss

ASSIGNMENT: Your boss, the president of Beowulf Basset Chow, sends you the following memo.

MEMORANDUM

TO: Employee X

FROM: Office of the President of Beowulf Basset Chow

I would like for you to take charge of the development of an ideal geometric shape for Beowulf Basset Chow. You were chosen for this assignment because of your background in geometry. Develop the new shape or shapes, and prepare a cost and profit report for next week's department meeting. Set your other projects aside, and give all your attention to this vital subject. We need to get a leg up on our competitors.

Compose a memo in response in which you sketch and defend your geometric shape, and develop a budget for this change. This is your opportunity to become known as something other than Employee X to the president. Assume his mathematical knowledge is limited. However, be clear, not condescending!

TO: Office of the President of Beowulf Basset Chow

FROM: [Your name and title]

Math Letters

NAME _____   DATE _____

ASSIGNMENT: Write a letter to your parents explaining why Modern Geometry is an important course for you regarding your future courses and career. In your letter, address at least three topics from the "Geometry Topics" list below. Your letter should be at least one page or four paragraphs in length. Consider your parents' mathematical and geometric knowledge as you choose words to describe or explain these topics. The letter must be typed and in a proper letter format. Consult an English textbook to remind you of this format.

Geometry Topics

triangle	scalene	isosceles	equilateral
polygon	pentagon	hexagon	octagon
spherical geometry	great circle	equator	longitude
graph theory	network	path	vertex
circle	diameter	radius	pi
sphere	cylinder	cone	frustum
symmetry	translation	reflection	rotation
glide reflection			

The final draft is due on _____.

Geometer Profiling

WHAT? Description

A profile is a short biographical character sketch or piece of writing detailing the relevant data concerning a particular person, place, or thing. Written profiles are often about persons, places, or activities in the community. Geometer profiles may focus on a person in the community who uses geometry in his or her work, a place where geometry is employed in its daily operations, or an activity where geometry is a vital component of the event. Just as criminal profiling is used as a method for uncovering the characteristics and, perhaps, the identity of a criminal, geometer profiling can be used to uncover the geometry used in a particular career or activity or the usefulness of a place or activity, or to help students make educated choices about their future careers. Geometers from the past may also be profiled; in this case, the interview is replaced by research using books and articles. These sources should be cited in a uniform manner.

Creating a geometer profile has several steps:

1. Find a topic for the profile, using the library, Internet, directories, persons, or resources in the community.
2. Make a plan of action by setting goals and establishing a time line.
3. Write out questions in advance for interviewing persons or researching activities.
4. Interview or collect information on the subject of interest.
5. Take notes.
6. Organize the information gathered, prepare an outline, and compose a rough draft.
7. Revise, edit, peer-review, and proofread the profile.
8. Read the profile out loud to yourself, and polish the final draft.

WHY? Objectives

Creating a math profile requires that the student:

• Research, write, and learn about a particular person, place, or event in the community.

- Prewrite, write, and rewrite a mathematical profile.
- Learn about and share the use of geometry in the community and possible career options or opportunities.

HOW? Examples

Here are some examples of persons, places, or activities for math profiles:

Person	Place	Activity
Mr. Streetwise, supervisor of road construction crew	Shawnee County Road Construction Office	The use of geometry in road construction
Dr. Math, math professor	Mathematics Department at Smalltown University	Pi Day, an outing that includes eating pies and exploring the circle and pi for area high school math students
Ms. Eureka, a local architect	Architecture for the Future, Inc.	News conference for the new dome-shaped school
Mr. Dollar, surveyor	Boundaries Are Us	Interview

Math profiles should contain the following information:

- The name of the person, place, or event and descriptive information
- The reason for profiling this person, place, or event
- The mathematics and geometry associated with this subject
- Any interesting anecdotes regarding the subject
- Any accomplishments or honors associated with the subject

Geometer Profiling

ASSIGNMENT: Use the worksheet to help compose your geometer profile. Be sure to fill in each category.

Profile topic (person, place, or activity)
Plan of action (brief description of your plan for researching and composing profile)
Deadlines Interview or observation day = _____ Rough draft due = _____ Peer review date = _____ Final draft due = _____
Interview or on-site questions
Research notes
Peer review comments *[see the peer review form]*
Final analysis or self-evaluation of profile

Geometer Profiling

NAME _____   DATE _____

ASSIGNMENT: Find a geometer, a city or country where a great geometric invention took place, or a geometric invention, discovery, or activity from the past for your geometer profile. Use the worksheet to help compose your geometer profile. Be sure to fill in each category.

Profile topic (person, place, or activity)
Plan of action (brief description of your plan for researching and composing profile)
Deadlines Interview or observation day = _____ Rough draft due = _____ Peer review date = _____ Final draft due = _____
Interview or on-site questions
Research notes
Peer review comments *[see the peer review form]*
Final analysis or self-evaluation of profile

Geometer Profiling: Peer Review Sheet

NAME _____   DATE _____

Peer reviewing is used to help the writer self-assess the profile. Fill in the table shown here, keeping in mind that your comments will assist the profiler in revising the piece.

Questions	Yes or No
Paper is well organized and neat.	
Subject is a good choice for a math profile.	
Paper is well written with few grammar and spelling errors.	
Paper contains all required components.	
Paper contains the appropriate mathematical connections.	
Paper is interesting.	

What I liked best about your profile was

_____

_____

One thing I would change is

_____

_____

Math Journals

WHAT? Description

A journal is a periodic record in which the writer documents experiences and chronicles his or her thoughts, feelings, and opinions regarding his or her activities. Entries in the journal are written daily, weekly, or monthly. The math journal is often a weekly log that serves as a forum for dialogue between student and teacher. The content to be recorded in a math journal differs from instructor to instructor. Some journal assignments ask for student reflection, some call for comments regarding content, and others ask for a combination of the two.

The reflective math journal gives students a forum for expressing positive and negative reactions to learning. Each week the assignment might be the same: students are to express their thoughts or feelings about the teaching and learning of geometry for that week only. Or the teacher may elect to use prompts to help direct the student writers to focus on one or more particular aspect—for example:

- How do you feel about taking this geometry course?
- Describe yourself as a learner of geometry.
- Evaluate your progress so far in this course.
- What problems did you encounter in class this week?
- Write about your mathematical strengths and weaknesses in geometry.
- Describe the effort you put into this geometry course this semester. Then rate your effort on a scale from 0 to 10, where 0 = no effort, 5 = average effort, and 10 = 100 percent effort.

A journal assignment that requires the writer to demonstrate understanding of geometric content allows the teacher to observe and respond to students' misconceptions or use of unique methods for problem solving. Here are several examples of prompts for students to refer to geometric content:

- Compare and contrast the formulas for finding the volume of cylinder and a cone. Write out your answer in at least two complete paragraphs. Then give an example of finding the volume of a cylinder and a cone with base area = 10 in.^{3} and height of 4 in.

- Write out in words a geometric proof for the Pythagorean theorem, that is, $a^2 + b^2 = c^2$, where a, b, and c are positive real numbers. Then give an explanation of why it is important to know that a, b, and c are positive.

- Sketch a concave polygon and discuss the concavity of a polygon. Use words and sketches, and be clear.

- Describe the usefulness of finding the frustum of a cone. Use a graphing calculator to find a particular case. Use whichever calculator (for example, TI 83) you usually use in class. Give all steps.

Here are some examples of prompts for combination journals:

- Writing about mathematics and geometry is considerably more difficult than ordinary writing. Do you agree? Defend your opinion.

- Write out your general process for constructing an equilateral triangle using only a straightedge and compass. Please write as if you were explaining the process to a student who was absent the day we covered this material in class.

All writing requirements for journal entries, such as length of response or use of complete sentences, should be given at the start of the course or the journal assignment.

Hints for Assigning a Math Journal for the First or Fiftieth Time

- Plan your time well; reading and responding to thirty journal entries each week takes time.

- Choose only one of your courses each semester to incorporate the math journal into the curriculum.

- If you ask students to comment on the course or the teaching, be prepared to read unflattering comments.

- Collect journals on Friday (or end of the week) and return them on Monday (or the beginning of the week). Be consistent so that students know you believe in the importance of this assignment.

- Have all students use the same type of book for the journal, such as a spiral notebook or a blue book. Avoid having students use papers placed in looseleaf binders because they tend to lose entries or mix class notes in with journal entries.

- Use a box with handles or a tote to collect and carry the journals.

- Give credit or points for journal entries. Often students consider ungraded assignments as busywork and respond in kind.

- Use journals only if you are a true believer that writing is a powerful teaching and learning tool in mathematics.

WHY? Objectives

Math journals allow the student writer to:

- Write about math on a regular basis.
- Share their feelings about the course and their progress in their courses.
- Answer questions posed by the instructor and note when they are struggling.
- Pose questions using this one-on-one method of communication.

HOW? Examples

The lessons that follow give examples of assignments and student journal entries.

Math Journals

ASSIGNMENT: Over the semester, you are to keep a journal for this geometry course. Each week you are to write a one- to two-page journal entry in a spiral notebook.

OBJECTIVE: The math journal will allow you a forum for having a dialogue with me over the semester. Please use the journal to ask questions of or give comments to me as needed.

DUE DATES: Every Wednesday, a journal prompt, in the form of a question(s), will be given. Write your response and hand in your notebook with each weekly entry in it on Friday. On the following Monday, all journals will be handed back. Due dates will be announced on shortened weeks or weeks containing holidays.

GRADING: Each entry is worth 5 points according to the following criteria:

Mechanics (grammar, spelling, transitions)	2 points
Accuracy (regarding content or use of math terms)	2 points
Follows guidelines (see rules below)	1 point
Total	5 points

Fifteen entries will be assigned over the semester. The math journal constitutes approximately one-eighth, or 12.5 percent, of the course grade.

JOURNAL ENTRY GUIDELINES: Each entry:

- Must be at least three-quarters of a page and at most two pages in length.
- Must contain complete sentences and at least two paragraphs.
- Must answer the questions or prompts completely. Often there will be two prompts. Answer both!
- Should contain as many geometry terms as possible.
- May include graphs, sketches, and geometric work in response to the question.
- Must be legible. Please print if your writing is hard to read.

Math Journals (continued)

FIRST ENTRY PROMPT: Please respond to both questions on separate pages. Write out the appropriate prompt at the top of each page.

1. Think back to your first experiences learning geometry in elementary school. Write out a description of yourself as an early learner of geometry or mathematics. Then describe yourself as a learner of geometry or mathematics today.

2. True or false: The triangle area formula is half of the rectangle's area formula. Defend your answer.

Math Journals

ASSIGNMENT: Each student is to keep a geometry journal in the blue examination books handed out the first day of class. The journal will consist of weekly entries, one to two pages in length each. All writing must be in complete sentences and contain as many geometry terms as possible. Each entry will contain responses to one or more of the following questions:

- Summarize in two or three paragraphs the geometry studied during the past week.

- Work out one problem from the homework assignment. Choose one that you need help on if possible.

- Give the reaction to the geometry studied this past week. Was it easy to understand? What was the hardest part of the week's lesson? How would you rate your progress and understanding? Write out any questions you have regarding this material.

DUE DATES

The journal questions will be given on Friday.

Each entry in the journal is to be handed in on Monday.

Journals will be handed back on Wednesday.

GRADING

Each entry is worth 3 points. The journal grade will comprise 20 percent of the course grade.

COMMENTS

- The ability to communicate effectively is one of the most valuable skills you possess. The math journal gives you a forum for honing this skill.

- Self-assessment is another valuable skill. Each entry calls for some form of self-assessment.

- Please consider the journal your opportunity to ask questions that you were unable to ask during class.

Math Journals

WHAT? The journal will be reflective, with weekly written reactions to readings from the book *A Beautiful Mind* (Nasar, 1998).

HOW? Each entry must be at least two paragraphs in length and contain complete and clear sentences with good transitions.

WHY? This excellent novel describes the life story of a gifted mathematician who was yet mentally ill. It also gives a superb overview of the mathematics of the twentieth century and insight into many gifted mathematicians' thinking. Look for and comment on these inferences when possible.

WHEN? Each entry is due on Monday and will be handed back the next class day.

HOW MUCH? The journal is worth 50 points or 10 percent of the course grade.

Math Journals

Students were asked to write about their understanding of functions. The following quotations are excerpts from these entries (Mower, 1995, pp. 52, 63, 54, 58):

- Students used the journal to pose questions:

  "I understood the examples of years in college increase your salary, or weight varies with age . . . could this be a function: Your interest in functions increases your understanding?"

  "I was a little confused about the horizontal asymptote . . . it would cover the whole line . . . from right to left, without any holes. . . . So, a line could cross the H.A., but would it be a point . . . or an open circle?"

- Some journal entries displayed students' moments of genius or at least of creativity. The following entries give definitions of a circle:

  "A neverending line that curves perfectly to meet at the start and continues in the same pattern."

  "A circle is a perfection, no end and no beginning. The shape of the largest objects in the universe. The sun, the stars. A perfect curve. A two-dimensional view of a sphere."

- Students often will use the journal to write about their feelings regarding the learning of geometry, using terms like *overwhelmed*, *wowed*, and *encouraged*. These comments can be used to amend the next lesson, by changing either the pace or direction of instruction.

Mathematical Investigator

WHAT? Description

Investigative writing begins with questioning and data collection and ends with a written report presenting this knowledge. During the investigation period, others' opinions or reactions are amassed; however, the writer usually abstains from giving his or her opinion on the subject of investigation. "Just the facts, ma'am!" Overall, the purpose of investigating is to discover facts, and the purpose of investigative writing is to present these facts. The very phrase "investigative reporting" brings to mind tabloid news or, at the very least, the uncovering of secrets. The study of geometry may seem to hold secrets to some. Certainly the number of people in the world who understand geometry at a level higher than high school geometry is relatively small. This is a wonderful fact to share with your students.

Investigative writing includes some or all of the following techniques:

- Choose a subject: a person, place, concept, or process having to do with geometry—for example, the Greeks' contribution to mathematics through the use of geometric proof.

- Ask and answer the "wh-" questions, such as what, where, when, and why.

- Summarize or take notes from sources, and record the bibliographical information about those sources in the appropriate format.

- Use a title and an introduction that grab the attention of the reader.

- State the main theme, hypothesis, or purpose of the investigation up front.

- Analyze (break it up into its parts), synthesize (put the parts back into a whole of your understanding), and summarize the unearthed facts and data regarding your geometric topic.

- Consider your audience, and write the report using vocabulary that is easily understood by this audience.

- Read your report out loud so as to catch and then correct grammar errors.

Remember that an investigative report is a news story detailing the known or, at times, surmised information regarding a topic. The report does not need to be written; it may take the form of an ad or a song or a more formal, research paper. An assignment sheet should be given to each student-writer detailing the writing expectations or grading criteria.

Note that the proof by a scientific investigation process (in geometry and algebra) is very similar to the reporting process described above. Proof by scientific investigation includes the following steps (the corresponding components of the process above are given in parentheses):

1. Investigating and observation (researching)
2. Conjecturing (formulating hypotheses)
3. Testing and belief (testing and choosing hypotheses)
4. Informal explanation (composing the outline or rough draft)
5. Proof (completing the final write-up)

WHY? Objectives

The mathematical investigator activity allows students to:

- Practice investigating and taking notes about geometric topics.
- Learn by practicing how to compose an investigative report.

HOW? Examples

The next two pages contain a list of suggested topics and an assignment sheet.

Mathematical Investigator

NAME _____   DATE _____

Geometric Topics	Tabloid Headlines (In other words, don't take this assignment so seriously!!!!!!)
Polygons	Concave or Convex? The True Question
Non–Euclidean Geometry	Geometry Unveiled! Was Euclid a Liar?
Sphere	The Only Real Sphere Lives in Your Imagination
Line	Man Goes to Infinity: One Endless Step for Mankind
Point	That Which Takes Up No Space! Do Points Really Exist?
Square	Pythagoras's Cult Strikes Again? Found Squaring the Circle
Symmetry	Twins Cloned; Symmetry Revealed!

Possible hypotheses or thesis statements:

- The empty set was created by a mathematician who had trouble solving math problems.
- Consider a line shooting off to infinity.
- Plato said the only true circle lives in man's imagination.
- Most models do not have faces with "real" reflection symmetry.

Mathematical Investigator

NAME _____ DATE _____

ASSIGNMENT: Choose a geometric concept to write a mathematical/scientific investigative report on. Remember you are the investigator. Investigate and take notes, as if you were a reporter uncovering a big story. You may use the matrix below to collect your facts. Then use this information to write a three- to four-paragraph report in response to your thesis statement. Consider your audience to be the subscribers to magazines or newspapers that uncover and report secrets or gossip.

Subject
What, when, where
Why
Hypothesis
Investigative notes
Thesis statement

7

Writing as Authentic Assessment

Quick Teaching Tip: Do not take things too personally.

When you ask students how they really feel about the course, they may tell you something that hurts or attacks your ego. Try to remember this is just one student on one day at that particular time. By showing anger or hurt, you take the chance of students not telling you the truth again.

Prelude

The strategies and activities in this chapter allow the student or the teacher to assess their progress in the course without consideration of assessing quantitatively. To assess student work typically is to assign value or credit to this work based on some sort of continuum, usually numerical. This assessment value is usually documented and reported to the student and other interested parties and is used in determining the student's immediate or future placement or graduation. To authentically assess, in contrast, is to assign qualitative worth to individual or group effort and work to see if the students are understanding the material.

Authentic means genuine or real. Authentic assessment of an individual student encompasses the painting of a portrait that reveals the student's learning goals, habits, skills, and interests—that is, a full picture of the real learner. Through the authentic assessment of individual students, teachers are able to pinpoint and address learning weaknesses and build on learning strengths. Moreover, through authentic assessment of larger groups of students, teachers are better able to plan effective approaches and time lines for the teaching and learning of geometry or certain geometric concepts. The NCTM cites that "communication can be used in many ways as a vehicle for assessment and learning" (NCTM, 2000, p. 351). This chapter presents eight activities; two of them (Muddiest Point and One-Minute Summary) can be used repeatedly to help students self-assess and allow teachers to see what the students understand and what they do not understand.

Students who learn to authentically assess themselves as learners also become better able to build on their strengths and address their weaknesses in learning. Authentic assessment of oneself or understanding how you think or learn is called *metacognition*. Students who reflect on themselves as learners of mathematics build metacognitive skills and become more productive learners.

The writing activities in this chapter address three types of authentic assessment, with some activities encompassing more than one of these types:

- The teacher's assessment of the progress of the geometry class as a whole, and thus a self-assessment as a teacher of geometry
- The teacher's assessment of and individual geometry student's learning progress
- A student's self-assessment as a learner of geometry and his or her progress in the course

Muddiest Point

WHAT? Description

The Muddiest Point (Angelo and Cross, 1993) is an activity that allows the teacher to assess student comprehension of the content addressed in a classroom discussion or lesson. Students are given a three- by five-inch index card at the end of a day's lesson and asked to write out the topic from that lesson that most confused them. They hand in the cards as they leave the classroom. The teacher reads the cards before preparing the next day's lesson. Often the cards reveal one or two topics that several students found unclear. The point or points of confusion may be addressed in the next lesson or, if time permits, a review of these topics may become the next lesson.

WHY? Objectives

The muddiest point activity permits the students to:

- Identify and write out the most unclear topic from the day's lesson.
- Give their instructors an idea of the most unclear topics from that day's lessons.

HOW? Examples

These examples are from students' muddiest points from a lesson on regular polygons:

- For me the most difficult topic in this unit is . . .
    Word problems
    Word problems
    Word problems!!
    Circles
    Circles finding area and radius

Constructing equilateral triangles

Finding the measure of angles with parallel lines and a transversal

Graphing calculator and sketching three-dimensional figures

- For me the easiest topic in this unit is . . .

Right triangles

Parallel and perpendicular lines

Right triangle applications

Pythagorean theorem

Muddiest Point

The muddiest point presented in class today was:

_____

_____

_____

The easiest thing presented in class today was:

_____

_____

_____

Geometry Analogies

WHAT? Description

Creating geometry analogies is an enjoyable and instructional activity that may be used to relieve students' learning anxiety. An analogy demonstrates a similarity between things that are normally considered dissimilar. On the first day of a geometry course, students might be asked to complete this statement: "Doing geometry is like . . ." Some responses might be "swimming upstream," "skipping on the beach," or "eating chocolate."

Having students share these responses with their peers is a novel way to start a course that some students might consider to be boring or difficult. Usually the analogies spark a lively discussion. The exploration of analogies can also reinforce student comprehension of geometric terms.

Students need to know the definition of terms before they are able to consider appropriate metaphors or analogies.

WHY? Objectives

The geometry analogy activity invites students to:

- Consider geometric concepts in a manner that they may not have considered before.
- Create math analogies.
- Think deeply regarding the definitions of concepts and listen to and consider peers' analogies.

HOW? Examples

Some examples can help get students started:

Earning an A in this course would be like _____.

Solving a geometry word problem is like _____.

Using a straightedge and compass to construct angles is like _____.

A triangle is to a polygon as a _____ is to a _____.

Parallel is to perpendicular as _____ is to _____.

A circle is to a sphere as a _____ is to a _____.

Taxicab geometry is to spherical geometry as _____ is to _____.

Geometry Analogies:
Points, Lines, and Planes

NAME _____ DATE _____

ASSIGNMENT: Fill in the blanks using the words below. In some cases, more than one word or expression will work. However, use only one word or expression for each blank.

square	orange	color
area	lemon	apple
polygon	cat	size
line segment	kitten	Fido
$a^2 + b^2 = c^2$	wedge	Sadie Sue
right angle	ladder	garage
degrees	house	paint brush
sphere	paw	roller
side	basset hound	number
circle	dog	zero
radius	symmetry	boy
ground	flat	woman

A line is to a point as a _____ is to a _____.

A slope is to a line as a _____ is to a _____.

The angle is to a triangle as a _____ is to a _____.

Parallel is to perpendicular as _____ is to _____.

Parallel lines are to equal slopes as perpendicular lines are to _____ slopes.

Analytical geometry is to synthetic geometry as _____ is to
_____.

A regular hexagon is to a nonregular hexagon as _____ is to
_____.

The third dimension is to the second dimension as _____ is to
_____.

A straightedge is to a ruler as a _____ is to a _____.

One-Minute Summary

WHAT? Description

The one-minute summary is a familiar assignment for English or writing teachers. Also called the *one-minute essay*, this brief writing yields a wealth of knowledge to the writer and the reader. The teacher asks the student to free-write (write without worrying about grammar or spelling errors) on a particular topic for one minute. One-minute summaries may be assigned at the beginning, middle, or end of a classroom lecture or demonstration. Often a teacher will assign this writing at the beginning and the end of a lesson. The student writer is then able to self-assess his or her progress in learning the lesson. One-minute summaries are handed in for the teacher to scan but usually are not graded.

WHY? Objectives

The one-minute summary assignment asks students to:

- Free-associate and free-write about a specified geometric topic in a limited amount of time.
- Self-assess their comprehension of a concept or lesson without worrying about grammar or spelling and grades.
- Demonstrate their comprehension of topics to the teacher.

HOW? Examples

The teacher might begin this activity by saying to the students, "Take out a clean sheet of paper. We are going to free-write for exactly one minute on one topic. To free-write means to write continuously without worrying about grammar rules or correct spellings. Just write everything you think or know about the following topic without stopping as you write."

Here are some sample topics:

slope

right triangle

sphere

regular polygon

vertex

Pythagorean theorem

lines

One-Minute Summary: Student Summaries of Triangles

Student Summaries

"Triangles have 3 sides and 3 angles. The angles add up to 180 degrees."

"There are acute, obtuse, equilateral, and isosceles triangles. They can be very big or small."

"Right angles have only one angle that is 90 degrees. The other angles add up to 90 degrees. Therefore, the sum of the two angles = to the right angle."

"*Triangles* mean three angles, *tri* for 3 and *angles* for angles. A triangle must be convex and can never be concave. I tried to draw one and could not."

Teacher Responses

"I think you mean the sum of the measures of the 3 angles is 180 degrees."

"Also, there are *scalene* triangles whose sides are all different lengths."

"Good observation!"

"That is called discovery learning. You made a conjecture and tried to find a counterexample but could not. Good work!"

Geometry as a Four-Letter Word!

WHAT? Description

This activity asks students to complete the following phrase with a four-letter word: "Geometry is (a) . . ." Students are then asked to explain their reasoning behind their choice of words. This is a good first-day-of-class assignment as it allows students to express their appreciation or anxiety regarding the learning of geometry. Sharing their metaphors and hearing others' make this an illuminating experience.

WHY? Objectives

The geometry as a four-letter word activity allows students to:

- Express negative or positive feelings regarding mathematics instruction.
- Experience lower anxiety through this self-expression.
- Share and hear others' interpretations of their metaphors.
- Think about geometry in another way, and identify and practice metacognitive skills.

HOW? Examples

Here are some responses that students have made:

"Math is *loud!* Loud because it keeps me awake at night, trying to solve problems that stumped me."

"Geometry is *rude!* The proofs are hard for me. I try but I can't see where I am going."

"Geometry is *cute.*"

"Geometry is a *bike.*"

"Geometry is my *love.*"

Geometry as a Four-Letter Word!

NAME _____   DATE _____

ASSIGNMENT: Complete the sentences, and explain what you mean.

Geometry is _____.

Explanation:

_____

_____

_____

_____

Geometry is _____.

Explanation:

_____

_____

_____

_____

E-Writing

WHAT? Description

E-mail is one of the primary modes of communication today. Having students communicate by e-mail gives one more forum for dialogue between student and instructor. This form of messaging is immediate, allowing geometry students to comment on class as soon as possible or refer to homework problems as they arise. Moreover, if a particular time is set for the instructor to respond to student e-mails, then the student and teacher can correspond at the same time, either through e-mail or instant messenger.

Computer systems at schools and colleges have software that allows the teacher to communicate with the whole class, individual students, and students' parents. Starting the course with an introduction by computer sets the atmosphere for the class and gives permission for students to send messages to the teacher.

Students may be asked to send e-mail responses to teacher-generated questions on a regular basis—perhaps once a week or even every day. The e-messages might be in response to questions about their progress in the course or questions calling for demonstrating their understanding of content. It is best to ask a clear and direct question for students to respond to—for example:

"What did you learn in class today?"

"Summarize the process for finding the slope of a line."

"What was the muddiest point in class today?"

"Write out how you solved the problem on page x from your homework assignment."

"What has been the greatest challenge for you in this class so far?"

"What has been the easiest concept for you to understand in this class so far?"

The ground rules for how the teacher expects student responses to look should be specified—for example, use complete sentences, give the correct spelling, and make frequent use of geometrical and mathematical terms. Teachers are then able to receive feedback before the next class and to correct problems or faulty use of mathematical vocabulary. Awarding points for the correct use of new geometry terms will encourage students to be careful.

WHY? Objectives

The e-writing activity gives the students:

- A forum for dialogue and immediate and direct feedback from the instructor about personal or class concerns.
- Another manner for communicating geometry or problems about geometry and receiving feedback about these concerns.

HOW? Example

The lesson gives a general e-writing assignment.

E-Writing

ASSIGNMENT: Each Friday your e-assignment will be posted on the board and in a general e-mail message. Please respond by Wednesday of the following week.

I will be online Monday evening from _____
to _____. Feel free to correspond with me at this time.

GUIDELINES

- Write out the weekly e-assignment first.
- Use at least two paragraphs.
- Use complete, clear sentences. Writing about mathematics should be concise, uncluttered, and clear.
- Include as many geometric terms as possible.

You may include other questions about homework or other comments. However, you must also respond to the weekly question using the guidelines above.

GRADING

Each e-mail is worth _____ points.
Extra points will be given for every new geometric term used correctly after the first two terms.

Geometry Similes, Metaphors, and Analogies

WHAT? Description

Similes, metaphors, and analogies are words and phrases that are used to conjure up vivid word pictures of related concepts. A *simile* is a comparison using the words *like* or *as*—for example, "Set P is like the set of polygons." A *metaphor* is a direct comparison suggesting that a concept is a word that quickly brings to mind a related picture—for example, "A circle is the shape of a pizza." An *analogy* is an enhanced simile or metaphor—for example, "Euclidean geometry is the study of points that take up no space, lines that go on forever and ever in space, and a plane that is a slice of space."

For the following activity, students were asked to reflect on concepts from the day's lesson and create a simile, a metaphor, and an analogy for each term. One student filled in the table in this way:

Concept	Simile	Metaphor	Analogy
Symmetry	Like an identical twin.	Symmetry is snake-eyes.	Symmetry is the outcome of the bisection of a proportionally perfect face.
Vertex	Like the corner of a coffee table.	A vertex is the very tip of a dog's tail.	A vertex is the joining of 6 regular hexagons on a tessellation of the same.
Polygon	Like the perimeter of a rectangular yard.	A polygon is the shape of a window.	A polygon is many-sided, as are many arguments.

WHY? Objectives

The similes, metaphors, and analogies activity asks students to:

- Consider the definitions and features of certain geometry concepts.
- Express geometry concepts in familiar terms.
- Learn more about geometry concepts through consideration of comparisons.
- Learn to identify and practice metacognitive skills.

HOW? Examples

Three example lessons follow.

Geometry Similes, Metaphors, and Analogies

NAME _____   DATE _____

ASSIGNMENT: Fill in the blank spaces in the table below with an appropriate simile, metaphor, and analogy. Recall that a *simile* is a comparison using the words *like* or *as*—for example, "A triangle is like a dinner bell." A *metaphor* is a direct comparison suggesting that a concept is a word that quickly brings to mind a related picture—for example, "Volume is the amount of a soft drink in a can." An *analogy* is an enhanced simile or metaphor—for example, "A translation is the hop of a rabbit in the middle of its journey across a field."

Use comparisons of things or words that you are familiar with. Be creative!

Concept	Simile	Metaphor	Analogy
Angle			
Radius			
Diameter			
Right angle			
Chord			

Geometry Out Loud

Geometry Similes, Metaphors, and Analogies

NAME _____   DATE _____

ASSIGNMENT: Fill in the blank spaces in the table below with an appropriate simile, metaphor, and analogy. Recall that a *simile* is a comparison using the words *like* or *as*—for example, "A triangle is like a builder's square." A *metaphor* is a direct comparison suggesting that a concept is a word that quickly brings to mind a related picture—for example, "Volume is the amount of a soft drink in a can." An *analogy* is an enhanced simile or metaphor—for example, "A translation is the hop of a rabbit in the middle of its fearless journey across a field."

Use comparisons of things or words that you are familiar with. Be creative!

Concept	Simile	Metaphor	Analogy
Symmetry			
Reflection			
Rotation			
Translation			
Mira			

Geometry Similes, Metaphors, and Analogies

NAME _____   DATE _____

ASSIGNMENT: Fill in the blank spaces below with an appropriate simile, metaphor, and analogy. Recall that a *simile* is a comparison using the words *like* or *as*—for example, "A triangle is like a dinner bell." A *metaphor* is a direct comparison suggesting that a concept is a word that quickly brings to mind a related picture—for example, "Volume is the amount of a soft drink in a can." An *analogy* is an enhanced simile or metaphor—for example, "A translation is the hop of a rabbit in the middle of its journey across a field."

Use comparisons of things or words that you are familiar with. Be creative!

Concept	Simile	Metaphor	Analogy
Polyhedron			
Cube			
Sphere			
Prism			
Pyramid			
Vertex			

Targeted Problem-Solving Assessments

WHAT? Description

The targeted problem-solving assessment activity allows teachers to assess students' understanding of certain problem-solving processes and make decisions about whether to spend more time on the targeted content. Teachers design a worksheet with three to five problems of the same type and give the sheet to students. Students are asked to name or describe the problem-solving process they will use on each problem and then solve each problem. This activity causes students to stop and think of which technique they should use before they leap into an incorrect process.

This activity is very similar to Angelo and Cross's documented problem solutions (1993). They suggest that the responses usually look similar to one of the following:

- Students who answered at least two problems correctly, named or described the process correctly, and clearly showed each step in the process
- Students who answered at least two problems correctly, but described and demonstrated the problem-solving process incorrectly and sloppily
- Students who obviously did not get it and were unable to name, describe, or demonstrate the correct problem-solving process (p. 223).

By examining the worksheets, the teacher is able to make decisions about time and coverage of content for this particular class.

WHY? Objectives

The targeted problem-solving assessment allows students to:

- Identify and practice metacognitive skills.
- Demonstrate problem-solving techniques for the teacher.
- Receive immediate feedback from the teacher regarding their problem-solving abilities.

HOW? Examples

The following lessons provide good examples.

Targeted Problem-Solving Assessments

NAME _____   DATE _____

ASSIGNMENT: Read and reflect on each problem. Name or describe the problem-solving process you will use to solve the problem in the space provided. Finally, solve the problem, showing each step clearly and completely. You may use another sheet of paper for this part.

1. Find $V = \pi r^2 h$ when $r = 3$ cm and $h = 10$ cm.

   Name or description of process to be used: _____

2. Find the angle measure of the side across from the longest side of a triangle with side lengths 6, 8, and 10 inches.

   Name or description of process to be used: _____

3. Find the surface area of a cube with side length of 5 cm.

   Name or description of process to be used: _____

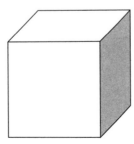

Targeted Problem-Solving Assessments

ASSESSMENT: Read and reflect on each problem. Name or describe the problem-solving process you will use to solve the problem in the space provided. Finally, solve the problem, showing each step clearly and completely. You may use another sheet of paper for this part.

1. Graph in the *xy* plane: A circle with center at (1, –2) and radius of 2 units.

   Name or description of process to be used: _____

2. Graph in the *xy* plane and find the area of a triangle with vertices at (1,1), (2,3), and (–1,4).

   Name or description of process to be used: _____

3. Sketch the following using synthetic geometry: A regular hexagon with regular triangles attached to each vertex. Let one of each of the regular triangles' vertices meet each vertex of the hexagon. Sketch the triangles as large as possible given your hexagon.

   Name or description of process to be used: _____

Targeted Problem-Solving Assessments

NAME _____   DATE _____

ASSIGNMENT: Read and reflect on each problem. Name or describe the problem-solving process you will use to solve the problem. Finally, solve the problem, showing each step clearly and completely.

1. Simplify: sin ½

   Name or description of process to be used: _____

2. Find the perpendicular bisector of the line segment below.

   Name or description of process to be used: _____

   _____

3. Simplify: $\sin^2 x + \cos^2 x - 1$

   Name or description of process to be used: _____

4. Simplify: Find the coordinates for the right triangle that has two vertices at the points (−1,2) and (3,5).

   Name or description of process to be used: _____

Self-Portrait as a Learner of Geometry

WHAT? Description

This activity asks students to paint a verbal portrait of themselves as a learner of geometry. Questions are written in such a way that they elicit descriptive responses from the student responder. Students who are artistically inclined may be asked to do a sketch of themselves as learners of geometry. Students whose interests or talents lie elsewhere are invited to use those interests to describe themselves as a learner of anything.

WHY? Objectives

The self-portrait as a learner of geometry activity requires students to:

- Complete a self-portrait of themselves as a geometer.
- Consider and document progress in their geometric skills and talents.

HOW? Example

The lesson that follows contains a sample questionnaire.

Self-Portrait as a Learner of Geometry

NAME _____   DATE _____

Part One: Type of Learner

I learn geometry best when I can

_____

_____

I learn geometry best when the teacher

_____

_____

Part Two: Description of Learner in Geometric Terms

Which of the following descriptors (math terms) best describe you as a learner of geometry? Check all that apply.

Maximum _____	Square _____	Linear _____
Minimum _____	Triangular _____	Parabolic _____
Infinite _____	Circular _____	Cubical _____
Finite _____	Hexagonal _____	Spherical _____

Self-Portrait as a Learner of Geometry (continued)

Part Three: Learner's Interest, Knowledge, and Skills*

Rate your interest, skills, and knowledge in the following geometry topics, using the chart below. Circle the numbers and letters that apply to you.

0 = No interest
1 = Some interest
2 = Interested in learning more
3 = Very interested

N = No skills, no knowledge
B = Basic skills and knowledge
H = Can do it and know about it adequately
W = Can do it well and know a lot about it

	Interest				Skills and Knowledge			
Symmetry	0	1	2	3	N	B	H	W
Triangle congruence	0	1	2	3	N	B	H	W
Similar triangles	0	1	2	3	N	B	H	W
Angle measure in polygons	0	1	2	3	N	B	H	W
Non–Euclidean geometry	0	1	2	3	N	B	H	W
Trigonometry	0	1	2	3	N	B	H	W

Part Four: Self-Sketch of the Learner

Create a sketch of yourself as a learner of geometry. Your sketch may be a drawing, a verbal description, a poem, a quantitative summary, or any other form that you feel adequately displays you as a geometer or a student of geometry. Use the back of this page or a sheet of graph paper.

*Part Three is adapted from Angelo and Cross (1993).

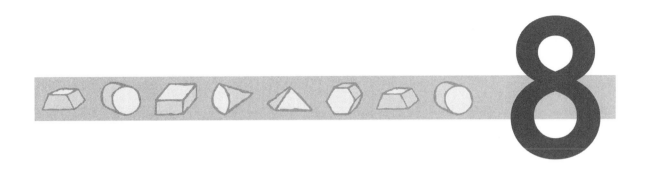

Writing for Assessment

Math Portfolios
Math Essays
Write Questions
The Geometry of Tessellations

Many of the activities in Chapter Five could also be used for assessment.

Quick Teaching Tip: Write out ten to fifteen topics you want all of your students to master.

Over the course of the school year or semester, note when each student shows mastery of each of the topics on an exam or quiz, answering a question in class, or during small or large group discussions.

Prelude

The strategies and activities in this chapter go beyond the usual types of exam writing questions—even those like the following that ask for more than the fill-in-the-blank or true-or-false questions:

- Compare and contrast a regular and nonregular hexagon.
- The shortest distance as the crow flies between New York City and Los Angeles is a line. True or false? If the answer is false, explain why.
- Explain the difference between a tangent line and a secant line.
- Plato once said that the only real circle lives in one's mind. What did he mean?
- What is the twelfth triangular number? Define a triangular number.
- What is another term for "regular polyhedra"? What are they, and how many are there?

The activities in this chapter are largely writing assignments and alternative ways of assessment for a test in a geometry course. Usually only one of this type of assessment is assigned each course and the topics reflect the course content. In fact the NCTM calls for us to use many different forms of assessment. The Assessment Principle from the NCTM's *Principles and Standards for School Mathematics of 2000* (2000) states: "Assessment should support the learning of important mathematics and furnish useful information to both teachers and students. . . . Assessment should not be done to students; rather, it should be done for students. . . . Assessment should become a routine part of the ongoing classroom activity rather than an interruption . . . assembling evidence from a variety of sources is more likely to yield an accurate picture" (pp. 22–24). In other words, assessment should be part of the learning process for both student and teacher, not merely a traffic light directing students to stop or go onward and upward.

Writing for assessment is one mode of evaluation that supports the NCTM's recommendations. Students demonstrate their understanding of mathematical concepts through their writings, and teachers give valuable feedback or add to the students' written understanding by responding with the teacher's written understanding. The Assessment Principle (NCTM, 2000) stresses two main ideas: that assessment should enhance students' learning and that it is a valuable tool for making instructional decisions.

The assessment activities are meant to be read and graded by the teacher. They should be assigned early in the course and their progress should be assessed at regular times during the entire course. Students' communication skills usually improve with practice. Also, writing for assessment is considered a writing strategy or a larger category of writing strategies by many writers.

Angelo and Cross (1993) suggest that for quality instruction, "faculty must first classify exactly what they want students in their courses to learn" (p. 13). In a geometry course, there is usually a list of fifty or more concepts that teachers want their students to know by the end of the course. Perhaps ten of these concepts are important enough that teachers would want students to be able to understand and explain them ten years from now. It is these concepts that writing-for-assessment activities can effectively target. For example, solving simple linear equations unites critical and logical thinking with the notion of generalization and a process that students may very well use in the future. Writing about this process helps solidify the process and applications of the process.

Math Portfolios

WHAT? Description

A portfolio is a dossier or a collection of materials that are representative of a person's work. A student's geometry portfolio contains examples of his or her writing assignments, exams, notes, or homework. Ideally, the portfolio contains papers that demonstrate the student's progress in a single mathematics course, such as geometry, or for all mathematics courses taken in high school or when earning a college degree.

Students might be asked to keep all of their writing-to-learn-geometry papers along with other more traditional assignments. Eventually the student chooses either the best pieces or the pieces that demonstrate growth or progress for the dossier. The student should append written reactions to the chosen pieces and, perhaps, the entire portfolio. Guidelines for the contents of the portfolio and assessment criteria should be given to the students.

WHY? Objectives

The math portfolios activity gives students the opportunity to:

- Demonstrate progress in a geometry course or over several courses in a math portfolio.
- Review and reflect on the geometry learned and search for materials that demonstrate personal growth in their understanding of geometry.
- Choose and organize appropriate material to demonstrate their progress.
- Show their teacher misconceptions or faulty thinking regarding the geometry explored in class.

HOW? Suggestions for the Portfolio

A variety of pieces could be included in a math portfolio—for example:

- An introductory essay detailing the writer's vision of the portfolio
- A Contents page
- All of the student's notes from one chapter of the textbook
- Ten homework assignments with the student's written reactions, including at least two construction assignments
- All writing-to-learn-geometry activities (for example, ads, poems, graph descriptions, and letters)
- At least two exams or quizzes that demonstrate improvement, along with the student's statements detailing this progress
- A geometric autobiography
- The student's philosophy of learning geometry
- A conclusion that describes or sums up the writer's mathematical experience in the course

Math Portfolio

NAME _____   DATE _____

ASSIGNMENT: Keep all writing in geometry pieces, notes, homework assignments, and exams in a dossier or binder. Eventually you will be asked to choose your best pieces from this collection for a math portfolio. Your portfolio must contain at least the following:

- A cover sheet and a Contents page
- All notes for one chapter of your choosing
- Ten hand-in homework assignments with your written reactions to your work attached to each; at least two must be construction assignments
- All writings composed for this course
- At least two exams or quizzes that demonstrate improvement with a statement detailing this progress
- A concluding essay that describes your experience learning geometry in this course

Portfolio Assessment Checklist

	Yes	No	Points
1. The portfolio contains all of the pieces listed:	_____	_____	_____/40
Cover sheet with Contents page	_____	_____	
All notes for one chapter	_____	_____	
Ten hand-in homework assignments	_____	_____	
All writings from this course	_____	_____	
Two exams or quizzes	_____	_____	
Concluding essay	_____	_____	
2. Homework assignments have satisfactory written reactions attached.	_____	_____	_____/10
3. Exams have clear statements that demonstrate progress.	_____	_____	_____/10
4. Concluding essay is clearly written and adequately describes your experience in the class.	_____	_____	_____/25
5. Overall appearance of the portfolio is neat and easy to follow.	_____	_____	_____/15
6. The portfolio is creative and clearly shows your personality.	_____	_____	_____/10

TOTAL POINTS EARNED _____/100

COMMENTS:

Math Portfolio

NAME _____   DATE _____

ASSIGNMENT: Keep all writing in mathematics pieces, notes, homework assignments, and exams from your geometry courses in a dossier or binder. Eventually you will be asked to choose your best pieces from this collection for a math portfolio. Your portfolio must contain at least the following pieces:

- A cover sheet and a Contents page.

- Any pieces of your work (at least one) on your favorite topics in geometry.

- Several hand-in homework assignments that show your progress in understanding geometry. Attach a written reaction to each piece. Include at least two construction assignments.

- All writings composed for the geometry course.

- At least two exams or quizzes that demonstrate improvement, along with your statement detailing this progress.

- A concluding essay that describes your mathematics experience in geometry.

Portfolio Assessment Checklist

	Yes	No	Points
1. The portfolio contains all of these pieces:	_____	_____	_____/40
Cover sheet with a Contents page	_____	_____	
At least one of your favorite pieces in the course	_____	_____	
Hand-in homework assignments	_____	_____	
All writings from this course	_____	_____	
Two exams or quizzes	_____	_____	
Concluding essay	_____	_____	
2. Homework assignments have satisfactory written reactions attached.	_____	_____	_____/10
3. Exams have clear statements that demonstrate progress.	_____	_____	_____/10
4. Concluding essay is clearly written and adequately describes your mathematical experience.	_____	_____	_____/25
5. Overall appearance of the portfolio is neat and easy to follow.	_____	_____	_____/15
6. The portfolio is creative and clearly shows your personality.	_____	_____	_____/10

TOTAL POINTS EARNED _____/100

COMMENTS:

Math Essays

WHAT? Description

One of the more common writing assignments for secondary and college students in disciplines other than mathematics or geometry is the essay. Essay writing can be a powerful assessment tool for both the teacher and students. The writing of an essay requires many of the same skills that geometric problem solving requires. Essays should be well thought out and well organized in a clear, step-by-step format. Also, the writing of an essay requires much thought and practice.

An essay is a short literary composition written to demonstrate the personal view of the writer. The five-paragraph essay provides a simple format for the student to follow and a good forum in which to display his or her opinion or thesis. The first paragraph introduces the thesis, the middle three paragraphs form the body of the essay and the supporting argument of the thesis, and the last paragraph contains the conclusion or summary of the essay.

The best math essays stem from well-written essay questions. Good essay questions present the topic and pose related questions. (See the HOW? section for examples.) Students need to know exactly what the teacher expects in terms of the topic and format of the essay. Are grammar and spelling as important as the content and argument for the thesis? Should the writer consider the teacher as the only audience? Is the essay to be typed or handwritten? What does an "A" essay look like? A grading rubric and a sample of an "A" paper may be shared with students to assist their efforts in composing a quality math essay.

The geometry instructor might assign a writing project on some topic in the history of geometry or on an application of geometry in today's world. In *Writing with a Purpose,* Trimmer (1995) suggests having the student answer several questions regarding determining her or his purpose of the writing project. The following questions are similar to Trimmer's yet adapted to the unique assignment of writing with purpose about a mathematics topic:

- What are the requirements regarding this assignment? How much mathematics should be included?

- What do I need to know about my topic? What sources will I get the information from? Do I know enough about the topic to get started right away?

- What will my hypothesis be? (Recall that a hypothesis is an unproven theory or supposition.) How many other hypotheses exist? Does my choice of hypothesis make sense?

- What purpose have I discovered for my writing project? Has it changed as I have researched my topic?

- What is my thesis? Does it make a clear, well-defined, and well-detailed summary about what my writing intends to show? Does it necessarily follow from my working hypothesis?

WHY? Objectives

The math essay activity requires students to:

- Research and reflect on a key mathematical concept.
- Clarify and present their views and understanding of the topic.
- Practice and refine writing and communication skills.

HOW? Examples

The two lessons for this activity provide good examples.

Math Essays: Geometric Constructions

NAME _____   DATE _____

ASSIGNMENT: Compose a well-organized essay describing geometric constructions. Use the five-paragraph format, and address the following questions in your essay:

- What is a geometric construction? What tools are used to construct geometric concepts, such as the perpendicular bisector of a line segment?
- Geometric constructions date back to 350 B.C. Describe this history and how the process has changed.
- Describe the steps for at least one construction.
- Discuss whether students should be allowed to use a graphing calculator to see the constructions.

Grading Rubric

- The format is worth 20 percent. The first paragraph should introduce your thesis. The next three paragraphs should support your thesis. The last paragraph should be the conclusion and should tie it all together.
- The accuracy of the facts and the substance and thoroughness of your argument for your thesis are worth 60 percent. This includes the answers to the questions posed above.
- Clarity and mechanics are worth 20 percent. Your essay must be word-processed and spell-checked. Complete and clear sentences are expected.

Grading Sheet

Points   **Comments**

Format: _____ (20%)

Content: _____ (60%)

Clarity and mechanics: _____ (20%)

Total grade = _____

Math Essays: Use of Technology in Geometry

NAME _____   DATE _____

ASSIGNMENT: In a well-organized essay, explain how the graphing calculator or computer programs assist in learning geometry. Be sure to answer these questions in your essay:

- Some people believe using a calculator is cheating. When is it cheating? When is it not?

- What features have you learned about directly from using your calculator? How has the calculator enhanced or diminished your understanding of mathematics?

- What software packages are available to help learn geometry? View one of these and critique it.

Grading Rubric

- The format is worth 20 percent. The first paragraph should introduce your thesis. The next three paragraphs should comprise your support of your thesis. The last paragraph should be the conclusion and should tie it all together.

- The accuracy of the facts and the substance and thoroughness of your argument for your thesis are worth 60 percent. This includes the answers to the questions posed above.

- Clarity and mechanics are worth 20 percent. Your essay must be word-processed and spell-checked. Complete and clear sentences are expected.

Grading Sheet

Points

Comments

Format: _____ (20%)
Content: _____ (60%)
Clarity and mechanics: _____ (20%)
Total grade = _____

Math Essays: Geometry, the Real World, and Me

NAME _____   DATE _____

ASSIGNMENT: Compose a clear and well-organized essay on the usefulness of geometry in the real world. State your opinion and defend it. Be sure to address these issues:

- Geometry is all about us.
- Certain learners prefer geometry to algebra courses because algebra is much more abstract than geometry.
- Understanding geometry reinforces critical thinking skills and problem solving in general.

Grading Rubric

- The format is worth 20 percent. The first paragraph should introduce your thesis. The next three paragraphs should support your thesis. The last paragraph should be the conclusion and should tie it all together.
- The accuracy of the facts and the substance and thoroughness of your argument for your thesis are worth 60 percent. This includes the answers to the issues above.
- Clarity and mechanics are worth 20 percent. Your essay must be word-processed and spell-checked. Complete and clear sentences are expected.

Grading Sheet

Points   **Comments**

Format: _____ (20%)

Content: _____ (60%)

Clarity and mechanics: _____ (20%)

Total grade = _____

Write Questions

WHAT? Description

Write questions are questions that require the geometry student to respond in writing rather than merely using computation or sketches. They are used in hand-in homework, quizzes, and exams. It is a good idea to introduce this type of question to the students as a part of their homework before using them on quizzes or exams. Students need time to practice writing and consider how writing about geometry compares or contrasts to other writing.

Write questions should require a short answer, usually two to three sentences. Students should be expected to give answers in paragraph form, the form that they probably will be expected to use in their future careers. The questions themselves usually begin in these ways:

Describe . . .

In your own words, write out the definition for . . .

Write out the method for . . .

Compare or contrast . . .

WHY? Objectives

The write question activity allows the students to:

• Practice communicating mathematically.

• Demonstrate how they understand geometry.

• Consider the features and fine points regarding a geometric concept.

HOW? Examples

This list gives some examples of write questions for assignments or on exams:

- Describe how a solid, such as a cylinder, can be formed using a graphing calculator. Use at least three complete and clear sentences in paragraph form.
- Write out the definition for a tessellation in your own words in paragraph form.
- Write out the method for constructing a perpendicular bisector for a line segment using only a straightedge and compass.
- Compare and contrast point slope form and slope intercept form of a linear equation. Use at least three complete and clear sentences in paragraph form.
- Give an application for a quadratic equation and explain how the equation can be used to solve this application. Use at least three sentences in the Pythagorean theorem paragraph form.

The lesson also provides an example of a write question.

Write Questions: Write Question of the Day

NAME _____   DATE _____

Write questions are designed to help you explore and understand the concepts discussed in class. Often these questions do not have a right or wrong answer but require you to take a stand.

Each question of the day is worth 5 points, and you can earn up to 50 points over the semester. You are required to respond to ten write questions this semester but may turn in more. Your lowest scores will be dropped if you elect to turn in more than ten write questions.

Each response must include at least three complete sentences of explanation. Examples, graphs, and pictures are also allowed and encouraged. The point is to make your answer clear! It may help to imagine you are explaining your answer to another student.

Responses will be graded on accuracy, clarity, and creativity. Clarity includes correct grammar and vocabulary.

Write Question

Is geometry invented or discovered? Defend your answer.

The Geometry of Tessellations

WHAT? Description

A tessellation is a tiling of nonoverlapping figures that cover a region entirely. Regular tessellations contain only one type of regular (congruent angle and sides) polygon, such as an equilateral triangle or a square. The sketch of squares below is an example of a regular tessellation:

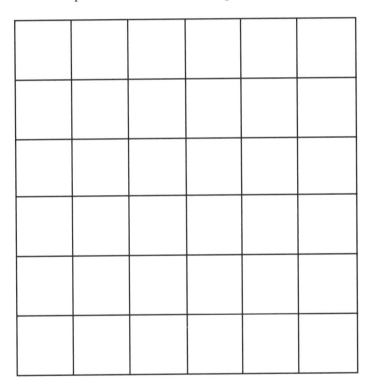

Each of any four connected squares in the figure above meets at one vertex or point, showing four 90-degree angles that sum up to 360 degrees. Only three regular polygons tessellate, or cover the plane with no gaps or overlaps: squares, equilateral triangles, and regular hexagons. Students should be encouraged to sketch each of the three regular tessellations and note that each central vertex has angle measures that add up to 360 degrees. Many tessellations are semiregular, meaning that they have a few different regular polygons that tessellate the region or many other tessellations contain a pattern of different shapes, like many Arabic rugs.

This activity can be performed in two parts: (1) the sketching and coloring of a tessellation and (2) a written title and description or explanation of the geometric patterns in the tessellation.

In a recent Mathematics for Elementary Education college course, students were asked to create colorful sketches of tessellations as they might assign their future elementary students to do. The sketches (some with titles and descriptors) are presented at the end of this chapter. The tessellations of the entire class grace a long bulletin board in a classroom at the college.

WHY? Objectives

The geometry of tessellations activity causes students to:

- Consider different figures that tessellate an 8.5 by 11-inch sheet of paper.
- Create a colorful sketch of a tiling much like they would ask their future students to create.
- Consider their tessellation and title it appropriately.
- Write out a description that clearly describes the tessellation using geometric terms.

HOW? Examples

The examples here are student-generated tessellations.

"Outerspace" by Erica Cowhick. This tessellation shows circles with rectangles traveling about an eight-sector outerspace.

By Lacie Mayes

"Stained Glass" by Hugo Cangiani. This tessellation contains triangles, squares, rectangles, and a stained-glass window with the sun shining through.

"Stars and Bowties" by Mandi Turner. This semi-regular tessellation displays hexagons and all sizes of equilateral triangles.

By Laura Wood

By Caroline Cezar

Geometry Out Loud

References

Angelo, T. A., & Cross, P. K. (1993). *Classroom assessment techniques, a handbook for college teachers* (2nd ed.). San Francisco: Jossey-Bass.

Baldwin, R. S., Ford, J. C., & Readance, J. E. (1981). Teaching word connotations: An alternative strategy. *Reading World, 21,* 103–108.

Barron, R. F. (1969). The use of vocabulary as advance organizer. In H. L. Herber & P. L. Sanders (Eds.), *Research in reading in the content areas: First report* (pp. 29–39). Syracuse, NY: Syracuse University Reading and Language Arts Center.

Bennett, A. B. Jr., & Nelson L. T. (2004). *Mathematics for elementary teachers: A conceptual approach* (6th ed.). New York: McGraw-Hill.

Blachowicz, C. (1986). Making connections: Alternatives to the vocabulary notebook. *Journal of Reading, 29,* 643–649.

Burton, D. (1994, 1999, 2003, 2005). *The history of mathematics: Fourth–Sixth editions.* Boston: WCB/McGraw-Hill.

Fleury, A. (2000). *Guided poetry.* Presentation at Washburn University.

Frayer, D. A., Frederick, W. C., & Klausmeier, H. J. (1969). *A schema for testing the level of concept mastery* (Tech. Rep. No. 16). Madison: University of Wisconsin Research and Development Center for Cognitive Learning.

Henderson, D. W., & Taimina D. (2005). *Experiencing geometry: Euclidean and non-Euclidean with history* (3rd ed.). Upper Saddle River, NJ: Pearson Education.

Herber, H. (1978). *Teaching reading in content areas* (2nd ed.). Upper Saddle River, NJ: Prentice-Hall.

Johnson, D. D., & Pearson, P. D. (1984). *Teaching reading vocabulary* (2nd ed.). New York: Holt.

Kiniry, M., & Rose, M. (1990). *Critical strategies for academic writing.* Boston: Bedford Books.

Langer, J. A. (1981). From theory to practice: A rereading plan. *Journal of Reading, 25,* 152–156.

MacBeth, S. J., and others. (1997). Internet article on cinquains.

Mower, P. (1995). *Writing to learn college algebra.* Unpublished doctoral dissertation, University of North Dakota.

Mower, P. (2003). *Algebra out loud.* San Francisco: Jossey-Bass.

Nasar, S. (1998). *A beautiful mind.* New York: Simon & Schuster.

National Council of Supervisors of Mathematics. (1988). *Essential mathematics for the 21st century.* Minneapolis: Mathematics Task Force.

National Council of Teachers of Mathematics. (2000). *Principles and standards for school mathematics of 2000.* Reston, VA: National Council of Teachers of Mathematics.

Ogle, D. M. (1986). The know, want to know, learning strategy. In K. D. Muth (Ed.), *Children's comprehension of text* (pp. 205–223). Newark, DE: International Reading Association.

Owen, S. (1998). Zero. In K. Brown (Ed.), *Verse and universe: Poems about science and mathematics.* Minneapolis: Milkweed Editions.

Polya, G. (1973). *How to solve it* (2nd ed.). Princeton, NJ: Princeton University Press. (Original work published in 1945)

Raphael, T. E. (1986). Teaching question-answer relationships, revisited. *Reading Teacher, 39,* 516–522.

Seydel, K. (1980). *Geometry: An exercise in reasoning.* Philadelphia: Saunders.

Thomas, D. A. (2002). *Modern geometry.* Pacific Grove, CA: Brooks/Cole.

Trimmer, J. F. (1995). *Writing with a purpose* (11th ed.). Boston: Houghton Mifflin.

Vacca, R. T., & Vacca, J .L. (1999). *Content area reading* (6th ed.). Reading, MA: Addison-Wesley.

Other Books of Interest

Algebra Out Loud:
Learning Mathematics Through Reading and Writing Activities

Pat Mower, Ph.D.

Paper   ISBN: 0-7879-6898-6

www.josseybass.com

Algebra Out Loud is a unique resource designed for mathematics instructors who are teaching Algebra I and II. This easy-to-use resource is filled with illustrative examples, strategies, activities, and lessons that will help students more easily understand mathematical text and learn the skills they need to effectively communicate mathematical concepts.

Algebra Out Loud specifically supports the NCTM Standards on mathematical communications. The book's strategies and activities will give students the edge in learning how to summarize, analyze, present, utilize, and retain mathematical content. The book offers proven writing activities that will engage the students in writing about algebraic vocabulary, processes, theorems, definitions, and graphs. The activities focus on such areas as word problems, proofs, statistical claims and tests, and algebra concepts.

Students will learn to:

- Organize and consolidate mathematical thinking
- Communicate their mathematical thinking coherently and clearly to peers, teachers, and others
- Analyze and evaluate mathematical thinking and strategies of others
- Use the language of mathematics to express mathematical ideas precisely . . . and more.

For quick access and use, the activities are printed in a full-page format and the book carries a lay-flat binding for ease in photocopying.

Other Books of Interest

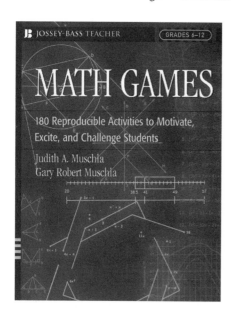

Math Games:
180 Reproducible Activities to Motivate, Excite, and Challenge Students, Grades 6–12

Judith A. Muschla and Gary Robert Muschla

Paper   ISBN: 0-7879-7081-6
www.josseybass.com

"For classroom teachers interested in successfully incorporating differentiated lessons into the existing curriculum, this book offers ready-to-use and relevant activities. And for students, it provides an enjoyable opportunity to challenge themselves while studying familiar concepts."

—*Michelle DiGiovanni, 7th-grade math and science teacher,*
Round Valley Middle School, Clinton Township, New Jersey

Math Games offers a dynamic collection of 180 reproducible activity sheets to stimulate and challenge your students in all areas of math—from whole numbers to data analysis—while emphasizing problem solving, critical thinking, and the use of technology for today's curriculum!

Each of the book's activities can help you teach students in grades 6 through 12 how to think with numbers, recognize relationships, and make connections between mathematical concepts. You pick the activity appropriate for their needs . . . encourage the use of a calculator . . . or provide further challenges with activities that have multiple answers.

Designed to be user friendly, all of the ready-to-use activities are organized into seven convenient sections and printed in a lay-flat format for ease of photocopying as many times as needed. Sections include whole numbers; fractions, decimals, percents; geometry; measurement; algebra; data analysis; and potpourri.

Judith A. Muschla has taught mathematics in South River, New Jersey, for over twenty-five years. **Gary Robert Muschla** taught reading and writing for more than twenty-five years in Spotswood, New Jersey. This is the seventh math resource coauthored by Judith Muschla and Gary Muschla. Their earlier books include: *The Math Teachers Book of Lists, Second Edition; Hands-On Math Projects with Real-Life Applications; Math Starters; Geometry Teacher's Activities Kit; Math Smart;* and *Algebra Teacher's Activities Kit,* all published by Jossey-Bass Publishers.

Other Books of Interest

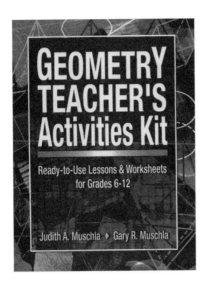

Geometry Teacher's Activities Kit:
Ready-to-Use Lessons & Worksheets for Grades 6–12

Judith A. Muschla and Gary R. Muschla

Paper   ISBN: 0-13-060038-5

www.josseybass.com

This unique resource gives teachers 130 lessons with accompanying activity sheets to help students understand geometric concepts and recognize, interpret, and appreciate geometry's relationship to the real world—from hexagonal snowflakes to the Golden Rectangle of art and architecture!

Each lesson features an objective, special materials, teaching notes with step-by-step directions, answer key when necessary, and worksheet. And for easy access and use, materials are organized into seven parts and printed in a big 8¼" x 11" lay-flat binding that folds flat for photocopying of any worksheet as many times as needed.

You'll find that lessons in Parts 1–6 are sequenced in order of difficulty—beginning with activities geared to middle school geometry and proceeding to activities designed for the high school curriculum. The activities in Part 7 can be used in any order you wish. What's more, many activities throughout the book are ideal for calculators and computer use.

Sections include:

- The Language of Geometry
- Polygons—The Foundations
- Polygons—Advanced
- Circles
- 3-D figures
- Applications
- Potpourri

In short, *Geometry Teacher's Activities Kit* gives you scores of stimulating ways to reinforce and extend the skills taught in your classroom while improving your students' ability to analyze, problem solve, and see geometry's vital role in the study of mathematics.

Other Books of Interest

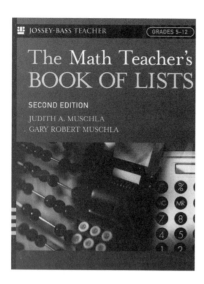

The Math Teacher's Book of Lists, Second Edition

Judith A. Muschla and Gary Robert Muschla

Paper   ISBN: 0-7879-7398-X

www.josseybass.com

"Through its assortment of informative lists, this book provides a clear and concise approach to mathematics. A practical reference for teachers, it will enable students to master a variety of topics within the parameters of both course and national standards."

—*Elizabeth Razzano, mathematics teacher,*
East Brunswick High School, East Brunswick, New Jersey

This second edition of the best-selling resource for mathematics teachers is a time-saving reference with over 300 useful lists for developing instructional materials and planning lessons for middle school and secondary students. Some of the lists supply teacher background; others are to copy for student use, and many offer new twists on traditional classroom topics. It includes comprehensive and updated content from general mathematics through algebra, geometry, trigonometry, and calculus, useful in grades 5–12 classrooms as well as community college classes.

For quick access and easy use, the lists are numbered consecutively, organized into sections focusing on the different areas of math, and printed in a large 8½" x 11" lay-flat format for easy photocopying.

Part I contains reproducible lists providing essential, challenging, and quick reference material on over 300 topics. **Part II** contains a variety of reproducible teaching aids and activities to support the instructional program.

For the second edition, the original lists have been updated and a new section, "Lists for Student Reference" has been added, along with approximately twelve totally new lists, including "Fractals," "Topics in Discrete Math," "Math Websites for Students," and "Math Websites for Teachers."

The Math Teacher's Book of Lists will save you time and help you instill in your students a genuine appreciation for the world of mathematics.

Other Books of Interest

Math Essentials, Middle School Level
Lessons and Activities for Test Preparation

Frances McBroom Thompson, Ph.D.

Paper	ISBN: 0-7879-6602-9
	www.josseybass.com

"A valuable resource for use by inservice teachers of middle school mathematics as well as preservice classrooms. The development lessons, followed by independent practice activities, and the inclusion of possible errors students may make provide the teacher with the tools necessary to help students succeed."

—*Ernest Oluwole Pratt, assistant professor,*
Department of Education, Mount Union College,
Alliance, Ohio

Math Essentials, Middle School Level gives middle school math teachers the tools they need to help prepare all types of students (including gifted and learning disabled) for mathematics testing and the National Council of Teachers of Mathematics (NCTM) standards. *Math Essentials* highlights Dr. Thompson's proven approach by incorporating manipulatives, diagrams, and independent practice. This dynamic book covers forty key objectives arranged in four sections. Each objective includes three activities (two developmental lessons and one independent practice) and a list of commonly made errors related to the objective.

Contents includes:

- Numeration and number properties
- Computational algorithms and estimation in problem solving
- Graphing, statistics, and probability
- Geometry and logical or spatial reasoning
- Measurement

The book's activities are designed to be flexible and can be used as a connected set or taught separately, depending on the learning needs of your students. Most activities and problems also include a worksheet and an answer key and each of the four sections contains a practice test with an answer key.

Other Books of Interest

Math Essentials, High School Level
Lessons and Activities for Test Preparation

Frances McBroom Thompson, Ed.D.

Paper   ISBN: 0-7879-6603-7

www.josseybass.com

"Secondary mathematics teachers will find the clearly described activities a sound supplement to standard textbook presentations. The well-designed sequences of activities proceeding from the concrete to pictorial to symbolic are especially suited for helping those who struggle with basic mathematics in high school."

—*Bill Juraschek, University of Colorado at Denver*

Math Essentials, High School Level gives high school math teachers the tools they need to help prepare all types of students (including gifted and learning disabled) for standards-based mathematics testing. It is designed to help teachers align their classroom instruction with their district and state mathematics guidelines, and it offers instruction for remediation and enrichment, provides necessary scaffolding to develop key skills, and measures student progress. All lessons are aligned with the NCTM standards.

This dynamic book covers key objectives found in a typical secondary mathematics curriculum, including algebraic thinking; graphs, statistics and probability; linear and quadratic functions and their properties; and geometry and measurement with applications. Each objective contains three lessons: manipulative, pictorial, and independent practice, along with a list of common errors made by students when working problems related to the objective. Lessons include worksheets or patterns and answer keys, and each section ends with a practice test and answer key.

Frances McBroom Thompson, Ed.D. is professor of mathematics at Texas Woman's University. She has taught mathematics in junior and senior high schools and served as a K–12 mathematics specialist, and she is now an educational consultant for grades K–12. Dr. Thompson received her doctorate in mathematics education from the University of Georgia, and she is the author of numerous books including *Hands-On Math!*, *Hands-On Algebra!*, and *Math Essentials, Middle School Level* (all published by Jossey-Bass).